Human Genetic Selection and Enhancement

Marta Soniewicka & Wojciech Lewandowski

Human Genetic Selection and Enhancement

Parental Perspectives and Law

Authors

Marta Soniewicka
Department of Philosophy of Law and Legal Ethics
Faculty of Law and Administration, Jagiellonian University,
Krakow, Poland

Wojciech Lewandowski
Department of Particular Ethics, Institute of Philosophy,
John Paul II Catholic University of Lublin, Poland

Editorial Secretary

Zofia Szafrańska-Czajka, PhD Candidate
Sociology, University of Lodz, Poland

Bibliographic Information published by the Deutsche Nationalbibliothek
The Deutsche Nationalbibliothek lists this publication in the Deutsche Nationalbibliografie; detailed bibliographic data is available online at http://dnb.d-nb.de.

Library of Congress Cataloging-in-Publication Data
A CIP catalog record for this book has been applied for at the Library of Congress.

This publication has been prepared within a research project financed by the Polish National Science Centre
(Dec-2013/10/E/HS5/00157).

Cover image: Norman Leto, Procreation, 2008, reproduced courtesy of East of Art Foundation, Cracow (Fundacja Wschód Sztuki, Kraków).

ISBN 978-3-631-74451-2 (Print)
E-ISBN 978-3-631-76815-0 (E-PDF)
E-ISBN 978-3-631-76816-7 (EPUB)
E-ISBN 978-3-631-76817-4 (MOBI)
DOI 10.3726/b14685

© Peter Lang GmbH
Internationaler Verlag der Wissenschaften
Berlin 2019

All rights reserved.

Peter Lang – Berlin · Bern · Bruxelles · New York ·
Oxford · Warszawa · Wien

All parts of this publication are protected by copyright. Any utilisation outside the strict limits of the copyright law, without the permission of the publisher, is forbidden and liable to prosecution. This applies in particular to reproductions, translations, microfilming, and storage and processing in electronic retrieval systems.

This publication has been peer reviewed.

www.peterlang.com

Contents

Acknowledgements 7

Marta Soniewicka
Introduction 9

Part I: Genetic Selection

    Marta Soniewicka
1 Ethical standards of genetic counselling and reproductive autonomy 21

    Wojciech Lewandowski
2 The criteria of rationality in genetic selection 35

    Marta Soniewicka
3 Sex as a criterion for progeny selection 51

    Marta Soniewicka
4 Reproductive harm 71

    Marta Soniewicka
5 Selective procreation and disability 101

    Wojciech Lewandowski
6 Parent-God analogy in procreative decisions 117

    Wojciech Lewandowski
7 Spare embryos and parental obligations 135

Part II: Genetic Enhancement

    Marta Soniewicka
8 The question of justice in the debate over human enhancement 155

    Marta Soniewicka
9 Human self-understanding in the debate over moral human
    enhancement: autonomy and authenticity 183

Wojciech Lewandowski
10 Genetic enhancement and moral perfection 229

Wojciech Lewandowski
11 Bioconservatism and the preference for *status quo* 247

Wojciech Lewandowski
12 Procreative autonomy in the context of person-affecting and impersonal reasons for human enhancement 259

Wojciech Lewandowski
13 Intrinsic and instrumental values in the assessment of human enhancement 271

Wojciech Lewandowski
Concluding remarks 287

Index 289

Acknowledgements

We owe special thanks to the reviewers of this book – Dr. Roberto Franzini Tibaldeo (UCL, Belgium) and Dr. Habil. Ewa Baum (University of Medical Sciences in Poznan, Poland) for their insightful remarks and critical comments which helped us to improve the final version of this book. Some parts of the book were previously published in Polish which we acknowledge in the end of the chapters. We are grateful to Philip Palmer for translating from Polish into English Chapters 3, 4, 8 and 9, as well as to Dr. Aeddan Shaw for translating chapters 2, 6, 7, 10, 11 and 12. Many thanks to Aeddan Shaw for his help in linguistic edition of the volume. We are also grateful to Zofia Szafrańska-Czajka for her help in technical pre-edition of the manuscript. We are indebted to Marcin S. Gołębiewski for his help in getting the rights to reproduce the picture by Norman Leto which graces the cover of the book. Last but not least, our word of thanks is to Beata Misiewicz for her excellent work on the cover design.

The preparation of this volume was financed by the Polish National Science Centre (Dec-2013/10/E/HS5/00157).

Marta Soniewicka

Introduction

The tremendous recent advances in biotechnology and knowledge derived from the Human Genome Project are expected to bring revolutionary changes to the practice of medicine and improve many aspects of our life, particularly with regard to our health. Many enthusiasts, on the one hand, expect that 21st century genomic medicine will open up new opportunities for us to live longer and healthier lives. Sceptics, on the other hand, point out that the analytical and clinical validity and utility of the genetic information obtained from the individual personal genome are still too weak. Nevertheless, there are certain aspects of human life in which genetic knowledge has gained special concern and has become crucial in making decisions of existential importance. Procreation is certainly one of them.

Reproductive genetic testing is the prominent branch of applied genetics in medicine which was primarily developed for the purpose of assessing reproductive risks by detecting foetal anomalies (Hodge 2003). One can distinguish three sorts of reproductive genetic testing: (1) preconception testing (carrier testing), aimed at identifying whether a patient is a carrier of a recessive disease gene that can be passed on to successive generations; (2) prenatal diagnosis of foetal cells (PND), aimed at identification of traits or conditions of a future child; and (3) preimplantation genetic diagnosis (PGD), aimed at the identification of traits or conditions of an embryo formed by in vitro fertilization. PGD can be also used to analyse ova before fertilization to produce an embryo with or without certain genetic traits or conditions. One may also use sperm sorting before fertilization to form an embryo with certain traits or conditions (Knoppers, Bordet & Isasi 2006; Quaid 2008).

Genetic knowledge, combined with assisted reproduction techniques, is supposed to enhance reproductive choices. By the enhancement of reproductive choices one usually means the increase of reproductive opportunities, in particular the opportunity to decide whether to become a parent of a child with a certain genetic makeup. Reproductive genetics enable selective reproduction which consists of deciding which children *will be born* (PGD) or which children *will not be born* (PND) on the basis of their genetic traits and conditions (Press &Ariail 2003). This book addresses the ethical controversies concerning this reproductive opportunity, in particular the problem of genetic selection (**Part**

I, Genetic Selection) and the idea of genetic enhancement (**Part II, Genetic Enhancement**).

Two general types of genetic selection can be distinguished: the negative and the positive. By negative genetic selection, one means weeding out a developing foetus, embryo or gamete with a diagnosed genetic disease or other unwanted trait (e.g. maleness or femaleness). By positive genetic selection one means choosing an embryo or gamete with a preferred diagnosed genetic trait. PGD may be used for positive selection for medical purposes when parents are screening for an embryo that would be a matching tissue donor for an ill child – the so-called saviour siblings. PGD may be also used to select for a genetic disorder or disability which the parents have and which they want to share with their progeny (e.g. hereditary deafness; Achondroplasia – dwarfism). Reproductive decisions based on positive genetic selection for disability are called dysgenic decisions or negative enhancement (Murray 2003).

By genetic selection based on medical traits and conditions, one usually means any kind of selection against or for a trait or a condition which is associated with a particular disease or a particular function/dysfunction of an organism and relevant to a medical purpose. One may name here sex selection for medical indicators, i.e. the identification of sex for the purpose of avoiding transfer of embryos with X-linked genetic diseases, such as haemophilia, Lesch-Nyhan syndrome etc. Sex selection to prevent X-linked diseases was the initial purpose of inventing and applying PGD to assisted reproduction. Now PGD can be used to detect monogenic diseases (such as Tay-Sachs, cystic fibrosis etc.) and to detect an abnormal number of chromosomes which are linked with genetic disorders (such as Turner syndrome, Down syndrome etc.). New uses of PGD include screening embryos for susceptibility to polygenic diseases (such as breast cancer), for late-onset diseases (such as Huntignton's disease), for HLA-matching for existing children. The number of conditions and the predisposition for diseases identifiable by PGD continues to increase and scientists speculate that, within a few years, it will be possible to identify genetic markers correlated with diabetes, mental illnesses, stroke, asthma, and all types of cancer. The distinction between medical and non-medical genetic traits seems for many authors crucial for the moral evaluation of genetic selection and intervention, yet it remains vague. There is a wide grey zone where the line between medical and non-medical traits is blurred since there is no clear distinction between a trait and a disorder, which blurs another distinction – between therapy and enhancement.

Current biotechnological developments are opening up new opportunities for genetic interventions that are aimed not only at preventing genetic disease, but also at improving the human mental and physical condition. By enhancement, one means: (1) correcting effects of disability or disease, e.g. an artificial leg or arm (treatment and enhancement – a vague distinction based on normal functioning); (2) increasing natural human potential (natural endowments of capabilities) within the range typical of the species homo sapiens, e.g. raising a person's IQ; (3) providing superhuman enhancements: increasing a person's capabilities beyond the range typical for homo sapiens, e.g. providing humans with gills (the capacity to breath under water) or bat sonar (Savulescu, Meulen, Kahane 2011). One may also distinguish between *ex-ante* enhancement (introduced before birth of an enhanced person, e.g. genetic intervention or genetic selection) and *ex-post* enhancement (introduced after birth, e.g. pharmacology, surgery, education) (Kamm 2013). None of these distinctions provide sufficient insights for either distinguishing enhancement from therapy, or for distinguishing permissible interventions from non-permissible.

Genetic human enhancement is to be achieved by means of genetic selection or genetic intervention (in particular germline gene therapy and CRISPR/Cas9). Genetic intervention resulting in heritable changes in the human species has become the subject of heated debate, especially since new methods of gene editing were developed that are much more flexible, cheaper and faster. These include Clustered Regularly Interspaced Short Palindromic Repeats (CRISPR), a technique that mimics nature (it is based on Cas9 – an RNA-guided enzyme that cuts DNA developed by bacteria), providing us with a new opportunity to not only combat genetic diseases (like HIV, Huntington's disease, sickle cell anemia, cystic fibrosis, muscular dystrophy etc.), but also to take further control over nature and evolution. With these new technologies at hand, we can promote our well-being by making potential improvements to our physical traits (e.g. musculature) and creating capacities that go beyond the level of a normal healthy individual.

This leads us to ponder the question of what it means to be human and how our self-understanding could potentially be affected by gene editing. The controversy this issue provokes has led to hundreds of scholars, scientists, policymakers and experts meeting together to discuss the ethical implications of using this revolutionary technology. They have produced reports containing guidelines and recommendations for legal regulations and called for the kind of public education and engagement which could aid assessment of the relevant issues and give due consideration to how individual and societal values could be applied to the risks and benefits of human genetic enhancement (report of the National Academy of Sciences and National Academy of Medicine 2017).

Our book is a response to this call. We would like to contribute to this ongoing debate by pondering the ethical and legal dimensions it involves. To realize this aim we present the philosophical doctrines which provide the justificatory frames and axiological sources for the future guidelines and precautionary measures. Since no single ethical position is fully adequate to guide our decisions in reproductive genetics, we believe that one should seek to formulate a pluralistic approach that captures the best elements of each of them. The present volume emphasizes the significance of both principles (norms) and virtues (character), as well as the relations and context in which reproductive decisions are made. We believe that our pluralistic approach, which accommodates insights from both virtue ethics and principle-based rationalistic doctrines, taking their consequences seriously, would serve as a unique guide to practical decision-making in reproductive genetics and a significant improvement over the predominant approaches in the field.

Reproductive genetics poses ethical and legal problems both old and new, which require the reconsideration of the scope and meaning of reproductive autonomy and responsibility for reproductive choices. Our book addresses the problems of reproduction by taking into account parental perspectives in resolving ethical and legal issues concerning new reproductive opportunities. The parental perspective introduced in the book embodies norms such as the norm of procreative beneficence (do good to your progeny), procreative nonmalaficence (do not harm your progeny), or such principles as the principle of reproductive autonomy, rationality, and, last but not least, parental love. We also emphasise that intentions and motives play a significant role in our moral thinking which cannot be simply reduced to the evaluation of the consequences of our actions or omissions. We attempt to elucidate that the core point of our moral thinking, specifically on reproduction, relies on our self-understanding, as well as the understanding of the meaning of life, death, and reproduction which we do not experience as mere facts. These significances have profound impact on 'our capacity to live [and to choose] well' as Cora Diamond claims (Diamond 1990, 173). Morality concerns the question of how to live well and how to treat other people (Dworkin 2011) and it should provide a 'connection between a sense of who we are, what kind of being, and the way we live' (Diamond 1990, 173).

According to Isaiah Berlin's famous distinction, philosophers may be described either as hedgehogs (unifiers) or foxes (multipliers) (Berlin 1969). Hedgehogs defend a unified theory of value according to which there are no irreconcilable conflicts among genuine values. They believe that we can solve all moral conflicts by applying a special procedure or an external independent point of view which guarantees the verification of values. Foxes, like Berlin, reject the ideal of monism and defend pluralism of values, where conflicts of values are inevitable. He claimed that there are some ultimate values which are incommensurable, i.e., there is no common moral currency in terms of which their conflict could be resolved with no loss of value. It not only contests utilitarian thinking with its common moral currency but also the Kantian or Lockean tradition in moral philosophy, where basic rights and liberties are placed beyond the conflict. In value-conflict situations, a pragmatic compromise is possible, but it is not a stable one. And for many people this is the reason that the debates over such intricate questions as abortion, stem-cell research, genetic selection etc., remain open and unsettled ones. People do not agree about these fundamental issues since they do not share an understanding of the normative status of foetus or embryo – their values are rooted in different philosophical and religious worldviews. Following Berlin we do not share the French Enlightenment's optimism that all values and rational goals can be ultimately humanized. Yet we attempt to explore moral horizons which set frames for these bioethical issues in order to provide a better and more profound understanding of the ongoing debate.

In one of the books on human enhancement, the authors mocked Michael Sandel's objections raised against biotechnological reproductive enhancements (Sandel 2007) by presenting how odd it would sound if the U.S. Food and Drug Administration (FDA) required appropriate labelling which were to include them:

> MAY CAUSE CONSTIPATION, DRY MOUTH, SKIN RASHES, AND LOSS OF OPENNESS TO THE UNBIDDEN. IF SYMPTOMS PERSIST AFTER 48 HRS, CONSULT YOUR PHYSICIAN AND/OR YOUR SPIRITUAL ADVISOR (Bostrom, Savulescu 2013).

There are many ethical concerns and moral threats that cannot be simply put in any prescriptions, yet we are aware of them and often find them much more important than any precautions concerning bodily harm alone. Take alcohol for instance. We can find labels on which we can read about alcohol's harmful effects on the liver or brain, yet we do not expect to find any label telling us that the abuse of alcohol may affect our relationships and harm our loved ones. Our philosophical considerations presented in this book address exactly such issues which are not to be covered by any medical labels or prescriptions since they go far beyond safety concerns.

***

In **Chapter 1, Ethical standards of genetic counselling and reproductive autonomy,** we present the principles and aims of genetic counselling and claim that the purely rationalistic philosophy of medicine based on either duties or principles presents an incomplete picture of moral life which is not sufficient to cover the complexity of the ethics of reproduction. We argue that the neo-Aristotelian virtue approach to ethics could significantly enhance the understanding of medical ethics and its application in the clinical context of genetic counselling.

In **Chapter 2, The criteria of rationality in genetic selection**, we address the requirements of rationality in reproductive choices. We discuss confrontational and non-confrontational conceptions of rationality in the context of genetic selection, and we attempt to formulate conditions for a universal conception of the plurality of reasons.

In **Chapter 3, Sex as a criterion for progeny selection**, we address the problem of sex selection for both medical and non-medical reasons. We discuss the arguments for the ban on elective sex selection, such as: the violation of sex balance in a society, sexual discrimination and the promotion of sexual stereotypes. Further, we present the arguments against the ban on elective sex selection, with an emphasis on family balancing, which are rooted in procreative autonomy. We argue that the ethical framework based on the principle of procreative liberty is not sufficient to discuss the problem unless we refer to values which are to be protected by this principle. We draw special attention to parental intentions and motives elucidating their significance for the understanding of procreation.

In **Chapter 4, Reproductive harm**, we pose the question of whether prospective parents are obliged to prevent so-called reproductive harm caused by genetically transmitted diseases. We analyse the harm principle and the legal concept of harm. Our philosophical considerations lead to the conclusion that a legal concept of reproductive harm is not fully justified and therefore the idea of a wrongful life action seems misleading. We claim that the idea of reproductive harm should be replaced by the idea of moral procreative responsibility in the given context.

Chapter 5, Selective procreation and disability, addresses the problem of disability in the context of reproductive decisions based on genetic information. We pose the question of whether selective procreation should be considered as a moral obligation of prospective parents. To answer this question, a number of different ethical approaches to the problem are presented and critically analysed: the utilitarian; Julian Savulescu's principle of procreative beneficence; and the rights-based. We claim that these approaches fail to provide any appealing principles on which reproductive decisions should be based. A full appreciation of the ethical significance of recognition in procreative decisions leads to a more nuanced and morally satisfying view than other leading alternatives presented in the chapter.

In **Chapter 6, Parent-God analogy in procreative decisions**, we present the implication of applying the Parent-God analogy to reproductive decisions with regard to the problem of permissible arbitrariness of choosing or accepting the birth of a disabled child.

In **Chapter 7, Spare embryos and parental obligations**, we present an analysis of the reasoning against embryo selection based on the assumption that the predicted existence of spare embryos puts parents in a moral dilemma. We analyse such premises of this reasoning as: 1) an embryo is an actual part of the parent-child relationship; 2) this relationship is a basis for parental obligation; 3) embryo genetic selection leads to conflicts in terms of parental obligations constituting a moral dilemma; 4) we should avoid decisions leading to moral dilemmas. The validity of these premises depends on the solution of some fundamental and practical problems, such as whether moral status is a necessary condition to be a part of a relationship; what constitutes parental obligations; and whether embryo adoption can be seen as an option which eliminates the moral dilemma.

New advanced technologies applied to medicine give people greater opportunities of enhancement than ever before, but these new genetic technologies are not available to a broad segment of the population. Thus, exclusive genomic medicine gives rise to new challenges in the fair distribution of health care resources within and among nations. We discuss these issues in **Chapter 8, The question of justice in the debate over human enhancement**. We draw attention to the main issues in which the idea of genetic human enhancement could conceivably completely change our previous understanding of justice or move reflections on justice on to a different level. We claim that the obligation to provide offspring with genetic enhancement not only fails to solve the problem of social injustice, but may become one of its most serious causes. We argue for a non-domination approach in defining justice which brings us to the conclusion that the very idea of exercising control using offspring enhancement reproductive technologies is a form of injustice. It enables those who perform the enhancement to dominate those who are enhanced by them, leading to the corruption of the parental relationship. It also enables the domination of some specific properties that are meant to guarantee access to the most valuable social goods.

Chapter 9, Human self-understanding in the debate over moral human enhancement: autonomy and authenticity, addresses the problem of the philosophical sources of the debate over moral human enhancement held between transhumanists and bioconservatives. The chapter is aimed at showing that the opposing positions in the debate are grounded in different philosophical traditions, namely naturalistic (Darwinian) and rationalistic (Kantian), which define human nature differently. The former emphasizes the passive nature of human beings and understands morality as experience; the latter focuses attention on autonomy and agency, emphasizing agency and intentionality as the crucial components of morality. Moral improvement is defined differently in these varying traditions and leads to alternative conclusions concerning the idea of human moral enhancement. We attempt to challenge the naturalistic assumptions by employing the Aristotelian understanding of virtue and the Kantian understanding of agency – both these approaches combine the notion of human moral integrity rooted in reflexivity and intentionality, which is insufficiently developed from a reductive naturalistic standpoint and the consequentialist ethical doctrines adopted by the transhumanists.

We discuss the problem of moral enhancement further in **Chapter 10, Genetic enhancement and moral perfection**, where we pose the question of whether it is possible to develop a compromise that would reconcile some versions of the moral enhancement project with the traditional vision of the individual and autonomous moral development. We analyse four problems related to the issue of moral excellence: the problem of the right to be imperfect, the problem of the justification of sacrifice, the problem of moral evaluation of an agent's traits and the problem of the aims of moral enhancement and moral perfection.

The bioconservative view holds that we should avoid biomedical interventions enhancing human capacities. One of the objections against this view claims that it is based on a *status quo* bias which gives unjustified preference to the existing state of affairs. We provide an in-depth discussion of this objection in **Chapter 11, Bioconservatism and the preference for *status quo***. The aim of this chapter is to show the possibility of an interpretation of a bioconservative view under which it is possible to avoid the *status quo* bias objection.

Conflicts between procreative autonomy and a future child's interests seem to persist because of the lack of a clear conception of whether moral principles concerning a future child have an impersonal or a person-affecting character. We address this problem in **Chapter 12, Procreative autonomy in the context of person-affecting and impersonal reasons for human enhancement**. We discuss the principle of procreative beneficence and we describe the non-identity problem in the context of enhancing interventions. We analyse the possibility of balancing person-affecting and impersonal reasons as a solution to the problem of conflict between parental autonomy and beneficence.

Chapter 13, Intrinsic and instrumental values in the assessment of human enhancement, addresses the problem of balancing competing reasons for undergoing some enhancing interventions. It is often claimed that reasons based on the instrumental value of some enhanced trait should be balanced against reasons based on the risk of an elimination of the already existing intrinsic value related to engagement in traditional human practices. This joins the instrumental values of human capacities with the preservation of intrinsic values as seen from an individual and anthropocentric point of view. This reasoning requires some type of model to compare outcomes with respect to an increase or decrease in intrinsic and instrumental values. In this chapter, we analyse the possibility of building such a model based on the combination of two criteria: the positive and negative outcomes of using a given capacity and compatibility with current human standards of valuation related to the intrinsic value of projects or interpersonal relationships. We argue that the application of a category of weak superiority between such described outcomes may help to resolve some problems with the assessment of human enhancement, although it cannot serve as the only basis for the moral evaluation of enhancing interventions.

References

Berlin I (1969) Four Essays on Liberty. Oxford University Press, Oxford.

Bostrom N, Savulescu J (2013) Introduction. Human Enhancement Ethics: The State of the Debate. In: Savulescu J, Bostrom N (eds) Human Enhancement. Oxford University Press, Oxford.

Diamond C (1990) How Many Legs. In: Gaita R (ed) Value and Understanding: Essays for Peter Winch. Routledge, New York & London, pp.149–178.

Dworkin R (2011) Justice for Hedgehogs. The Belknap Press of Harvard University Press, Cambridge, MA&London.

Hodge JG Jr (2003) Genetic Testing and Screening. In: Post SG (ed) Encyclopedia of Bioethics, vol 2, 3rd ed. Thompson & Gale, New York, pp.1016–1020.

Kamm FM (2013) Bioethical Prescriptions To Create, End, Choose, and Improve Lives. Oxford University Press, Oxford&NewYork.

Knoppers BM, Bordet S, Isasi RM (2006) Preimplantation Genetic Diagnosis: An Overview of Socio-Ethical and Legal Considerations. Annual Review of Genomics and Human Genetics 7(1):201–221.

Murray RF Jr (2003) Genetic Counseling, Ethical Issues. In: Post SG (ed) Encyclopedia of Bioethics, vol 2, 3rd ed. Thompson & Gale, New York, pp. 948–952.

National Academy of Sciences and National Academy of Medicine (2017) Human Genome Editing. Science, Ethics, and Governance. Committee on Human Gene Editing: Scientific, Medical, and Ethical Considerations.

A Report of The National Academies of Sciences, Engineering, Medicine, The National Academies Press, Washington, DC. https://www.nap.edu/catalog/24623/human-genome-editing-science-ethics-and-governance (accessed: 1 July 2017)

Press N, Ariail K (2003) Genetic testing and screening. In: Post SG (ed) Encyclopedia of Bioethics, vol 2, 3rd ed. Thompson & Gale, New York, p 1002.

Quaid KA (2008) Predictive genetic Testing. In: Beauchamp TL et al. (eds) Contemporary Issues in Bioethics. Thomson Wadsworth, Belmont, pp. 243–247.

Sandel M (2007) The Case against Perfection. Ethics in the Age of Genetic Engineering. The Belknap Press of Harvard University Press, Cambridge MA-London.

Savulescu J, ter Meulen R., Kahane G. (eds) (2011) Enhancing Human Capacities. Wiley–Blackwell, Chichester; Malden, MA.

Part I: Genetic Selection

Marta Soniewicka

1 Ethical standards of genetic counselling and reproductive autonomy

There is a gap between sequencing and analysing data; as Esther Dyson neatly summarized the problematic nature of sequencing the genome: 'We know ninety words of Russian and we've been handed *War and Peace*' (Dyson in Angrist 2010, 206). Even when we get genetic information, we usually do not know how to understand it and use it to improve health. What is more, the ability to predict diseases outstrips our ability to treat them. By taking reproductive choices, the parents are facing irreversible and difficult life-altering decisions, in particular when an abnormality of the foetus is detected. In order to enhance their ability for reproductive choices, genetic counselling has been established and its scope was extended to other branches of genetic testing (Biesecker 2003).[1]

1.1 The aims and the principles of genetic counselling

The main goals of genetic counselling are: (1) providing useful information (to deliver genetic information to the parents to help them make reproductive choices; to help them understand and personalize technical and probabilistic genetic information; to elucidate the consequences of their choice based on genetic information); (2) providing medical help (enhancing parental ability to adopt to the consequences of their choice including information about medical help and treatment); (3) providing education (exploring the meaning of the information in the light of personal values and beliefs of the parents promoting parental preferences and self-determination in exercising reproductive choice); (4) providing psychological assistance (helping to minimize psychological stress of the parents and to increase personal control of the parents) (Biesecker 2003; Murray 2003). Besides, one could name the goal (5) to provide assistance to the prospective parents in coping with the moral problem which may occur if the values on which their decision is made are in conflict (helping the parents to identify the moral problem and to understand it according to their intuitions).

---

[1] In some countries genetic counselling is provided by physicians while in others it is a separate profession. In this chapter I will use the term 'genetic counsellor' as being equivalent to the term physician and vice versa.

To understand genetic information, one has to think in probabilities and not every patient is able to do so. Patients are not interested in the information about the probability of the risk of the onset of a disease, but they rather want to know if they should start preventive treatment. It is like with a weather forecast – you check it to get to know whether to take an umbrella or not with you while leaving home (Davies 2010). The genetic information provided by the counsellor must not only be understandable but also of a high quality and usefulness. By the quality of genetic information, one may mean analytical validity (guaranteeing accuracy and avoiding errors) and clinical validity (identifying the level of risk, preventing misinterpretation and misunderstanding), as well as clinical utility (the calculation of the risks and benefits of performing genetic testing) of the information. Genetic information of clinical utility is the information which can be used in order to improve health condition of the patient. It means that genetic testing should be generally performed in order to detect diseases that are treatable or of which symptoms can be alleviated (Davies 2010). Otherwise, there is a risk that the costs and harm (e.g. mental) of genetic testing would outweigh the benefits. Of course, there are also some people who may want to know about their genetic conditions or susceptibility for untreatable diseases in order to take important reproductive and life decisions.

Genetic counselling promotes the idea of the self-determination of patients, especially in their reproductive choices and is primarily aimed at providing neutral, useful, reliable and understandable information to make the decisions of prospective parents possible on the grounds of their own beliefs and sets of values. One may identify the following principles which were established to guarantee the realization of this aim: (1) nondirectiveness (promoting autonomy); (2) nonmaleficence and beneficence; (3) confidentiality and protecting privacy; (4) veracity and truth-telling (Murray 2003; cf. Beauchamp & Childress 1989; Engelhardt 1996). Let us consider them briefly.

1.1.1 Nondirectiveness and reproductive autonomy

The principle of nondirectiveness forbids the placing of any pressure on the patient that would result in influencing her decision (Wachbroit & Wasserman 2006). Genetic counsellors should not suggest (directly or indirectly) that the patient either perform particular genetic testing, or take any particular decisions based on the results of genetic testing. Furthermore, they should not implement their own moral values in any such decisions or manner that would determine the decision.

Yet it is worth emphasising that the principle of nondirectiveness has no absolute character. There are some situations in which the genetic counsellor may give priority to other principles if they remain in conflict with each other which always requires a justification. The most frequently given example is the conflict between the principle of nondirectiveness and the principle of nonmaleficence when the autonomous decision of the patient would harm others, what is particularly significant in the context of the parent-child relationship. For instance, one may consider a situation when the parents decide to perform a genetic test on their newborn child to determine whether the child has the requisite conditions for Huntington's disease (a very serious untreatable inherited disorder which results in the death of brain cells and which manifests its symptoms usually at the adult age of approx. 40–50 years). Such a decision may be ethically controversial since it is recommended not to perform genetic testing which does not evidently and directly benefit a child and may only result in harm (the knowledge about an untreatable disease may bring about a mental burden and stress) (Andorno 2004). The parents have the rights to control and determine the life of their children. Yet, according to such philosophers as Joel Feinberg, parental rights should be limited by the so-called rights-in-trust of their children, which means that the future rights of their children are entrusted for the time of their infancy to the parents who are supposed to protect these rights taking into account the good of their children (Feinberg 1982). By the good of the child Feinberg understands guaranteeing the child's future as being as open as possible (i.e. guaranteeing the widest scope of opportunities left for the decision of the child when it becomes adult), respecting the future autonomy of the child, and promoting the child's self-fulfilment. Assuming that everybody not only has the right to know, but also the right not to know about her genetic untreatable conditions, one may argue that genetic testing of a child for late-onset disease would limit its future autonomy, providing the child with genetic knowledge that one would not necessarily like to have (Andorno 2004).

The principle of nondirectiveness gains special significance in the context of reproduction where the stress on autonomy is stronger than in any other branches of medicine (see Chapters 3 & 12). A constitutional right of reproductive autonomy is defined by Ronald Dworkin as a right of women 'to control their own role in procreation unless the state has a compelling reason for denying them that control' (Dworkin 1994, 148). Procreative freedom has transformed its merely negative meaning (*liberty from* the intervention of others, including a state, in one's own reproduction) to a much broader positive meaning (*freedom to* procreate). The concept of reproductive autonomy was extended from a right to control unwanted fertility, to a right to control unwanted infertility (O'Neill

2005). Thus, Buchanan and others understand reproductive autonomy as the choice of whether to procreate, with whom, when, and by what means, determining also the choice of *what kind of children to have*, and of whether to have children biologically related or not etc. (Buchanan et al. 2007). This evolution in thinking about reproductive freedom consists in the fact that one not only wants to control the quantity of wanted children, but also *the quality of wanted children* (Davis 1997). In particular, the latter aspect may be morally problematic leading to moral conflicts in genetic counselling.

1.1.2 Nonmaleficence, beneficence

The principle 'first, do not harm' (*primum non nocere*) is one of the most fundamental principles of medical ethics and also plays a significant role in genetic counselling. One may expect that genetic counsellor will not harm the patients, quite the contrary, counselling should benefit the patient, according the principle of beneficence. In order to meet these expectations, one has to specify what benefits the patient and what may harm her. In the case of genetic counselling, it is hard to answer these questions because of two main reasons. Firstly, genetic information usually has a prognostic or predictive character and is based on probabilities which means that, in contrast to traditional medical information, they are concerned to a much higher degree with an unsure future prognosis regarding a health condition (e.g. susceptibility testing such as breast cancer and ovarian cancer tests based on prognostic markers; carrier testing which identifies healthy 'carriers' of a copy of a recessive disease gene that may result in a disease of the future child). Secondly, genetic information, in particular in the context of reproductive genetics, concerns other parties (future children, the other parent, the closest relatives, society), not only the one who is taking the decision (in the reproductive context this is usually the prospective mother). The good of the future child may be differently interpreted and will depend on the assumption of the normative status of a foetus or of an embryo which may bring about intricate questions in genetic counselling.

1.1.3 Confidentiality and protecting privacy

On the grounds of genetic counselling, the principle of the confidentiality of medical information and to protect the privacy of the patients gain a specific meaning too. The principle of confidentiality obliges the genetic counsellor to get the permission of the patient in any case in which the information is to be revealed to third parties. The physician is allowed to violate the principle of confidentiality only in exceptional cases, usually strictly regulated by the law, including the cases of high public interest (e.g. information required for a criminal procedure or in the case of epidemic) and the cases in which the information is essential for the life or the health of the third party (e.g. the information about HIV status may be essential for the health of a sexual partner).

Genetic information is shared by close relatives (siblings, parents, grandparents and children) and may be of significance for them too. For instance, the information about carrying the gene implicated in Tay-Sachs disease may benefit others when shared with siblings and other relatives to discover their genetic status; the information about the genetic condition for heart muscle disease may be important for the institution in which the patient is employed if the onset of this disease may constitute a risk for others (e.g. in the case of a pilot of a civil plane). Yet it is highly controversial whether genetic information may constitute a situation in which the physician has the right to inform a third party, or much more – the obligation, to inform about the shared risk. Assuming the probabilistic meaning of the information which does not provide certainty about the onset of a disease, one may claim that withholding such information cannot directly affect the life or the health of the third parties.

To illustrate this problem, let us consider a case in which a patient performs genetic carrier testing for CF. If the result of the genetic testing of both prospective parents is positive, i.e. if each of them is carrying a copy of a recessive gene, there is a risk that their child will be born with a disease. Let us assume that a prospective father got a positive result and told the genetic counsellor that he would keep the information secret from his wife, being afraid that she would leave him or refuse to have children with him. The risk that his wife is also a carrier of the recessive gene for CF is quite rare (it is estimated that one person in 25 can be a carrier for CF). What is more, even if she were a carrier, the risk of having an unhealthy child (assuming that they would not use PGD) for them is 25% (25% chance of having a healthy child, and 50% that the child would be a carrier). In this case, the genetic counsellor would have to decide which principle has the priority – the autonomy and privacy of the patient or the reproductive autonomy of his partner. Giving the probabilistic nature of the information, the limitation of reproductive autonomy does not constitute a direct risk to health or life, thus it seems unjustified to violate the principle of confidentiality in such a case.

1.1.4 Veracity and truth-telling

Finally, the last principle of veracity and truth-telling means that the genetic counsellor should neither lie to the patient nor hide any medical information from him, even for the good of the patient. In some exceptional cases, the physician may refrain from revealing the accidentally found genetic information which could bring mental harm and distress (e.g. accidentally found information about the condition for Alzheimer's) or which may result in breaking family bonds (e.g. accidentally found information that a parent is not genetically related to a child).

1.2 Moral challenges to genetic counselling

The genetic disorders covered by reproductive genetic testing may significantly differ in many ways. There is a big variety in the probabilities of the onset of the diseases – the onset of quite rare monogenic diseases (e.g. Huntington's disease) may be predicted with a probability close to certainty, while with most diseases (which are polygenic or multifactorial) the prediction of a manifestation of a disease in an individual case is very complicated and far from certainty (it may also depend on environmental issues and their correlations with particular genotypes). Genetic defects also differ in respect to the health burden they may provide; some of them with morbidity, some with imparity, and some affect health condition in a lesser degree. What is more, some genetic diseases manifest their symptoms later in life (so-called late-onset diseases). Therefore, the distinction between serious and not serious conditions or predispositions is very vague and thus may give rise not only to ethical questions but also to legal ones.[2] Thus, some argue that drawing a line between serious and trivial medical conditions is necessary and should be introduced to clinical practice by setting

---

[2] For instance, according to Polish law, a woman has the right to terminate a pregnancy if 'prenatal tests or other medical findings indicate a high risk that the foetus will be severely and irreversibly damaged or suffering from an incurable life-threatening disease' (Art. 4a of the 1993 Family Planning, Protection of the Human Foetus and Conditions Permitting Pregnancy Termination Act). The condition is limited in time until the foetus is capable of surviving outside the mother's body. The question is how one ought to interpret the meaning of 'severely and irreversibly damaged' foetus? Which condition counts as serious enough? The extreme negative examples seem easier to interpret. Terminal diseases such as Tay-Sachs or anencephaly may count as severe and irreversible damages as well as incurable life-threatening diseases. Yet there are conditions or predispositions that refer to disorders which are not terminal and do not cause suffering which could not be alleviated, such as haemophilia, most kinds of Down syndrome etc. In some cases, even if suffering may be alleviated, the lifespan of a person with a certain disease (like CF) may be limited; in others the disease may manifest its symptoms in older age, guaranteeing a healthy 40-50 years of life (Huntington's disease). Thus, the controversy about the interpretation of this condition for legal

ethical or legal standards (Botkin 1995; Botkin 1998). Others argue that drawing such a line would bring about eugenic polices by providing a distinction of who is genetically fit enough to be welcomed into the world and who is not (Parens & Asch 2003).

The ideal of neutrality seems to be undermined by offering the prospective parents the wide range of prenatal genetic testing for hundreds of conditions (usually from commercial reasons). The introduction of almost routine genetic testing set new standards for 'responsible reproduction'. It has a significant impact on shaping the attitude of parents toward their future children, as well as on their understanding of reproduction and parenthood.

One may also pose the opposite question, whether not providing the information about the IVF option by the physician would violate the principle of autonomy of the patients by limiting their scope of choice. One may argue that the principle of autonomy is not absolute and that it could be limited when the autonomous decision would harm others. Assuming that the physician considers that the embryo has moral status and should not be destroyed, she could find the negative selection of the embryos in such a case as inconsistent with her moral views. Would it be a conflict of the principle of autonomy with the principle of nonmaleficence in this case? Since there is no moral consensus about the moral status of an embryo and therefore no consensus concerning the right to be born or the right not to be born, it is more likely to interpret this conflict as a moral conflict between the autonomy of the physician and the autonomy of the patient if their moral views on reproduction differ significantly; in some cases it could also be considered as the conflict between autonomy and justice (Pellegrino & Thomasma 1993).

One can also use PGD for positive selection, and instead of weeding out a certain medical condition, one may choose to opt for it. For instance, there are some parents who are born deaf and understand their deafness as a significant part of their identity and culture and want their children to share it with them, so they use sperm sorting or PGD to select for deafness (Davis 1997; Davis 2010). Although such cases as a deliberate conception of a child with disability are a relatively rare practice thus far, they have already occurred and give rise to deep ethical controversies. One may pose the question of whether giving the patients value-free information in genetic counselling is ever fully possible in the reproductive context:

---

termination of pregnancy brought about legal suits (see *R.R. v. Poland*, application no. 27617/04, ECHR, the judgement of May 26, 2011).

Although deeply committed to the model of nondirective counseling, most genetic counselors enter the profession with certain assumptions about health and disability--for example, that it is preferable to be a hearing person than a deaf person. Thus, most genetic counselors are deeply troubled when parents with certain disabilities ask for assistance in having a child who shares their disability (Davis 1997, 7).

Some may argue that in such cases some degree of persuasion of prospective parents by the genetic counsellors is justified (Davis 1997; Davis 2010), while the others argue that such reproductive choices should be restricted by the law as harmful (Buchanan et al. 2007).

Assisting the parents in their idea of creating a disabled child must be a great moral challenge for genetic counselling deeply devoted to the model of nondirectiveness and reproductive autonomy. As Dena Davis argues:

> This way of looking at moral issues in genetic counselling often leaves both the counselors and commentators frustrated, for two reasons. First, by elevating respect for patient autonomy above all other values, it may be difficult to give proper weight to other factors, such as human suffering. Second, by privileging patient autonomy and by defining the patient as the person or couple who has come for counselling, there seems no 'space' in which to give proper attention to the moral claims of the future child who is the endpoint of many counselling interaction (Davis 1997, 7).

Davis considers this kind of conflict not as the conflict between beneficence and autonomy, but rather as the conflict between parental autonomy and the child's future autonomy. Yet her argumentation is not free of objections since if the parents decided to have a non-disabled child instead of a disabled one, it would be of no benefit for the latter one which was never born (Parfit 1987). By giving birth to a deaf child, they do not limit this particular child's open future (as it would be by refusing hearing implant for instance) since the only alternative for this child is not to be born (there is no such alternative for this child as to be born healthy, see Chapters 4, 5 and 12).

1.3 Virtue-based theory and genetic counselling

The moral problems or dilemmas that we face in reproductive genetics do not arise from biotechnological development but rather from problems with understanding the medical profession and its aims (Pellegrino & Thomasma 1993), as well as from the problem with defining such significant human practices as reproduction (Sandel 2007).

The relationship between the physician and the patient plays a significant role in understanding the meaning and the value of the medical profession. The physician-patient relationship is usually understood in two different ways, as: (a) the doctor-centred paternalistic model; (b) the patient-centred model based on autonomy. A paternalistic model of the physician-patient relationship is based on the assumption that medical professionals know better what is good for the progeny than parents; thus, they use the information asymmetry and the power of knowledge in the relationship with prospective parents in order to decide on their behalf. This model has been strongly challenged in Western societies in recent decades, especially in the context of reproduction as it was mentioned above. One of the reasons for giving priority to the reproductive autonomy in genetic counselling was the desire to disassociate current genomic medicine from the authoritarian eugenic polices that have been vehemently disavowed in modern liberal societies (Sorenson 1993, Caplan 1993; Davis 1997).

The opposite model of the physician-patient relationship leaves the unrestricted decision fully with parents. Reproductive autonomy gains the highest respect within this model but in the same time it may lead to liberal eugenics (Habermas 2003). This model is based on the assumption that the parents always want the best for their children. Yet, one has to remember that knowing what is the best does not result from wanting the best for the progeny. The role of the medical professionals is to provide the prospective parents with the best possible information that may help them to take the right and fully informed reproductive decision. Absolute reproductive autonomy shifts ethical responsibility for a medical decision from physicians to prospective parents, while healthcare professionals withdraw into a position of technical responsibility (Helén 2004). Thus, this model may lead to some ethical concerns too.

To address the problems of responsibility, Pellegrino and Thomasma provide another distinction between contractualist and an end-oriented beneficence model (Pellegrino & Thomasma 1993). The former one may appear as (a) consumer (where healthcare is defined as commodity, the physician is defined as the healthcare provider and the patient as the client) or as (b) a negotiated contract model (where equality and partnership between the physician and the patient is emphasised). The consumer or negotiated contract models are usually patient-centred in which the physician is reduced to the technical role of healthcare provider; they promote autonomy as the primary value. This approach can be characterized as mainly procedural, instrumental, legalistic, economic, technical, and based on minimal trust or even on a mistrustful attitude. Pellegrino and Thomasma criticize this approach as misleading since the relationship between the physician and the patient is not equal; the vulnerability and dependence of the patient is neglected in this model, as well as the asymmetry of knowledge. They also claim that the approach undermines trust, thus it may be also dangerous for the physician-patient relationship since it corrupts the meaning of the medical practice which rests on trust. In the contractualist model, the physician is aimed solely at fulfilling the terms of the agreement which does not cover such important aspects of medical practice as beneficence, compassion, fidelity to trust, self-effacement, etc.

Thus, the authors argue for the end-oriented beneficence model which is based on the covenant of the fidelity to trust. This approach emphasizes the significance of caring experience and the special, higher responsibility of the medical practitioners. The ends of the medical profession (such as: health, cure, technically correct and morally good decisions) are embedded in the practice, give medicine its distinctive character, structure the relationship, and determine the ethos of medical practice. Within this model, patients also have duties toward physicians (such as truth-telling, respecting the autonomy of the physician etc.). The physician is not an instrument to satisfy the desires and interests of the patient, but also first and foremost a moral agent too (an integral moral being), holding special responsibility attached to his profession and technical power. This model is supported by the virtue-based approach to ethics which can enhance, but not replace, the principle-based doctrine in medicine (Pellegrino & Thomasma 1993; Soniewicka 2018).

One cannot understand the meaning of the good physician independently of the characterisation of the medical virtues. Pellegrino and Thomasma term such medical virtues as: fidelity to trust, compassion, *phronesis* (prudence), justice, fortitude, temperance, integrity (Pellegrino & Thomasma 1993; see also Gelhaus 2012a; Gelhaus 2012b; Gelhaus 2013). These virtues are derivable from the ends of the profession and are linked with duties and principles; they rest upon the caring bond and the public trust (commitment to care) which constitutes the meaning of the medical practice.

The virtue-based approach constitutes maximalist (perfectionist) ethics in contrast to the minimalistic (contractualist) ethics. A virtuous person is habitually disposed to respect principles which she considers to be a part of who she is – thus, she could not do otherwise. Consider such issues as reproductive cloning or producing human-animal mixtures (hybrids and chimeras) – one may argue that a virtuous person would never consider such practices if they were inconsistent with her understanding of humanity and reproduction (cf. Kass 1997; Sandel 2007). According to this approach, ethics cannot be reduced to a dilemma-solving exercise, since 'One may develop substantial and skilful arguments leading to conclusions that no person of good character can accept' as Minor Hippias claimed (Minor Hippias in Pellegrino & Thomasma 1993, 20). Therefore, the medical ethos, as well as the character of the physician are so significant in medical ethics:

The character of the physician is an irreducible factor in the healing relationship. How he or she interprets the moral principles, selects the values that will predominate, and shape self-interest will be more important than how the moral principles are formulated (Pellegrino & Thomasma 1993, 29).

Assuming that medical practice is primarily aimed at the good of the patient and reproductive counselling also includes the good of the progeny, we have to remember that this aim cannot be reduced to its negative aspect – respecting the autonomy of the patient (nondirectiveness). The good of the patient encompasses the whole well-being of the patient, not only what is medically good, but also what is defined as good by the patient, and what is understood as the good for human beings as such and human beings as spiritual beings (Pellegrino & Thomasma 1993). What is more, this aim is person-oriented, thus one cannot give priority to the abstract sum of welfare or healthy genes in the population genetic pool over the good of particular human beings. Medical prudence requires the right balance between technical competences and moral judgements, acting with respect to other virtues and aims of medicine. If a medical intervention cannot benefit any particular human being but rather prevent its birth, one may question its moral justification (see Chapter 5).

The main objection to the virtue approach is that it is not sufficient for medical ethics since in a pluralistic modern society we are unable to define the objective good (flourishing) of the patient and thus this approach may lead to subjectivism and relativism (cf. McDougall 2007, Saenz 2010;[3] Holland 2011[4]). Principles, on the other hand, are universal and general. To refute that objection one may claim for combining both views: virtue ethics with principles and duties, claiming that they do not compete or replace each other, but they rather complement each

---

3   Rosalind McDougall claimed in her paper that the virtue-based approach to the ethics of reproduction justifies genetic selection for deafness and other impairments if they are shared by the parents since flourishing of a child may be differently defined depending on the environment-specific characteristics. Carla Saenz, in her response to McDougall, aptly points out that this argumentation does not do justice to virtue ethics at all (McDougall's line of argumentation is based on 'minimal requirement test', while virtue ethics requires excellence); Saenz concludes that virtue ethics is not sufficient to justification of moral permissibility of reproductive choices, claiming for prima facie principles instead.
4   Stephen Holland addresses the important distinction between application of virtue ethics to the personal morality of an individual and to societal decisions of legalization certain practices or medical procedures; he discusses the main objections to the latter and ponders the rejoinders to critics which could help in enhancing the methodology of virtue ethics.

other, constituting a more complete picture of moral life (I develop this position further in Soniewicka 2018). As Pellegrino and Thomasma write:

> Without principles, the moral life would rest on sand. There is too much variability in modern, secular, pluralistic society to trust that every person would act virtuously, or even that we could agree on what virtuous activity would entail in such an environment. Yet the adverse is also true. Ethics is far more than obeying rules (Pellegrino & Thomasma 1993, 165).

1.4 Concluding remarks

One may significantly enhance medical ethics, as well as improve our understanding of moral thought, by putting principles and duties into a broader picture of moral reasoning which is rooted in the character of the moral person and determined by the physician-patient relationship based on caring and trust (cf. Jonas 1974 & 1987). This offers the virtue-based approach to medical practice which was considered as the paradigm of virtue ethics by Aristotle (Aristotle 2011; Jaeger 1971; Pellegrino & Thomasma 1981; Pellegrino & Thomasma 1993). The virtue approach to medical ethics, in contrast to rationalist principle-based approach, does not promise any simple, universal and general solution to the reproductive problems considered in this book. The interpretation and application of the principles of genetic counselling are determined by our understanding of the aim of medicine and may differ and evolve depending on those who participate in the social practices which are at stake here.

References

Andorno R (2004) The Right Not to Know: an Autonomy Based Approach. Journal of Medical Ethics 30:435–440.

Angrist M (2010) Here Is a Human Being. At the Dawn of Personal Genomics. Harper Perennial, New York.

Aristotle (2011) Nicomachean Ethics (trans: BartlettRC, CollinsSD). Chicago University Press, Chicago & London.

Beauchamp T, Childress J (1989) Principles of Biomedical Ethics, 3rd ed. Oxford University Press, New York.

Biesecker BB (2003) Genetic Counseling, Practice Of. In: Post SG (ed) Encyclopedia of Bioethics, vol 2, 3rd ed. Thompson & Gale, New York, pp. 952–955.

Botkin JR (1995) Fetal Privacy and Confidentiality. Hastings Center Report 25(5):32–39.

Botkin JR (1998) Ethical Issues and Practical Problems in Preimplantation Genetic Diagnosis. The American Journal of Law, Medicine and Ethics 26:17–28.

Buchanan A, Brock DW, Daniels N, Wikler D (2007) From Chance to Choice: Genetics and Justice. Cambridge University Press, Cambridge & New York.

Caplan AL (1993) Neutrality is not morality: the ethics of genetic counseling. In: Bartels DM, LeRoy BS, Caplan AL (eds) Prescribing our future: ethical challenges in genetic counseling. Aldine de Gruyter, New York, pp. 149–165.

Davies K (2010) The $1,000 Genome. The Revolution in DNA Sequencing and the New Era of Personalized Medicine. Free Press, New York & London.

Davis DS (1997) Genetic Dilemmas and the Child's Right to an Open Future. Hastings Center Report 27(2):7–15.

Davis DS (2010) Genetic Dilemmas: Reproductive Technology, Parental Choices, and Children's Futures. Oxford University Press, Oxford.

Dworkin R (1994) Life's Dominion. An Argument about Abortion, Euthanasia, and Individual Freedom. Vintage Books, New York.

Engelhardt HT Jr (1996) The Foundations of Bioethics. Oxford University Press, New York.

Feinberg J (1982) The Child's Right to an Open Future. In: Aiken W, LaFollette H (eds) Whose Child? Children's Rights, Parental Authority, and State Power. Totowa, New Jersey, pp. 124–153.

Gelhaus P (2012a) The Desired Moral Attitude of the Physician: (I) Empathy. Medical Health Care and Philosophy 15(2):103–113.

Gelhaus P (2012b) The Desired Moral Attitude of the Physician: (II) Compassion. Medical Health Care and Philosophy 15(4):397–419.

Gelhaus P (2013) The Desired Moral Attitude of the Physician: (III) Care. Medical Health Care and Philosophy 16(2):125–139.

Habermas J (2003) The Future of Human Nature. Polity Press, Oxford.

Helén I (2004) Technics over life: risk, ethics and the existential condition in high-tech antenatal care. Economia e Sociedade 33:28–51.

Holland S (2011) The Virtue Ethics Approach to Bioethics. Bioethics 25:192–201.

Jaeger W (1971) Paidea: The Ideals of Greek Culture, vol 3. Oxford University Press, New York & Oxford.

Jonas H (1974) Philosophical Essays: From Ancient Creed to Technological Man. Atropos Press, New York.

Jonas H (1987) Technik, Medizin und Ethik: Zur Praxis des Prinzips Verantwortung. Suhkamp, Frankfurt am Main.

Kass LR (1997) The wisdom of repugnance. The New Republic 2(6):17–26.

McDougall R (2007) Parental Virtue: a New Way of Thinking about the Morality of Reproductive Actions. Bioethics 21:181–190.

Murray RF Jr (2003) Genetic Counseling, Ethical Issues. In: Post SG (ed) Encyclopedia of Bioethics, vol 2, 3rd ed. Thompson & Gale, New York, pp. 948–952.

O'Neill O (2005) Autonomy and Trust. Cambridge University Press, Cambridge.

Parens E, Asch A (2003) Disability Rights Critique of Prenatal Genetic testing: Reflections and Recommendations. Mental Retardation and Developmental Disabilities Research Reviews 9:40–47.

Parfit D (1987) Reasons and Persons. Clarendon Press, Oxford.

Pellegrino ED, Thomasma DC (1981) A Philosophical Basis of Medical Practice. Oxford University Press, New York & Oxford.

Pellegrino ED, Thomasma DC (1993) The Virtues in Medical Practice. Oxford University Press, New York & Oxford.

Saenz C (2010) Virtue Ethics and the Selection of Children with Impairments: a Reply to Rosalind McDougall. Bioethics 24:299–506.

Sandel M (2007) The Case against Perfection. Ethics in the Age of Genetic Engineering. The Belknap Press of Harvard University Press, Cambridge, MA & London.

Soniewicka M (2018) The Moral Philosophy of Genetic Counseling: Principles, Virtues and Utility Reconsidered. In: Soniewicka M (ed) The Ethics of Reproductive Genetics – Between Utility, Principles, and Virtues. Springer International Publishing AG part of Spinger Nature, Cham, pp. 33–47.

Sorenson JR (1993) Genetic Counseling: Values that have Mattered. In: Bartels DM, LeRoy BS, Caplan AL (eds) Prescribing our future: ethical challenges in genetic counseling. Aldine de Gruyter, New York, pp. 3–14.

Wachbroit R, Wasserman D (2006) Patient Autonomy and Value-Neutrality in Nondirective Genetic Counseling. In: Kuhse H, Singer P (eds) Bioethics. An Anthology. Blackwell Publishing, Oxford, pp. 237–245.

Wojciech Lewandowski

2 The criteria of rationality in genetic selection

Future parents are faced with many choices and decisions. The most common of these are when to have a child, how many to have, our short and long-term plans concerning how we plan to assure the child of the requisite conditions needed to guarantee a better life, their health and their vision of the family. The number of such decisions grows considerably when assisted procreation is concerned and includes the choice of clinic, donor, surrogate or embryo. Each of these decisions may be regarded as existential ones since it is upon these that questions such as those concerning whether the child will exist and what their life will be like are decided. It is of the utmost importance that such decisions are taken rationally.

Does a moral obligation exist which states that the decision to have a baby must be a rational one? Since there is a chance that one may become a parent in an unplanned, accidental manner, there is a chance that this requirement may not be fulfilled. From the popular perspective, the rational requirement in relation to natural childbirth tends to be lower. This usually means that it suffices for certain conditions to be met: the rational potential of the parents usually means they are adults, capable of living independently, are free of any transmittable diseases which might adversely affect the health of the child and a willingness to bring them up and ensure that they have a good start in life. In such cases, even when the child is unplanned, it is possible to claim that the parent has used their procreative autonomy in a rational manner. The moral requirements connected with rationality increase with assisted procreation and may not only encompass the necessity of considering the genetic factors which may influence the life of the child but also the selection of such attributes which would minimize the risk of suffering and permit the parents to choose and realize certain preferences which do not conflict or collide with the autonomy and future rights of the child. These include the right to an open future or the need to take into consideration the interests of other people and impact on the future condition of society.

The discussion concerning the concept of rationality in respect to the criteria for genetic selection is part of a broader debate concerning rationality in ethics and whose fundamental problem may be best summarized in the form of a question: does an ahistorical and independent rationality exist which is free from cultural and linguistic conditioning and which cannot be reduced to some form of community traditions, including philosophical ones, that would allow a moral subject to control their lives. The positions in such a debate range widely, from the radical negation of the existence of such a possibility through accepting one dominant rationality to the recognition of a pluralism of mutually complementary rationalities. The context of being a parent and making such decisions in which emotions play an equal role to convictions and reasoning, results in a discussion which is increasingly difficult to manage. Do disabled parents act rationally in using genetic selection to ensure that their child is also disabled? Is the adoption of unused embryos after in vitro treatment also rational? These competing conceptions of rationality must contain a position concerning the moral status of embryos and the relationship between axiological and normative judgements.

In this text, I will attempt to analyse this discussion in terms of the confrontational and non-confrontational conceptions of rationality which surround genetic selection. The first two parts will concern the confrontation between the instrumental and substantive conceptions of rationality which claim that the agent deciding upon the matter at hand uses different criteria than those found in the given conception is acting under the influence of a prejudice or self-deception. In the third part I will examine the non-confrontational conception which contains the possibility of assuaging or eliminating allegations of irrationality on the basis of incompatible criteria.

2.1 Bayesian and non-Bayesian parents

Max Weber is one of the most important sources in the discussion concerning the criteria of rationality. He divides social activity into the rational, traditional and affective (Weber 1978). He includes in the list of rational actions those which are based on instrumental rationality or the autotelic. In the first case, rational choice means the calculation of costs and benefits whilst the other means striving for the goal regardless of the costs. Traditional activity is not based on reasons but rather on the social customs familiar to the agent whilst affective actions are an expression of the mental state experienced by the agent. Applying such a simple model to the matter of decisions concerning genetic selection allows the consideration of all the current positions in the debate. The consequentialist position would make the greatest use of instrumental rationality whilst those in favour of the sanctity of life would appeal to autotelic rationality. The contemporary ethical debate tends to privilege instrumental rationality criteria in the sense that they are used in the theoretical decisions. Unfortunately, the use of the above model lies beyond the bounds of possibility afforded by rational justification based on communitarian principles whilst the fear of change is the accusation most frequently laid at the door of bio-conservatives. The main strategies for defending these positions against accusations of irrationality is often shown by the fact that at their heart lies a substantive conception of rationality assumes that the autotelic reasons have priority over instrumental ones.

Rationality based on calculation is obviously connected with the selection of embryos. Instrumental rationality consists not only of assessing the embryos but also the invasive and non-invasive means of their selection. The basic goal of selection is the precise identification of the embryos whose selection will lead to the birth of a healthy child. Inaccuracies or errors in the application of this assessment may lead to, amongst others, a multiple pregnancy, premature birth or birth of a child with genetic defects (Makrakis et al. 2016). Thanks to the growing knowledge about the genetic basis for many illnesses, PGD is also moving closer to the possibility of being able to make even more precise diagnoses of the health of a child after birth and other traits which will influence their quality of life.

In terms of the choice between natural procreation and IVF together with genetic selection, the decision lies in the probability of obtaining a healthy child. Both in the case of natural procreation and assisted, the possible scenarios for parents may be summarized in a simplified form as the following:

1) A healthy child is born
2) Due to genetic defect of the embryo the implantation does not take place; the mother miscarries or chooses to have an abortion.
3) The embryo is healthy, but the implantation does not take place or the mother miscarries
4) A child is born with a genetic defect

One might maintain that at first glance, most people would not have a problem with the above list, although it should be noted that the list is neither sharply defined nor complete. Many parents would maintain that an abortion would be less preferable to a miscarriage or giving birth to a child with genetic defects. For others, giving birth to a child with genetic defects would be preferable to not having a child at all. Ordering such preferences would depend on the type of defect and the chances of having another child if the pregnancy is not taken to term. The incomplete nature of the list lies in the fact that it does not account for the possibility of multiple pregnancies and possible scenarios which may occur after the child has been born, for example the potential external support available for caring for and raising the child.

The dominant Bayesian conception entails that the subject should act in such a way that maximises their subjective expectations of utility. Bayesian theory allows the subject to achieve a coherence between the preferences possessed, their convictions with regard expected results and the subjective probability of their occurrence. What ultimately determines the rationality or irrationality of a given choice are ultimately the beliefs and desires of the person taking the decision, since the probability and utility functions are dependent on them. The facts concerning the external world and the objective concept of probability do not have an effect on the assessment as to the rationality of the decision. The likelihood of being a happy and good parent in the case of giving birth to a sick or healthy child may only be defined and determined by the parent taking the decision and, thus, any calculation concerning the influence that giving birth to a healthy or a sick child may have on the quality of life of the parents need not be judged according to the rationality of the decision. A general criticism of Bayesian theory is that in the case of the ideal subject making the decision, it does not supply any normative indications. The original ordering of preferences is enough to allow them to decide in a risky situation. In terms of the non-ideal agent who possesses an incomplete order of preferences, utility and probability, Bayesian theory is also a subject of criticism. Firstly, it shows that the assumption that the theory permits the non-ideal agent to complete all the gaps in their initial order of preferences is far too optimistic (Peterson 2008, 207). In terms of the preferences of parents – even if they possess very concrete expectations, they frequently do not consider all the potential scenarios associated with bringing up a child. Bayesian theory may therefore be insufficient in order to complete an initially incomplete set of preferences. Furthermore, the theory does not give a complete enough justification in the eyes of its critics for the initial order of preferences either, ultimately leaving substantive rationality to be a matter of taste (Peterson 2008, 207). Utility and probability, in the opinion of Peterson, may be used not to help define preferences in uncertain situations but rather as the basis of a probabilistic theory of uncertain preferences[1].

The most famous example of the application of a non-Bayesian conception of rationality in ethics is John Rawls' theory of justice which maintains that actions take place in accordance with the Maximin principle which calls for choosing the option which gives the greatest pay-off in the worst case scenario.[2] Such an

---

[1] The criteria of rationality in non-ideal subject were formulated by, amongst others,: Paul Weirich (Weirich 2004), John Pollock (Pollock 2006).

[2] As well as Rawls, non-Bayesian decision theory in ethics is utilized by David Gauthier (1986) and John Broome (1991).

ethical theory does not refer to subjective probability but is connected to the conception of rationality which is based on values, maintaining that Maximin would be a principle adopted in order to safeguard opportunities to attain fundamental goods.[3] The rationality of individual decisions is transferred to the level of the rationality of social choice. This part of the theory of Rawls' has been applied to genetic selection by authors such as Buchanan, Brock, Daniels and Wikler (Buchanan et al. 2000). According to this framework, if every rational subject were to direct themselves according to the Maximin principle in fulfilling the demands of justice, the result would be to guarantee each the possibility to participate in the 'dominant cooperative framework'. On the one hand this conception gives a rather broad room for manoeuvre in terms of the permissible rational choice between natural procreation and assisted, as well as decisions made with regard to genetic selection itself. Here it constitutes the basic limit of the acceptance of such a state which gives a reasonable probability that the new person will be able to enjoy participation in social life. Attention should be paid, however, to the fact that rationality based on the Maximin principle, when applied directly to the individual choices of parents, would warrant the use of preimplantation genetic diagnosis to minimize the risk of having a baby with genetic defects or, if the selection was nontherapeutic, to minimize the risk that the parents' choice of features would be incompatible with possible life plans of the child (Agar 1999, 178).

The main accusation laid against the Maximin rule is the necessity of taking into account all the negative consequences of our choices, even the least likely. According to John Harsanyi 'it is extremely irrational to make your behaviour wholly dependent on some highly unlikely unfavourable contingencies regardless of how little probability you are willing to assign them' (Harsanyi 1975, 595). One should, however, note that the participation in the 'dominant cooperative framework' depends not only on the health of the child but also upon the society's ability to adapt and adjust itself to the presence within it of less privileged people (Kamm 2013, 256). The evaluation of the application of the Maximin principle by parents regarding the birth of a disabled child would depend on the substantive concept of the rational life plan (Sparrow 2011), a conviction of the social obligation to guarantee support and care for the worst-off and a general conception

---

3   The conditions of the rationality used in Maximin are, for Rawls, a justified skepticism about the ability to properly estimate the probability of each option, the acceptability of losses due to the lack of other options and the unacceptable nature of certain effects which would carry with them other options (Rawls 1971, 154–155).

of the value of life[4]. Whether the parents' decision is based on heuristics or error depends not only on the concept of instrumental rationality, but primarily on the concept of substantive rationality.

2.2 Substantive rationality

Whilst in the case of instrumental rationality the problem is to determine the optimal strategy in a situation of risk and uncertainty, the divisions between competing concepts are even greater with respect to substantive rationality. This problem may be overcome by basing the criteria for PGD solely on instrumental rationality. This strategy is adopted by Tomasz Żuradzki, in whose opinion the justification of the application of PGD in order to choose the best embryo for implantation does not necessarily rely upon any conception of substantive rationality. The criteria for the rationality of decision making under uncertainty and risk, together with the principle of respect for patient autonomy, are entirely sufficient as the basis for this obligation. Firstly, the intuitive rule of Bayesian decision theory gives us a variety of options, in which the probability of winning is greater. Since all rational agents which the selection concerns, including embryos, to the extent that they are able to make decisions, accepted this rule, the principle of patient autonomy requires one to act in accordance with it (Żuradzki 2014). As a justification Żuradzki appeals to the example of two siblings in a life-threatening situation. Terrorists are threatening to kill one of them and only they can choose which one is killed. If they knew that one of them might be the bearer of an incurable genetic disorder which will result in their death within a year, and they have the ability to take a test which will reveal which of the siblings has it, then for both it would be a rational decision to take the test and sacrifice themselves in the case of a positive result.

Żuradzki's argument is founded on the assumption that it may be applied regardless of the conception of substantive rationality since in every such conception, life is regarded as essential to the achievement of any goal (Żuradzki 2014, 14). It seems, however, that for this kind of argument to work, it is necessary to appeal to at least some consequentialist assumptions. First, it should be assumed that there is no any non-consequential value that the condemned brother may achieve in the last year of his life. Secondly, if healthy sibling decides

---

[4] The assumption taken by David Benatar, that every life is not worth living allows to recognise that applying both Bayesian rules, and the Maximin principle allows to justify the rationality of refraining from procreation in any given case (Benatar 2006, 181–182).

to sacrifice her life, there are excluded any non-consequential considerations about value of this sacrifice, such as fulfilling oneself as a person through making one's life a gift to another person.[5] Thirdly, Żuradzki's argument is correct only assuming the possibility of interpersonal comparisons between different people's lives, and calls for the adoption of an assumption that it is morally acceptable not only to sacrifice one's own life, but also to sacrifice the life of another person in similar circumstances. The assumption about the hypothetical consent of a person whose life is taken is based on the calculation of life's length and quality.

The example above shows that if the reference to at least some assumptions of substantive rationality is necessary, then consequentialism seems to be the theory that is the easiest to reconcile with the decision theory. Both these theories share the concept of utility, and thus the criterion of substantive rationality will be based on the concept of utility. According to John Harsanyi, the Bayesian conception of rationality, in conjunction with Pareto efficiency, leads to an almost mathematical necessity to accept utilitarian ethics (Harsanyi 1978, 223).[6] Although this argument has not won widespread acceptance, especially in the context of assisted procreation, the consequentialist conception has become the primary example of using rationality when faced with the problem of selecting embryos. The individual aspect of the parents' decision as to the child's genetic endowment can be quite easily aligned with the social choice theory, as good health is both consistent with the parents' wishes, and comprises value to society. According to consequentialists, referring to a specific, tangible impact of undertaken actions on other people is a rational justification of the moral evaluation of genetic selection. To allow an assessment of this impact, there are three degrees of the value of human life resulting from our decisions: 'a life more worth living', 'a life less worth living', and 'a life not worth living'. In this perspective, a genetic procedure is considered acceptable if it does not lead to giving birth to persons living 'a life not worth living', and if it leads to improving the quality of life of all people it has an impact on, when compared with any alternative course of action.

The consequentialist conception does not fall within Weber's category of autotelic rationality. Although the quality of human life is an internal value, it is denumerable, allowing to consider the worthwhileness of having a child with a certain quality of life, taking into account the costs and possible alternative options. In most cases, natural procreation could be justified by low costs and

---

5   This condition is related with the condition that excludes taking one's own life directly, which, however, does not occur in the present example.
6   According to Harsanyi, the utilitarianism of principles avoids the famous Arrow's impossibility theorem (Harsanyi 1979).

a relatively low probability of having a child with genetic defects. In the case of assisted procreation, when there is no other alternative or if genetic selection provided a real possibility of improving the future quality of life of the child or other people, failure to take advantage of it or relying on blind luck would be irrational (see Chapters 4, 5, 9 and 12). One of the main arguments against consequential criterion is that significant cost reductions and improving the effectiveness of assisted procreation procedures would lead to the recognition that natural procreation will no longer be a rational choice in the future. However, isn't the reluctance to recognise this conclusion merely the result of the evolutionary adaptation of the human species, for whom natural procreation was the only way of passing on genes?

Leon Kass is one of the authors who defend the rationality criterion based on natural human dispositions. The justification for the 'wisdom of repugnance' is one of the elements of this defence. According to Kass, some of our emotional responses are an expression of deep wisdom, which not always can be articulated in terms of reason (Kass 2002, 150). The concept of rationality, however, cannot be based only on this element. If there is no criterion to distinguish emotional responses expressing that wisdom from fear of change, aversion to risk or other emotions together referred to as 'the yuck factor', then when it comes to genetic selection, an agent acting in line with this concept is not able to fend off allegations of irrationality. The criterion provided by Kass refers to the natural inclination to procreate and bring up offspring, which have a profound relation to personal development. Biological facts about human procreation, associated with every man's unique genetic endowment derived from both parents are inseparably joined with the individuality and equality of all people, equally coming upon the world in a familial nexus of origin and fulfilling their humanity in the limited time given before death (Kass 2002, 53–4). The criterion of compatibility with natural human inclinations precludes selection and is met only by natural procreation. The response to this position may rely on demonstrating that natural human inclinations do not exclude selection. Among the examples discussed in contemporary ethics, one may point to those, where choosing one child is the only chance of saving one of them when it is not possible to save both, such as the example of the Siamese twins Mary and Jodie (Harris 2001) or the Sophie's choice, which is already a classic in the discussion of moral dilemmas (Styron 1976). Assuming the moral status of embryos, genetic selection would be analogous to those dramatic choices and could cause similar emotional reactions.[7] It does not change the fact, however, that these emotions cannot constitute a criterion of rational choice, whereas the reasons for choosing the child with the greatest chance of survival in a good condition would not be eliminated. Harris illustrates this argument with different variants of situations concerning a woman named Martha (Harris 1998). He differentiates between being wronged and being harmed as a result of coming into the world. In the first case, a child is born burdened with diseases resulting in a negative quality of life (i.e. it would be rational to choose non-existence rather than life in this state), whereas in the second – life has a positive quality, but it is burdened with a disability. According to Harris, it is wrong when parents deliberately bring avoidable suffering into the world. The exception to this rule is a situation, when Martha has no other option of bringing a child into the world, that is to say, each of her possible children would have the same disability. According to the criteria of instrumental rationality, refraining from having biological offspring would allow to avoid such a situation, however Harris's exception is based on the assumption that the chance of having a biologically related child is almost universally acknowledged to be one of the most worthwhile experiences and important benefits of life (Harris 1985, 152). The refusal to recognise this possibility of any person is considered serious harm. Introducing this element of substantive rationality brings Harris and Kass's position closer, however in the former parents could not calculate the value of having a child and the quality of its life, unless the quality was positive.[8] Harris's attempt to reconcile calculation with autotelic values seems problematic. The lower the child's quality of life, the more controversial the introduced exception becomes in terms of consequentialist assumptions. The possibility of having a child with a quality of life only a little higher that the bare minimum would not differ significantly from Kass's position in respect of a situation, in which the child's quality of life falls slightly below this level.

For authors such as Kass and Sandel, the main way of defending against the allegation of irrationality is to demonstrate that tradition and emotions do not constitute the ultimate criterion of rationality, but allow to discover innumerable values. For Kass and Sandel, the question about the essential purpose and meaning of human life is the starting point for deciding about these issues. Sandel, however, interprets human life as a gift. Those brought to the world should be treated as a gift, and thus – surrounded by unconditional love, precluding any

---

7   The analysis of the problem of parental attachment and responsibility can be found in Chapter 7.
8   The category of 'rational irrationality', introduced by Bryan Caplan, may form a basis for this strategy (Caplan 2001).

exploitation. According to this approach, all forms of designing future humans or embryo selection are wrong, because they cannot be reconciled with unconditional parental love. These values have priority both over denumerable values subject to instrumental rationality, as well as over individual preferences and desires of the parents. This assumption implies that parents can act rationally even without using decision theory. The fundamental values to which parents refer would constitute the primary limitation in decisions regarding genetic selection. Intentionally selecting an embryo that has the lowest chance of survival or whose likelihood of living in enormous suffering is very high can be justified as wrong even without referring to the quality of life criterion, but to the ideal parent-child relationship or to the rights resulting from the embryo's personal dignity. The argument about the non-countability of values goes hand in hand with the normative order to protect these values. Each embryo created in the IVF programme has equal right to life, and therefore, instrumental rationality can only help in choosing those measures that may optimally serve to protect this right.

The problem associated with utilising substantive rationality is its radical prospectiveness. According to Jürgen Habermas, each of these values is deeply rooted in culture and constitutes the identity of individuals and societies. The range of possible values and beliefs that parents refer to is so wide that it is difficult to identify a common standard of substantive rationality. Refusal to take advantage of genetic diagnostics will be considered irrational from the point of view of a person who adopts naturalistic assumptions about human existence and the value of human life, but from the perspective of parents convinced of the absolute and equal moral status of human embryos, it would be irrational to make the decision on their implantation dependent on their genetic endowment. According to Weber's analogy, each of those perspectives constitutes a separate sphere of values, each governed by a different god (Weber 1946, 148). In such a case, rationality's only requirement would be the requirement for internal consistency. According to Habermas, this way of thinking does not reach the level of moral reasoning, which must be included in the most general structures of human communication. Another problem in applying substantive rationality is that innumerable values are difficult to formalize in terms of modern decision theory. The criteria of rationality do not apply to the results of actions, but to their compliance with standards that protect individual values. On the one hand, this allows divalent evaluation of actions, but on the other, there is a whole range of circumstances affecting whether, and to what extent, a given action respects a given value. The above issues form the basis for seeking non-confrontational criteria of rationality.

2.3 Non-confrontational criteria of rationality

There are three main ways to eliminate allegations of irrationality formulated on the basis of confrontational criteria of rationality: referring to discourse, referring to the hope of technological progress, which will eliminate the subject of the dispute, and referring to the criterion of cohesion as the minimum criterion of rationality.

In the first case, practical discourse on the standards that protect generalised interests would be a test for the rationality of the parents' decision. The rationality of communication introduced by Habermas is, on the one hand, distinct from instrumental rationality, and on the other – from substantive rationality, constituting a higher level of reflection. Exploring the context of social decisions allows to reconstruct how the competing criteria of rationality can be connected by convincing arguments on the development of society (Habermas 1985, 121). According to Habermas, decentralisation, reflection and distinction between spheres of values constitute the criteria of rationality. Formal terms of communication rationality applied to bioethical issues lead to the recognition that only those interventions that do not restrict autonomy are permissible. Assuming that everyone has the need to autonomously shape their identity and the awareness that what remains out of control within it has been formed by natural processes, and not designed by other people. Future people would not agree for procedures that restrict their autonomy, and therefore it is a reason for considering them to be wrong (Habermas 2003). According to the critics of this approach, although it is formulated in such a way as to constitute a second-order theory, allowing to achieve neutrality between clashing concepts, the accepted assumptions concerning the autonomy and self-understanding of the human species allow to qualify it among the confrontational theories of rationality when it comes to genetic selection (Häyry 2010, 36–40).

The second way of ensuring complementarity between the various criteria of rationality is through invoking hope offered by technological progress. According to Dena Devis, what is worrying in genetic selection is not the calculation of the parents' preferences and the child's future itself, but the risk that the more time, money, and effort is invested by parents in measures leading to the birth of a healthy baby with the selected characteristics, e.g. sex, the less likely it is for them to support a child devoid of these features (Davis 2010, 42). Access to means of achieving parental preferences that are cheap, easy, and compatible with natural procreation could eliminate moral problems associated with selection. In accordance with the criteria based on this assumption, it would be rational to strive for having a child naturally, utilising measures where the selection of gametes and embryos takes place without the participation of the parents or medical personnel, and which provide results most similar to artificial selection. With the current lack of non-controversial measures or in the case of measures that make it necessary to balance the preference between calculation or naturalness, the above solution requires a secondary criterion. In addition, Davis's assumption that the probability of not accepting a child possessing undesirable characteristics is proportional to the effort that has gone into the attempts to create these features may be waived by another assumption that 'parental love always prevails' (see Chapter 6).

The third way of dealing with hidden religious or ideological assumptions and different conceptions of values is proposed by Matti Häyry. While referring to the enthusiastic adoption of the competing concepts of rationality concerning the use of genetics to improve human life by various groups, he assumes that there is no Archimedean point that allows to compare different criteria. Taking into account the advantages of each of these concepts, i.e. potential calculation, reference to absolute values, and universal acceptance, it would be difficult to formulate a coherent, non-arbitrary criterion of rationality for parents, covering the most important aspects of their life and the life of the child. Therefore, he proposes his own, non-confrontational concept of rationality:

> *Non-confrontational notion of rationality* – a decision is rational insofar as it is based on beliefs that form a coherent whole and are consistent with how things are in the world; and it is aimed at optimising the immediate or long-term impacts on entities that matter (Häyry 2010, 43).

In accordance with this definition, it is possible to recognise different decisions as rational. A decision's degree of rationality depends on the degree of internal and external consistency. The same criteria should bear similar results in similar cases. Häyry's non-confrontational criterion of rationality, therefore, seems to assume the atomism of reasons, claiming that if some characteristic operates as a reason in one case, then it must likewise operate as a reason in every other case (Dancy 2004, 7). What is more, the adoption of this non-confrontational notion of rationality allows one to say that there are many rational solutions to the problem of genetic selection, which serve as a good foundation for answering the challenges of genetics, so far as they remain internally consistent and acknowledge facts. Häyry proposes the adoption of the polite bystander's perspective, which assumes that competitive positions are internally consistent and may form a rational solution to a given problem. The polite bystander assumes reflective equipoise of the individual criteria of rationality, noting that each of them has significant support among professionals dealing with philosophy, bioethics, and other relevant disciplines. The category of reflective equipoise is formulated based on the analogy with clinical equipoise as a condition for the permissibility of clinical trials. In accordance with this criterion, clinical trials of a new treatment are permissible if there is a state of uncertainty about the relative merits of two different treatments (Freedman 1987, 141–5). The purpose of applying the clinical equipoise condition is to make the most effective therapies available without exposing the participants of clinical trials to unnecessary risks. Applying this analogy allows to place the opponents of genetic selection on a different level than the representatives of anti-vaccination movements or proponents of homeopathic medicines, where the equipoise criterion cannot be used.

The second element that characterises the polite bystander position is the pursuit towards achieving reflective equipoise, so that the problem' solution consists in a stable balance between general principles and specific judgements. Therefore, the 'polite bystander' position assumes refraining from the adoption of any of these posts, with the exception of those solutions that seem to be shared by all parties. Philosophical reflection can only demonstrate the deficiency of certain arguments and leave others open to discussion. However, it cannot provide universal evidence of validity or invalidity of a certain genetic procedure. In accordance with this concept, the parents' choice would satisfy the requirement of rationality if it were made on the basis of one of the criteria present in decision theory, reflecting their beliefs, preferences, subjectively or objectively assessed probability concerning the entire life of the child and being a parent, as well as objective facts about the world and society, in which the child will live. a practical consequence of this approach is found in the non-directivity postulate in genetic counselling (see Chapter 1). The non-confrontational notion of rationality allows to include multiple positions only because it contains the general formula of 'that, what is important from a moral perspective', allowing the parents to substitute this variable with what they deem important. As in the case of Bayesian rationality, we will not find any reasons for the original ordering of preferences here. According to Peter Herrisone-Kelly, Häyry's atomism excludes the possibility of silencing reasons (Herrisone-Kelly 2011). Paradoxically, one may formulate a position of non-confrontational rationality competitive to Häyry's criterion, one that assumes reason-holism, which states that if a feature operates as a reason in one case, it does not have to operate as a reason in a different one, or be an opposite reason.

The criticism of Habermas and Häyry shows that each non-confrontational criterion of rationality at the n level becomes confrontational from the point of view of level $n+1$. The above attempts to gather parental decisions in a single concept of rationality delineates an alternative, that it will either be prospective rationality, devoid of universality and potentially conflicting impartial principles, or it will appeal to more general criteria of neutrality. None of these options allows parents to fully discover what is important from the moral point of view in the context of procreation. A solution to this alternative could be found in replacing the pluralism of rationality with a pluralism of reasons, together with rules allowing for their comparison. This way, we avoid the need for searching for a higher-order criterion of rationality. Indicating different types of reasons formulated from different perspectives, finding the links between them and highlighting the one having priority over the others.[9] Another possibility is to determine the lexical priority between moral and non-moral reasons, as well as between instrumental and intrinsic values. This strategy requires to determine whether strong or weak lexical priority should be applied. Strong – where it comes to an incomparable intrinsic value, such as human dignity. Weak – where a given intrinsic value can be graded. The necessary condition for the application of this criterion to the problem of selecting human embryos is to solve the problem of their moral status. Finally, it is necessary to indicate the circumstances that influence the potency of reasons and discover, whether such facts exist, that may revert a given reason. In this area, the main focus is to determine whether the existence and potency of a reason may depend on its formulation from the first- or third-person perspective.

Acknowledgements

Translated from Polish into English by Aeddan Shaw.

References

Agar N (1999) Liberal eugenics. In: Kuhse H, Singer P (eds) Bioethics: an anthology. Blackwell, Oxford, pp. 171–181.

Benatar D (2006) Better never to have been: the harm of coming into existence. Clarendon Press, Oxford, Oxford University Press, New York.

Broome J (1991) Weighing goods. Basil Blackwell, Cambridge, MA.

Buchanan A, Brock DW, Daniels N, Wikler D (2000) From chance to choice. Cambridge University Press, Cambridge.

Caplan B (2001) Rational ignorance versus rational irrationality. Kyklos 54:3–26.

---

[9] The possible types of reasons and the analysis of the potential relations and rules of priority between them will be presented in the following chapters.

Dancy J (2004) Ethics without principles. Clarendon Press, Oxford, Oxford University Press, New York.

Davis DS (2010) Genetic Dilemmas. Oxford University Press, Oxford, New York.

Freedman B (1987) Equipoise and the ethics of clinical research. The New England Journal of Medicine 317:141–145.

Gauthier DP (1986) Morals by agreement. Clarendon Press, Oxford, Oxford University Press, New York.

Habermas J (1985) The theory of communicative action, vol 1. Reason and the rationalisation of society (trans: McCarthy T). Beacon Press, Boston.

Habermas J (2003) The future of human nature. Polity Press, Cambridge.

Harris J (1985) The value of life. Routledge Kegan Paul, London.

Harris J (1998) Clones, genes and immortality: ethics and the genetic revolution. Oxford University Press, Oxford, New York.

Harris J (2001) Human beings, persons and conjoined twins: an ethical analysis of the judgment in Re A. Harris J. Medical Law Review 9(3):221–236.

Harsanyi J (1975) Can the maximin principle serve as abasis for morality? acritique of John Rawls' theory. The American Political Science Review 69(2):594–605.

Harsanyi J (1978) Bayesian decision theory and utilitarian ethics. American Economic Review 68:223–228.

Harsanyi J (1979) Bayesian decision theory, rule utilitarianism, and Arrow's impossibility theorem. Theory and decision 11(3):289–317.

Häyry M (2010) Rationality and the genetic challenge: making people better? Cambridge University Press, Cambridge, UK, New York.

Häyry M (2013) Rationality and the genetic challenge revisited. Cambridge Quarterly of Healthcare Ethics 20(3):468–483.

Herissone-Kelly P (2011) Reasons, rationalities and procreative beneficence: need Häyry stand politely by while Savulescu and Herrisone-Kelly disagree? Cambridge Quarterly of Healthcare Ethics 20(2):258–267.

Kamm FM (2013) Bioethical prescriptions: to create, end, choose, and improve lives. Oxford University Press, Oxford.

Kass L (2002) Life, liberty and the defence of dignity. Encounter Books, San Francisco.

Makrakis E, Dinopoulou V, Giannaris D (2016) The path of embryo selection for improving IVF success rates. Endocrinology & Metabolism International Journal 3(2):00041. doi: 10.15406/emij.2016.03.00041.

Peterson M (2008) Non-bayesian decision theory: beliefs and desires as reasons for action. Springer, Dordrecht.

Pollock JL (2006) Thinking about acting: logical foundations for rational decision making. Oxford University Press, Oxford, New York.

Rawls J (1971) A Theory of Justice. Belknap Press, Cambridge, MA.

Sparrow R (2011) Liberalism and eugenics. Australasian Journal of Philosophy 89(3):499–517.

Styron W (1976) Sophie's Choice. Random House, New York.

Weber M (1946) Science as vocation. In: Gerth HH, Wright Mills C (trans and eds) From Max Weber: Essays in Sociology. Oxford University Press, New York, pp. 129–156.

Weber M (1978) Economy and society [1921]. In: Guenther R, Wittich C (trans and eds). University of California Press, Berkeley, CA.

Weirich P (2004) Realistic decision theory: rules for non-ideal agents in non-ideal circumstances. Oxford University Press, Oxford, New York.

Żuradzki T (2014) Pre-implantation genetic diagnosis and rational choice under risk or uncertainty. Journal of Medical Ethics 40(11):747–778.

Marta Soniewicka

3 Sex as a criterion for progeny selection

The issue of progeny selection according to the criterion of sex is often labelled in the literature as sex selection. Yet what is at issue here is not the selection of a certain trait, in this case, sex, but rather the selection of progeny of a specific sex. There are currently different ways of performing sex selection, of which the following methods are often singled out: a) postnatal; b) prenatal; c) preimplantation; d) preconception.

Selection following birth either involves infanticide or the abandonment of children of an unwanted sex, as has long been practised in Asian countries (mainly China and India), and, despite the appearance of prenatal methods, the scale of this phenomenon has not greatly changed (Sen 2009). This method is the most repulsive from an ethical standpoint and widely condemned.

Prenatal methods involve establishing a child's sex during pregnancy using Prenatal Diagnosis (PND) and taking a decision, based on this information, to remove the foetus in the event that the sex turns out to be not what was desired. For obvious reasons, this is a very controversial method criticised by both opponents of abortion in general and opponents of using the sex criterion as a basis, specifically, for abortion. In countries in which abortion is permitted on request, like, for example, the USA, it is difficult to introduce comprehensive regulations prohibiting abortion on the grounds of sex, because there would be a need, on a case by case basis, to acquire reliable information on the motives for every abortion (President's Council on Bioethics 2003). For these reasons, in countries such as India, where the practice of abortion on the grounds of sex was quite widespread, regulations were introduced making it impossible to attain information on the sex of a child during pregnancy (Wilkinson 2010). The application of both the first methods to eliminate children of a particular sex has been termed *gendercide* (Warren 1985).

The third method involves the use of Preimplantation Genetic Diagnosis (PGD) during in vitro fertilisation that enables the establishment of the sex of embryos and the selection for implantation of those that meet the requirements of a favoured sex. This method may provoke controversy, not only because of the actual criterion of selection, but also because the embryos of the unwanted sex are destroyed. In the case of this method, much like that of the previous one, tests are used that were invented for a different purpose – to detect congenital embryo defects.

The fourth method involves selecting suitable gametes for fertilisation to obtain the wanted sex (sorting sperm with X or Y chromosomes). Accurately selected male gametes can be used in either in vivo (sperm inseminated directly into the woman's body) or in vitro (outside the woman's body) artificial insemination. The sperm sorting method was invented by the American Department of Agriculture in the 1980s for the purposes of animal husbandry before being patented and used with people as well in artificial insemination clinics (President's Council on Bioethics 2003). The American firm Fairfax began offering this method employing MicroSort technology in Virginia. It turned out to have a 93% success rate at selecting for female sex and 85%, for male sex. It also turned out to be quite a profitable venture. In Europe, the firm is based in Switzerland, but the MicroSort technology is available in many clinics offering artificial insemination. The firm's website claims that it only offers its methods to couples at risk of X-linked disorders and those seeking to balance out the genders in their families (family balancing).[1] Anyone wishing to take advantage of the firm's services for this second purpose needs to meet the criterion of possessing at least one child, and the sorting process is meant to be carried in a manner favouring the gender that is underrepresented in the family.

The fourth method, termed Preconception Gender Selection (PGS), though it is the least frequently used, is best equipped to emphasise ethical problems specific to selection of progeny of a specific sex, because this same method would appear, especially in the case of the in vivo option, to be ethically neutral. In the other cases, which require the removal of the child, the removal of a foetus or the destruction of embryos of an unwanted sex, these practices, both the methods themselves and their objective may be questioned. I shall be focusing in depth on the aim of these methods – selecting of progeny of a specific sex – by primarily limiting my reflections to the selection of progeny by sex for non-medical reasons using the least controversial fourth method (the second section of the chapter). However, before I move on to this, I shall briefly discuss the issue of sex selection to avoid the birth of a child afflicted with X-linked diseases, which is usually carried out using the third method (negative selection of embryos).

---

[1] MicroSort – Genetics & IVF Institute (GIVF): http://www.microsort.com/?page_id=319 (accessed in June 2017).

3.1 Medical reasons for selecting progeny of a particular sex

X-linked diseases are genetic diseases that occur in representatives of a particular sex, because they are linked to changes in or mutations of the X chromosome. When genetic tests are not available that are able to confirm the presence of a given genetic mutation causing an illness, sex becomes the only indicator of the possibility of the onset of that disease. Women who possess a single copy of the mutated recessive gene on the X chromosome can be carriers of these diseases, even though the symptoms fail to manifest themselves. The symptoms of the disease would emerge in women possessing two copies of the defective recessive gene, while in men, one copy of the mutated recessive gene is sufficient for the disease to reveal its symptoms. For these reasons, it is men who most often suffer from these diseases, while women usually only carry them, meaning that they can pass them on genetically to their progeny. Such diseases include haemophilia or Duchenne muscular dystrophy (DMD).

It is most often suggested to women who know, on the basis of genetic tests, that they are carriers of defective recessive genes responsible for X-linked diseases that they should use in vitro fertilisation to avoid the birth of a sick child. At first glance, this situation would appear to be analogous to the destruction of an embryo possessing genetic defects, which, in many legal systems, is permissible. However, the practice described in this chapter differs from the negative selection of embryos for congenital defects (see Chapter 5) in one important respect. In cases when progeny selection is guided by the criterion of a specific sex being linked to potential genetic disease, the decision is being taken for a *potentially* healthy child not to be born. I shall illustrate this problem using the case of haemophilia.

After the birth of their first son who was diagnosed with haemophilia, his parents underwent genetic testing, which determined that his mother was a carrier of the disease, while his father was healthy. The parents planned to expand their family. Statistically, there is a 50% chance that a boy will be born and a 50% chance that a girl will be born following a natural birth. Statistically, every boy that is conceived has a 50% chance of being born healthy and a 50% chance of being born sick, while each girl may turn out, in 50% of cases, to be a carrier of the disease. In other words, statistically, there is a 25% risk that a son afflicted with haemophilia will be born following a natural birth and a 25% risk that a girl will be born who is a carrier of haemophilia. If the parents opt for in vitro fertilisation and PGD, they can eliminate male embryos and then be certain that a girl will be born. Statistically, therefore, half of the destroyed male embryos could be healthy (unafflicted with haemophilia).

This raises the important ethical question of whether the risk of being sick, when determined to a certain degree of probability, can be treated as fulfilling the same diagnosed genetic defect criterion. The answer to this question could depend on the degree of probability. However, in the situation being discussed here, it would appear to be evident that a 50% risk of becoming ill cannot be treated the same as an almost 100% certainty of a genetic defect being diagnosed. Another question that arises here is whether, in that case, the goal of avoiding the birth of a sick child will justify the sacrificing of any possibility of potentially healthy children of the male sex being born. Any answer to this question will of course depend on what moral value we ascribe to a human embryo. However, no matter whatever standpoint we adopt on this question, it is worth bearing in mind what outcome will be achieved when reproductive decisions of this type are guided purely by the criterion of maximising the probability of giving birth to completely healthy offspring. According to this utilitarian line of reasoning, we not only have a moral right (or even duty; see Chapter 5) to reject an embryo linked to a 50% risk of disease, but we would also have the same right to choose an embryo free of any detectable predisposition toward or genetic susceptibility to illness (including increased susceptibility to diseases such as cancer or Alzheimer's disease). Even if the probability of such illnesses appearing in adult individuals is not large, utilitarian reasoning dictates that we should continue to eliminate the likelihood of future illness by eliminating such an embryo (cf. HFEA 2005). If genetic tests of this type were routinely carried out during every pregnancy, resulting in the application of this type of reasoning, most of us would never have been born, for it is not difficult to find a person possessing predispositions, often not activated, toward *certain* diseases or also increased susceptibility toward *certain* diseases. However, even if these diseases were activated, not every one of these illnesses would appear to provide sufficient cause to not be born (see Chapters 4 and 5).[2] It should also be added at this juncture that

---

2   An interesting example of this type of problem can be found in Alexander Sanger's book relating the case of his wife, Jeanette, who has congenital hip dysplasia. During the fourth month of pregnancy, she went for a USG scan to check if her pregnancy was proceeding normally, at which point a doctor told her that genetic testing would certainly shortly be available (a conversation that took place in 1981) to discover, in early pregnancy, if a foetus carried this genetic defect. The shocked woman replied to the doctor: 'I would never kill my baby because he had hip dysplasia.' (Sanger 2004, 3). At the same time, the author presents a pro-choice stance in his book, but, by citing his wife's case, he shows how arbitrary the criteria for terminating a pregnancy due to foetal defects can be. Assumedly, a person who was not born with a similar congenital defect and does not know anything about how such a defect affects quality of life

the currently available genetic tests, both diagnostic and predictive, are limited in their application, not covering many existing, often serious diseases. It may therefore be imagined that, when selecting for an embryo that does not exhibit increased susceptibility to cancer, an embryo is, at the same time, being chosen that will produce a child afflicted by serious heart defects.

It should be stressed that progeny selection within the context being discussed here is not selection against the possession of a child of a certain sex, but against the possession of a sick child. If PGD for the presence of the gender-linked diseases such as haemophilia was used, the problem of negative selection for sex would not occur. However, the issue of what type of genetic defects provide sufficient grounds to prevent the birth of a child afflicted with them remains open to question. Within the context of haemophilia, which today is a disease that can be fully controlled without causing excessive suffering and without reducing life expectancy, many people claim that it should not constitute a criterion either for abortion or negative embryo selection (cf. Galjaard & Noor, 2004). Problems of this type will be tackled in later chapters, especially Chapter 5.

3.2 Non-medical reasons for selecting progeny of a particular sex: family balancing

Selecting progeny for sex in itself rather than for sex as a predictor of illness provokes massive controversy and is termed elective selection, selection for social or non-medical reasons. It should be noted at the very outset that selecting progeny for sex for social reasons is the only method currently applied to parental decisions relating to a child's important identity traits. This also explains why the outcome of the debate over whether permission should be granted to select a child of a particular sex for non-medical reasons may also have a bearing on any stance adopted on the issue of the selection of other traits in progeny unconnected with health (cf. Holm 2004), which could actually be possible in the not-too-distant future, and this will be the focus of our reflections in the second part of the book. Within the context of other traits not directly connected with health, so-called offspring enhancement is the most frequent topic of debate. However, the term 'enhancement' is not used within the context of selecting progeny of a specific sex, because that would imply the assumption that one sex is of more value than the other. However, it should be remembered that what we term enhancement will always depend on the values we are guided by as parents

---

would be more inclined to regard this defect as sufficient grounds for terminating a pregnancy.

(Buchanan et al. 2007). The term 'enhancement' may also be encountered within the context of any opportunities widening choice and parental control over procreation (see Chapter 5).

Many legal regulations prohibit sex selection (e.g. Convention for the Protection of Human Rights and Dignity of the Human Being with Regards to the Application of Biology and Medicine: Convention on Human Rights and Biomedicine), and many organisations and circles openly criticise it (HFEA 2002a, b; ASRM 2004; ACOG 2007; FIGO 2006). The position critical of sex selection of progeny is often moderated in cases when the purpose of such selection is the balancing of families in which there is a predominance of offspring of a particular sex (ASRM 2001; HEFA 2002a, b).

First, I shall take a look at the main arguments invoked in the debate on procreational sex selection by its opponents (Levy 2007; Berkowitz & Snyder 1998), and then I shall present the counterarguments of bioethicists who regard restrictions on gender-related reproductive decisions as unjustified (Dahl 2005, 2007; Harris 1998; Robertson 2001; Savulescu 2006; Wilkinson 2010). Finally, I shall attempt to show that any moral assessment of the arguments in this debate is dependent on the conceptual framework, or horizon of values, implicitly contained within the stances adopted by the opposing sides at the outset. When these values are openly articulated, a better understanding can be gained not only of the discussion itself, but also the main subject of dispute.

The arguments given to justify the legal restriction of sex selection of offspring can be divided into consequential reasoning contesting that this practice leads to undesirable outcomes for society and deontological reasoning regarding this type of practice as morally wrong in itself. The first category includes 1) the charge that the balance of the sexes in society would be infringed. The second category includes charges relating to parental intentions and motivations, including: 2a) sexual discrimination; 2b) the promotion of sexual stereotypes. These arguments are most frequently set in opposition to 3) an argument based on procreative freedom, sometimes supported by reference to the principle of consistency.

3.2.1 The violation of the sex balance in society

Studies show that, if everybody had equal access to sources of nutrition and healthcare, the global sex ratio would amount to 102.2 women to 100 men (Drèze, Sen 1989, 1995). In some societies or communities, the local rate departs markedly from the norm, seriously upsetting the sex balance. In some Asian countries (mainly, China and India) as well as Caucasian countries (Armenia, Azerbaijan, Georgia), this rate departs markedly from the norm. In these countries, there are many more men than women, with the ratio of the male to female sex even reaching 130 men to 100 women (President's Council on Bioethics 2003; Buchanan et al. 2007; Wilkinson 2010).

An appropriate sex balance is in the interests of society, because if this fails to exist, it may lead to many undesirable consequences, including a scarcity of potential partners accompanied by a procreation crisis in a given society or a crisis in and need to redefine the family. Other consequences of the violation of the sex balance in a society are also highlighted, including increased violence due to the surfeit of men or the domination of the majority sex over the opposite sex.

Many bioethicists claim that this argument means little in Western societies, in which such an imbalance has not been observed, while any sex imbalance among ethnic subgroups residing in western countries may in effect contribute to their openness, forced on them by a scarcity of partners, to representatives of groups outside their own (Wilkinson 2010). It would appear unlikely that the social implication of the aggregate individual parental decisions would violate the sex balance in liberal societies, because this would require a single overriding preference with regard to sex, which is something practically unheard of in western societies (cf. Holm 2004). However, even if the majority of parents making a sex selection happened to have similar preferences and choices of this type were being made on a mass scale, it would then be possible to introduce various legislative solutions preventing any imbalance in the sexes. Examples of such solutions include proposals to monitor sex selections carried out within a country and introduce appropriate restrictions when faced with an immediate need (Wilkinson 2010). Without going any further into the details of these proposed solutions, the consequential argumentation against sex selection is weak, because it fails to address sex selection itself, concentrating instead on its consequences, which could be prevented in other ways not requiring a ban on sex selection itself. I shall therefore move on to discuss the stronger argumentation being applied to the practice of sex selection.

3.2.2 Sexual discrimination and sexism

The fundamental and most commonly cited argument related to the sex selection of progeny is the issue of parental motivation based on attitudes of discrimination. The problem is associated with the phenomenon of sexual discrimination (in this case, against the female sex), mainly practised in the countries of Central Asia.[3] The source of this problem is the attribution of a higher rank to the male

---

3 Western liberal culture based on the premise of socio-legal equality between men and

sex. This may be linked to the higher social position of men in a particular culture, opportunities to fulfil certain social functions and access to most professions or a broader range of education. In societies based on values guaranteeing men a higher status, parents may prefer to possess offspring of the male sex to provide them with a sense of pride, privilege or, ultimately, essential economic assistance.

It should be asked at this juncture who the objects of sexual discrimination within the sex selection context actually are. The problematic issue of determining the normative status of an embryo or foetus can be avoided by using the sperm sorting method to argue that such a practice is not discriminatory, because it is impossible to discriminate against someone who has not yet been conceived (e.g. a girl, if this method led to a boy being conceived). However, the sexual discrimination invoked in the case of these practices does not apply to discrimination against those whose birth or conception were prevented, but rather living representatives of a sex regarded as inferior in a particular society, if parents were guided by this when selecting the progeny of a specific sex. The stance that parents are expressing a certain attitude through the reproductive choices they make is known as the expressivist argument (see Chapter 5). According to this argument, if parents are investing so much effort into ensuring that a boy, rather than a girl, will be born to them, they are in effect sending the message that girls are not worth as much as boys. This argumentation is only sustainable, in Kamm's view, if the choice made by parents is indeed motivated by a conviction that daughters are worth less (Kamm 2013).

However, sexual discrimination need not always be bound up with a situation where a higher value is ascribed to one of the sexes, for it can also apply to situations in which parents are guided by other sexual prejudices, in particular, stereotypes relating to social roles associated with a particular sex. These types of stereotype are exemplified by parents' need, embedded in some cultures, to possess a son, preferably a firstborn, to feel that they are leading a fulfilled life. Attitudes of this type cannot be interpreted in isolation from the aforementioned socioeconomic and legal context, where the role of a firstborn son is of a special nature, being bound up with the acquisition of certain family rights.[4]

---

women is a relatively new phenomenon. Not until the 19th and 20th centuries was there any change in the position of women in the western world, who earlier did not possess full capacity for legal actions (they could not represent themselves in an official capacity or inherit or manage property without supervision or assistance), active and passive electoral rights, access to education or the right to hold public posts.

4   Yet such strong preferences for the firstborn child being male are also broadly distributed across Western societies (Holm 2004).

In societies or communities based on powerful gender stereotypes, sex selection performed by parents may be the outcome of social pressure, a wish to adapt to family or societal expectations or wish to guarantee progeny a good start in life. The latter argument is often invoked to show that parents practising selection need not always be directed by their own desires, but may also be wishing the best for their child, for, if access to valuable social goods is dependent in a certain society on being of particular sex, then selecting a child of that sex is tantamount to guaranteeing it a privileged social position. Argumentation of this type is problematic for many reasons. First, selecting offspring according to harmful social stereotypes deepens and reinforces those stereotypes. As Kamm argues:

> The traits parents choose may make their children more 'successful' within a sex-stereotyped system when it might be better to question that system itself (Kamm 2013, 258).

Second, if we accept that no one can gain any advantage from not being born, then the decision to give birth to a child of *any* sex will be just as good for that particular child if the alternative would be to not be born at all (see Chapter 4). Third, it is pointed out that the desire to guarantee progeny a 'positional advantage' by means of reproductive decisions enabling the selection of a child with certain competitive traits, such as, for example, being tall, may turn out to be self-defeating (Buchanan et al. 2007; Singer 2013). For if a large proportion of families in a certain society are guided by the same aim, for example, only bringing boys into the world, the resultant scarcity of girls would mean that the boys' position would no longer be privileged. On the contrary, they would be faced with increased competition for important positions as well as greater difficulties finding a wife and building a family, assuming, that is, that such values are equally vital in these communities to life success.

There is a quite rarely encountered consensus among bioethicists investigating this topic that using the sex selection of progeny for promoting discriminatory or sexist attitudes can be harmful for society. The crux of the disagreement is actually the problem of determining when we are dealing with attitudes of this type and whether sex selection for non-medical reasons should be totally prohibited if we are to achieve our goal of combating discrimination and sexism. Opponents of any prohibition of elective sex selection adopt two stances. Some believe that any prohibition of this practice should not be total, as they wish to allow for the possibility of sex selection for the purposes of family balancing, building on the premise that, in this case, parents are not being guided by discriminatory or sexist attitudes. Others believe that in western societies, attitudes of this type are rarely a problem, so prohibition is not justified at all and discriminatory attitudes can be combated using other methods that do not restrict procreative freedom.

As Søren Holm aptly points out, the term 'family balancing' is a term with powerful rhetorical properties which is creating a new 'unbalanced family syndrome':

> It is a term that not only describes a particular situation but also implies a potential problem and allows new forms of social identification. The term is thus not only descriptive but also creates a new social reality. Who would like to belong to an 'unbalanced family'? Before reading this term I had never realised that I had a potential problem in coming from an unbalanced family (being an only child), and that everyone else growing up in families with children of only one sex shared this problem with me (Holm 2004, 31).

Stephen Wilkinson correctly notes, the very notion of 'family balancing' is fuzzy, and can be interpreted in a number of ways. For example, family balancing could be understood to be a situation where parents possess at least two children of one sex and no children of the opposite sex (HFEA 2003; Wilkinson 2010). This would then mean that a 'gender imbalance' in the family entails not having a child of one sex as well as a specific quantitative difference in the arrangement of sexes (or the numerical advantage of at least two children of a given sex over a wished-for child of the opposite sex). The previously mentioned Fairfax firm defines 'family balancing' much more broadly, defining the possession of only one child as the essential requirement, while any sex selection must be to the advantage of the sex that is underrepresented in the family. Therefore, if the 'family balancing' requirements laid down by Fairfax are to be met, parents may have two boys and a girl and carry out sex selection favouring another girl, or have only one girl and carry out sex selection favouring a boy.

No matter how we define 'family balancing', we are not able to use this term to completely prevent discriminatory or sexist attitudes, because neither the number nor sex of the children that parents possess tell us anything unequivocal about their attitude to a social role or gender value. The parents of two daughters may select the sex of the next child to have a more balanced family, or they may just as well want to have a son, because they regard the possession of a son as more socially valuable. As Inmaculada de Melo-Martin correctly points out, we are dealing here with an epistemological problem – we are not able to establish with any degree of certitude by what motives the parents were guided when making the sex selection (de Melo-Martin 2013). We should therefore concur with Holm and Wilkinson that the privileged treatment of sex selection on the grounds of 'family balancing' is based on appearances rather than solid arguments (Holm 2004; Wilkinson 2010).

It is often stressed that sex selection for the purposes of family balancing is motivated by parents' desire to experience the raising of a child of a different sex to the sex of the children they already have (Steinbock 2002; Wilkinson 2010). The statements parents make justifying their wish to select the sex of their future offspring include a desire to possess a daughter who they could go shopping with or son who could be taught how to play football. These parents have nothing against either of the sexes. Nevertheless, all these statements are based on assumptions adopted by the parents linking a sex with a particular social role – they may therefore be regarded as sexist, if sexism is understood to be any *a priori* linking of a specific sex with a social role. Combating sexism, conceived in such broad terms, would require as to ascribe to an ideal based on a genderless society in which children are brought up in a manner stripped of any reference to gender roles, allowing every child to choose their own gender roles. Such a dualist approach in which a complete distinction is made between the biological sex we are born with and social gender we either choose ourselves or society imposes on us is difficult to sustain. Invoking some 'asexual I' that becomes gendered in society is nothing more than a fiction (President's Council on Bioethics 2003). Our social understanding of ourselves and our roles always presupposes some context. Rather than occurring within a neutral vacuum, it takes place within an existing culture and our relations with others. In particular, the lack of any conceptual framework, as it were, for the definition of social roles could turn out to be harmful for us, because one of the basic human needs is the recognition on the part of others, and every instance of recognition requires us to refer to a role of some kind (see Chapters 5 and 9). It is therefore hardly surprising that sex and its social meaning, or gender, are of importance to us. It is no coincidence that clinics offering sex selection based on artificial insemination use the term 'gender selection' rather than 'sex selection', because future parents are actually motivated by their child possessing a more or less stereotypical set of psychological traits comprised of its gender identity rather than certain purely biological traits (President's Council on Bioethics 2003). When guided by a desire to experience the raising of a girl or boy, parents have to adopt the assumption that there is a difference between raising boys and girls, and also that gender is bound up with differences in character that are of importance to them (de Melo-Martin 2013). In other words, all parents selecting progeny of a specific sex, including those wishing to achieve 'family balancing', base their decision on the ascription of a specific value to a given sex. They need not in the least be guided by the assumption that daughters are worse than sons. Nevertheless, every time they make a decision on sex selection, they are assigning a value to sex by acknowledging that sex is a trait that is worth more to them in a given context (cf. Kamm 2013). Such a context could be the possession of three sons, causing parents to assign more value to the possession of a daughter than a fourth boy, which does not mean that the existing three boys are less valuable than the girl who is to be born. Such a valuation of sex within a reproductive context is not completely free of ethical concerns, but it is different in nature to the charge of sexism discussed in this section. I will be returning to this in the last section of this chapter.

3.2.3 Procreative freedom

Those advocating the lifting of all restrictions on the sex selection of progeny, most often invoke the principle of procreative freedom, arguing that any restrictions placed on this are only justified by preventing harm to others (see Chapter 4). The burden of proving that harm has been caused by a reproductive decision is shifted on to those who argue for restrictions on reproductive freedom. However, as de Melo-Martin aptly notes, argumentation favouring sex selection that invokes procreative freedom needs to demonstrate that sex selection is an essential aspect serving the realisation of the values protected by this principle. Most authors defending sex selection make no attempt to demonstrate this, since they regard the link between this practice and procreative freedom to be self-evident. It is worth considering whether this is indeed the case.

As the members of the President's Council on Bioethics note:

> [S]ex selection is defended on grounds that it could increase the happiness of the parents by enabling them to fulfill their desire for one or more sons or daughters (President's Council on Bioethics 2003, 64).

In the case of sex selection, it is self-evident that parents are making a choice while bearing their own preferences in mind.[5] The pro-choice stance, which is based on the procreative freedom principle, gives priority to parental 'wants'. Adopting a stance maximising parental choices in the area of procreation is tantamount to acknowledging that any or most forms of reproductive selection are justifiable. However, procreative freedom need not be understood in this consumer manner. Procreative freedom can be understood as a right guaranteeing

---

5   It is true that some argue that they want to select progeny of a specific sex to provide their existing children with the experience of possessing a sibling of the opposite sex, but in principle, most parents stress that they are realising their own desires.

the realisation of such values as the value of procreation itself (the priceless experience of passing on life) or the creation of valuable family relationships. Selecting a child of a particular sex, rather than promoting the value of procreation as such, is either promoting the value of choosing in itself, which is bound up with the libertarian or utilitarian conception of procreative freedom, or promoting the value of a particular sex.

Robertson attempts to demonstrate the link between the principle of procreative freedom and sex selection by arguing that justifying sex selection as a mere parental preference is not enough. For it to be fully justified, it needs to be a necessary condition for procreation. Reproductive choice, as Robertson writes:

> [S]erves the needs of couples who have strong preferences about the gender of their offspring and who would not reproduce unless they could realize those preferences (Robertson 2001, 3).

Apart from the aforementioned problem of establishing parents' true preferences, the author makes no attempt to demonstrate that the right to sexual selection can be inferred from the right to procreative freedom, but simply assumes this. For he presupposes that procreative freedom not only incorporates the right to decide to have children, but also the right to decide what (sex) these children should be, if the latter is a condition of the former. This type of conditionality is, however, completely subjective, for some parents could just as well decide that they will not have children if they cannot choose their skin colour (Berkowitz & Snyder 1998), sexual orientation (Stein 1998; see Chapter 5) or level of intelligence. As some authors correctly note, the right to possess children certainly does not, in itself, give parents' the automatic right to possess children of a particular sex, or with specific traits (President's Council on Bioethics 2003; de Melo-Martin 2013).

Procreative freedom is not an absolute right, for many restrictions are placed on it, within the contexts, for example, of adoption or reproductive cloning. Advocates of sex selection understand procreative freedom to be a right guaranteeing increased control, not only over the time, place and method of procreation, but also on its outcome, including both the quantity and quality of any children that are possessed (Davis 2010). It should be noted that the freedom to procreate was initially understood in legal terms as a negative freedom – *freedom from* state interference in the sphere of procreation. Subsequently, this right began to be interpreted as a positive freedom (*freedom to*) incorporating the right to access various artificial procreation technologies (O'Neill 2005). While this notion was created during the abortion debate to guarantee the right to control unwanted fertility (Dworkin 1994), its application was later expanded, along with advances in biotechnology, to incorporate the right to control unwanted infertility. The most widely understood right to procreative freedom began to incorporate all reproductive choices and also the introduction onto the market of human gametes, embryos and reproductive services (like surrogacy; Fabre 2008). It is highly controversial to derive a positive conception of the right from the negative conception of it, and even if one were adopted, legal interference in the positive conception of freedom can be subject to much greater restrictions than the negative conception of freedom.

Some bioethicists here reference the right to self-determination and right to choose. The basic problem with argumentation of this type lies in the fact that reproductive autonomy is understood to be an extension of individual autonomy, when it applies, by its very definition, to more than one party. Procreation is not an individual undertaking. One of the reasons for restricting autonomy can be its influence on the lives of others, and deciding about child's sexual identity undoubtedly exerts an influence on a third party – the child (President's Council on Bioethics 2003). There is no need to invoke the notion of harm to question such far-reaching parental control over a child. This can be achieved by invoking the protection of the parent-child relationship and autonomy of offspring, as we shall be discussing in the following chapters.

Some authors, such as Julian Savulescu, argue that tolerating sex selection is a requirement if we are to maintain consistency in the face of widespread acceptance of folk methods for achieving the same goal (Savulescu 2006). He cites paying attention to diet, becoming pregnant at a certain time and opting for particular sexual positions as examples of attempts to influence what sex a child will be born, and they are all consistent with folk beliefs. As the author argues, the only difference between these methods is that the new methods applied during ART are much more effective. However, the consistency of argumentation against sex selection can be defended on moral grounds. Even if all attempts at sex selection, whether more or less effective, are regarded as immoral, there is no need at all to call for their prohibition. The fact that lying is normally regarded as immoral does not mean that every kind of lying is legally sanctioned. Much the same applies to marital infidelity – even if it is regarded as morally wrong, there is no need at all to call for unfaithful spouses to be punished by the state. Folk methods of procreation differ from artificial methods of procreation in that the latter are not in fact 'folk' methods, and therefore go beyond the scope of negative freedom. They are practised within the framework of the legally regulated sphere of social life containing healthcare and may have restrictions placed on them to protect those values on which that social life is based.

3.3 Concluding remarks: a conceptual framework for the dispute and the meaning of procreation

The decision over whether the principle of procreative freedom should incorporate or exclude sex selection requires a specific interpretation of this principle which is usually implicitly accepted without providing additional arguments. Procreative freedom incorporating sex selection is not just promoting the value of procreation in itself, but also such values as: maximising parental reproductive preferences and the absolute or relative value of a given sex. It is difficult to concur with the utilitarian stance based on these values that the purpose of procreation is to promote the strongest reproductive preferences guaranteeing the greatest sum of an abstract conception of happiness. Procreation is in fact commonly perceived as an intimate practice expressing interpersonal ties, and a child is both part and the outcome of these. What is at issue here then is not the outcome of procreation *per se* or procreation as a practice continuing the species, but rather participation in the creation and realisation of significant relationships. Undoubtedly, the desire to possess offspring is a strong preference for many people, but the decision to possess offspring should not be purely perceived as the fulfilment of egoistical desires. It should rather be perceived as the desire to *pass on* life bound up with a readiness to take responsibility for the life, which in turn requires the development of the love-based relationship. The term 'passing on life' places a different emphasis on the practice to the term 'possessing a child'. Procreation involves more than simple self-fulfilment gained through a child. It also involves adopting the role of mediator in giving life. This role carries the implication that we will open ourselves out to a life that is distinct from us and can only appear in the world through our efforts rather than being an expression of the projects of our will. The desire of parents to control the outcome of procreation by deciding on important aspects of a child's identity distorts this role and undermines a relationship that should be based on unconditional acceptance of our progeny (Sandel 2007).

The libertarian conception of procreative freedom presupposes that freedom of self-possession is a natural right that has absolute priority over other rights, and procreation is one of its manifestations. This standpoint fails to take into account the specific nature of procreation, which neither equates to individual freedom nor incorporates every aspect of positive freedom. De Melo-Martin would certainly appear to have a point when she notes:

> [E]ven if one were to accept that procreative liberty is a fundamental moral or legal right, no compelling reasons have been provided for believing that sex selection falls

within the scope of procreative liberty. Proponents of this position either beg the question or force us to accept absurd activities as being constitutive of particular rights. But if sex selection cannot be properly said to fall within the scope of procreative liberty, then advocates of sex selection fail to persuade when they claim that the only legitimate reason to interfere with the use of this practice is the causing of harm to others (de Melo-Martin 2013, 13).

It is difficult to concur that procreation is one of many forms of self-expression, as this would reduce the parent-child relationship to that of producer-product. Since procreation is a field of human freedom that, by definition, includes a third party (the child), we should be seriously considering whether the conditionality, commercialisation and commodification of this practice is impacting negatively on the parent-child relationship. The conditionality of reproduction, as exemplified by sex selection, relies on the assumption that the decision to bring a child into the world is dependent on the meeting of parental expectations. This leads to children becoming the product of contracts that parents enter into with clinics that are meant to implement that process according to their preferences, which would appear to undermine the foundations of our understanding of both procreation and parenthood (President's Council on Bioethics 2003).

Argumentation based on parent-child relationship draws attention to the fact that we are attempting to understand what procreation is by referring to the intentions and motivations of parents and the targets they set themselves when making decisions about their progeny. The motivations of parents can influence the meaning ascribed to the relationship that arises from procreation. Parental motivations that are sexist are perceived as harmful and they enable restrictions to be placed on freedom of procreation. Sexism is harmful when based on certain values that make such a stance harmful to others (de Melo-Martin 2013). Likewise, the conditional procreation stance can be perceived as harmful due to the aforementioned values. The principle-based approach to reproduction is not sufficient, as a conceptual framework, to resolve the issue of how to justify sex selection (de Melo-Martin 2013). Such a resolution needs to pay reference to a definition of procreative freedom that will be based on specific values. Purely utilitarian values or the value of individual freedom do not appear to do full justice to the meaning that procreation has for the parties concerned.

Acknowledgements

This is a modified version of the text which was originally prepared in Polish and published as a part of chapter 3 in: Soniewicka M (2018) Selekcja genetyczna w prokreacji medycznie wspomaganej. Etyczne i prawne kryteria. Wolters Kluwer, Warszawa. Translated from Polish into English by Philip Palmer.

References

ACOG (American College of Obstetricians and Gynecologists), Committee on Ethics (2007) ACOG Committee Opinion No. 360: Sex Selection. Obestetrics and Gynecology 109:475–478.

ASRM (American Society of Reproductive Medicine), Ethics Committee (2001) Preconception Gender Selection for Nonmedical Reasons. Fertility and Sterility 82 Suppl 1:245–248.

ASRM (American Society of Reproductive Medicine), Ethics Committee (2004) Sex Selection and Preimplantation Genetic Diagnosis. Fertility and Sterility 75:5.

Berkowitz J, Snyder JW (1998) Racism and Sexism in Medically Assisted Conception. Bioethics 12(1): 25–44.

Buchanan A, Brock DW, Daniels N, Wikler D (2007) From Chance to Choice: Genetics and Justice. Cambridge University Press, Cambridge & New York.

Dahl E (2005) Sex Selection: Laissez Faire or Family Balancing? Health Care Analysis 13(1):87–90.

Dahl E (2007) Sex Selection: Morality, Harm, and the Law. Southern Medical Journal 100(1):105–106.

Davis DS (2010) Genetic Dilemmas: Reproductive Technology, Parental Choices, and Children's Futures. Oxford University Press, Oxford.

de Melo-Martin I (2013) Sex Selection and the Procreative Liberty Framework. Kennedy Institute of Ethics Journal 23(1):1–18.

Drèze J, Sen A (1989) Hunger and Public Action. Oxford University Press, Oxford.

Drèze J, Sen A (1995) India: Economic Development and Social Opportunity. Clarendon Press, Oxford.

Dworkin R (1994) Life's Dominion. An Argument about Abortion, Euthanasia, and Individual Freedom. Vintage Books, New York.

Fabre C (2008) Whose Body is it Anyway? Justice and the Integrity of the Person. Clarendon Press, Oxford.

FIGO (International Federation of Gynecology and Obstetrics), Committee for the Ethical Aspects of Human Reproduction and Women's Health (2006) Ethical Guidelines on Sex Selection for Non-Medical Purposes. International Journal of Gynecology and Obstetrics 92:329–330.

Galjaard H, Noor LHW (2004) Prenatal testing. New developments and ethical dilemmas. Proceedings of a symposium organized by the Science and Ethics Advisory Committee of the Royal Netherlands Academy of Arts and Sciences, the Netherlands on June 18, 2003. Royal Netherlands Academy of Arts and Sciences, Amsterdam.

Harris J (1998) Rights and Reproductive Choice. In: Harris J, Holm S (eds) The Future of Human Reproduction. Oxford University Press, Oxford.

HFEA (Human Fertilisation and Embryology Authority) (2002a) Sex Selection: Choice and Responsibility in Human Reproduction. Consultation document, London.

HFEA (Human Fertilisation and Embryology Authority) (2002b) Sex Selection: Options for Regulation. A Report, London.

HFEA (Human Fertilisation and Embryology Authority) (2003) Sex Selection: Options for Regulation. A Report, London.

HFEA (Human Fertilisation and Embryology Authority) (2005) Choices and Boundaries: Should People be able to Select Embryos Free from an Inherited Susceptibility to Cancer. Consultation document, London.

Holm S (2004) Like a Frog in Boiling Water: The Public, The HFEA and Sex Selection. Health Care Analysis 12(1):26–39.

Kamm FM (2013) Bioethical Prescriptions to Create, End, Choose, and Improve Lives. Oxford University Press, Oxford & New York.

Levy N (2007) Against Sex Selection. Southern Medical Journal 100(1):107–109.

O'Neill O (2005) Autonomy and Trust. Cambridge University Press, Cambridge.

President's Council on Bioethics (2003) Beyond Therapy: Biotechnology and the Pursuit of Happiness. President's Council on Bioethics, Washington, DC.

Robertson JA (2001) Preconception Gender Selection. American Journal of Bioethics 1(1):1–9.

Sandel M (2007) The Case against Perfection. Ethics in the Age of Genetic Engineering. The Belknap Press of Harvard University Press, Cambridge, MA & London.

Sanger A (2004) Beyond Choice. Reproductive Freedom in the 21st Century. Public Affairs, New York.

Savulescu J (2006) Sex Selection: The Case For. In: Kuhse H, Singer P (eds) Bioethics: An Anthology. Blackwell Publishing, Oxford, pp. 145–149.

Sen G (2009) Gender biased sex selection. Key issues for action. Development Alternatives with Women for a New Era, Sexual and Reproductive Health and Rights (SRHR). http://www.dawnnet.org/feminist-resources/content/gender-biased-sex-selection-key-issues-action-gita-sen (accessed: 11 June 2018).

Singer P (2013) Parental Choice and Human Improvement. In: Savulescu J, Bostrom N (eds) Human Enhancement. Oxford University Press, Oxford.

Stein E (1998) Choosing the Sexual Orientation of Children. Bioethics 12(1): 1–24.

Steinbock B (2002) Sex selection: Not Obviously Wrong. Hastings Center Report 32(1):23–28.

Warren MA (1985) Gendercide: The Implications of Sex Selection. Rowman & Allanheld: Totowa, NJ.

Wilkinson S (2010) Choosing tomorrow's children. The ethics of selective reproduction. Clarendon Press, Oxford.

Marta Soniewicka

4 Reproductive harm

4.1 Introduction: the 'harm principle'

One of the core values in liberal-democratic societies is freedom (or autonomy). This accounts for the appearance, within the domain of reproduction, of arguments focusing on the protection of reproductive autonomy (see Chapters 1 and 12) as a key principle defining the boundaries of legal interventions within the sphere of procreation. By acknowledging that every legal intervention in our lives, by definition, limits our freedom, and, further, that the legal interventions that can be justified are those whose sole end is to prevent people from being harmed by others, we are in effect agreeing with a principle formulated by John Stuart Mill which, in his view, was entitled to:

> [G]overn absolutely the dealings of society with the individual in the way of compulsion and control, whether the means used be physical force in the form of legal penalties, or the moral coercion of public opinion. That principle is, that the sole end for which mankind are warranted, individually or collectively, in interfering with the liberty of action of any of their number, is self-protection. That the only purpose for which power can be rightfully exercised over any member of a civilised community, against his will, is to prevent harm to others. (…) A person may cause evil to others not only by his actions but by his inaction, and in either case he is justly accountable to them for the injury. (…) To make any one answerable for doing evil to others is the rule; to make him answerable for not preventing evil is, comparatively speaking, the exception. Yet there are many cases clear enough and grave enough to justify that exception. In all things which regard the external relations of the individual, he is *de jure* amenable to those whose interests are concerned, and, if need be, to society as their protector. There are often good reasons for not holding him to the responsibility; but these reasons must arise from the special expediencies of the case: either because it is a kind of case in which he is on the whole likely to act better, when left to his own discretion, than when controlled in any way in which society have it in their power to control him; or because the attempt to exercise control would produce other evils, greater than those which it would prevent. When such reasons as these preclude the enforcement of responsibility, the conscience of the agent himself should step into the vacant judgment seat, and protect those interests of others which have no external protection (Mill 2003, 94–96).

The harm principle does not have a universal application, for there are acts that are wrong and punishable yet have no relation to harming anyone (e.g. littering in public park or jumping a red light when the road is clear). There are also actions that may be perceived as harmful from the perspective of individuals, but they are permitted or legally enforced for the good of society (e.g. prescription in case of possession in bad faith or the forced quarantine of people suffering from contagious diseases). Mill's principle does apply to actions, as well as inactions or omissions, that may harm others. The obligation to prevent harm that does not result from action or inaction is a very controversial question. In most legal systems, there is a complex system of civil liability arising from the risk connected with, for example, introducing unsafe products onto the market or property ownership. In this case, strict liability is independent of culpability and can incorporate the behaviour or inaction of others, as well as the behaviour of animals or events caused by forces of nature. Controversy is also aroused by the failure to prevent wrongdoing. After all, not everyone would agree that a principle imposing the obligation to prevent others from being harmed can be naturally derived from a principle prohibiting the causing of harm. Whereas continental law often provides punishment for failure to assist people whose life or health is at risk or failure to notify the law enforcement agencies of a crime, thus equating such inaction with criminal liability, there are no similar regulations in the Anglo-Saxon legal system.[1] It is also open to question whether the conclusion can be drawn from Mill's principle that state intervention aimed at protecting individuals from any harm that they may do to themselves is also justifiable (the problem of so-called paternalistic legal norms).

As can be read in the passage quoted above, doing harm constitutes a legal infringement upon the legally protected interests of people on whose behalf social organs can act and under whose protection these individuals find themselves. Exclusion from liability for causing harm can be justified in some areas of life by special circumstances that dictate that an individual not controlled by society would act better than in a situation when a system of control existed or when social control in a specific area could contribute to a greater evil than the actual harm that would be prevented. This is sometimes used to justify permissive approaches to, for example, prostitution, employing the argument that even if we assume that we are dealing with the exploitation of people forced to sell sexual services in difficult living conditions (and therefore, harm), nevertheless, legal instruments prohibiting these types of practice are not necessarily best suited to the protection of exploited people. Excessive state interference within the sphere of family relations is also sometimes perceived as ill-advised, because

---

1   The American legal system only contains the Good Samaritan Law, according to which the person providing assistance is exempted from liability for damages in the event that the person receiving the assistance comes to harm as a result of this assistance being provided.

it can cause even more harm (e.g. depriving someone of parental rights as the result of a minor case of negligence, or any forms of child punishment).

Assuming that Mill's harm principle should be the primary justification for legal interference in citizens' lives, we should then ask whether we are dealing with harm within the context of reproductive decisions taken on the basis of genetic tests. And if we are, what type of harm we are dealing with, who is harming whom and whether this should result in the attribution of legal liability.

In law, a distinction is made between civil liability and criminal liability. The latter mostly applies to physical persons (in exceptional circumstances, some legal systems attribute criminal liability to legal persons) who bear sole responsibility for their own actions carried out deliberately or otherwise (wilful or unintentional fault). Criminal liability is attributed to the perpetrator of an act prohibited by the law in force at the time when the offence was committed, irrespective of whether that offence resulted in economic harm. However, civil liability can be attributed both to perpetrators of a culpable act, including failure to act, and non-culpable behaviour, including the above-mentioned behaviour of others and unforeseeable circumstances. Civil liability, which is economic in nature, is attributed when harm has occurred. The primary focus of this chapter is the issue of harm, as interpreted by civil law, within the context of reproductive decisions.

4.2 The notion of harm

Liability for damages can be based on a tort (always the case when personal rights have been violated and in situations when harm has been caused to property by an unlawful act) and breach of contract (this only applies to property-related harm resulting from failure to perform obligations arising from contractual relationships) as well as insurance and warranty issues.

Liability for damages only arises from the act of the violation of the legally protected personal rights of a person who, as an outcome of this violation, suffers harm to their person or property. Personal rights mostly apply to life, health and freedom. The general formula for attributing liability for damages under civil law therefore incorporates three basic elements: (1) a legal fact (an instance of behaviour, inaction or event); (2) harm; (3) an adequate causal link between conditions (1) and (2). This means that liability is only attributed to the normal consequences of that legal fact. Additional variable conditions can include: guilt, risk and principles of social coexistence. In other words, *A harms B if, as a result of A's indefensible action (or inaction), B's personal rights are violated, leading to an adverse effect manifested as harm* to B's *person or property*. Economic harm incorporates both losses and lost gains, so, when assessing the occurrence of harm, both a 'worsening test' and 'counterfactual test' should be conducted, as Joel Feinberg writes (Feinberg 1992, 6–11). The worsening test helps to determine whether B *was better off* before A's action. The counterfactual test investigates whether B *would be better off* had A not acted in a certain way. Harming can therefore occur when we are not making anyone worse off through our actions and even when we are making them better off. If a doctor saves the life of a dying patient using a certain medical procedure, but administers it without due care, causing permanent insufficiency in the patient's organism, it can then be said that the patient is better off than before the doctor's action yet worse off with regard to what could have occurred if the doctor had administered the procedure with due care (or as it should have been administered). We therefore apply the 'good doctor' standard, which has not been met in this case, to the assessment of such a situation.

We may also be dealing with harm when the injured party is worse off, even though the conditions of the counterfactual test have not been met. There are cases when B is worse off, but would be even more worse off if A had taken no action. Here, Feinberg gives the example of a taxi driver who causes an accident when driving a businessman to the airport that results in the businessman missing his plane. The seriously injured businessman ends up in hospital, and meanwhile the plane he had meant to take crashes shortly after take-off and all the passengers on it die. Although the accident caused by the negligent driver has saved the businessman's life, common sense dictates, as Feinberg notes, that this circumstance does not absolve the taxi driver from liability for the harm done to the businessman as a result of the accident. Irrespective of whether the lesser evil has rescued him from a greater evil, the liability for causing this harm cannot be compensated for in this way.

Finally, very rare cases may arise that fail to pass both the counterfactual test and the worsening test. For example, a situation in which an athlete was barred from taking part in a competitive event due to the actions of another party which deprived him of the opportunity to win a prize, yet rescued him from assassins who wanted to kill him at this event. If the person preventing the athlete from taking part in the event took no action to save his life (but did this, for example, to make it possible for another competitor to win the prize) he bears responsibility for the harm caused to the athlete even if that harm saved his life. Feinberg therefore proposes the counterfactual test be reformulated to a doubly counterfactual test which would apply to tort liability:

A harms B only if his wrongful act leaves B worse off then he would be otherwise in the normal course of events insofar as they were reasonably foreseeable in the circumstances (Feinberg 1992, 11).

4.3 Kinds of harm in the context of reproduction

As regards reproductive decisions, a distinction can be made between three basic types of harm: (1) harm caused to a future child (the legally protected interest is the well-being of the child); (2) harm caused to the parents, especially the mother (the legally protected interests of the mother include her right to privacy, reproductive autonomy, health and bodily integrity); (3) social harm (security or the well-being of a society can be a legally protected interest).

4.3.1 Prenatal and preconception harm

As far as harm caused to a future child is concerned, many legal systems introduce the concept of prenatal and preconception injuries (Justyński 2003). Prenatal injury is understood to be a situation in which action or inaction causing harm to a future child occurs between the child's conception and birth. For example, a situation in which a pregnant woman has been infected with rubella during a hospital stay, resulting in the birth of a disabled child. In this case, both the mother and child may claim compensation from the hospital for the negligence from which the infection arose. A similar outcome may arise when a pregnant woman has taken medication without a pharmaceutical firm informing her of potential risks she may face during the course of her pregnancy.[2] In this case, both the mother and child are entitled to make claims against the pharmaceutical firm. Preconception harm is understood to be situation in which an action causing harm to a future child has occurred before conception. Modifying the example above, a situation could be imagined in which a woman has been infected during a hospital stay by rubella before she becomes pregnant, is not informed of this, becomes pregnant and gives birth to a disabled child. The legal consequences here would be the same as in the previous examples.

No consensus has been reached in jurisprudence, legal doctrine and among bioethicists regarding the normative status of human life in the various developmental stages preceding birth. However, regardless of whether we grant legal

---

2   A good example of this is the famous case of thalidomide – an over-the-counter pain reliever sold in the 1950s and 1960s that had undesirable teratogenic side effects (causing severe damage to a foetus). See Ito et al. 2010.

personality to the unborn child, we can, in the above cases, make a case for granting the protection of personal rights before the appearance of a physical person. We can do this because personal rights can be violated as a result of action or inaction taking place before these rights emerge. In legal doctrine, we refer to this as 'retroactive protection of an individual's rights and interests' (Justyński 2003). In such cases, we adopt the notion of the 'delayed action' of causal behaviour whose outcome only becomes apparent after the emergence of a subjective right. In German doctrine, this is explained by distinguishing between violation in a factual sense (i.e. when the event causing the harm occurs) and violation in a legal sense (which occurs when subjective law begins to take effect). We can indeed be harmed as a result of actions preceding our existence, as Feinberg illustrates using the example of a time bomb placed in a kindergarten, which explodes after 6 years, injuring a 4-year-old child (Feinberg 1992). We could also imagine the example of a firm producing a toxic paint being used to paint the walls in a kindergarten, causing children attending the school over the following years to become ill. The aggrieved parties may then be children who did not exist when the action was taken that resulted in the occurrence of the harm. Of course, the question arises of how far back in time one can go to claim such compensation. This could be answered as followed: as far back as it is still possible to prove an adequate causal link between the action and harm, although this will usually be limited by the fact that the notion of preconception harm is generally applied to situations in which the action causing the harm occurred shortly before conception. The problem of demonstrating an adequate causal relationship does, however, raise well-founded interpretive controversies that not only apply to preconception or prenatal harm, but also postnatal harm.

The notion of retroactive protection of the rights of the individual is suited to the discussed cases, with the proviso that a claim for compensation can only be made by the child once it is born. We find similar provisos in Polish law of succession, which, on the model of Roman law, provides for the possibility that a child conceived but not yet born (termed as *nasciturus*) can be an heir on condition that it is born alive. In the event of injuries caused before birth, in addition to *nasciturus*, another legal abstraction known as *concipiendus* (the unborn and unconceived child) is introduced to accommodate situations when an event causing harm to the child has occurred before conception (Justyński 2003). The appearance of this new, somewhat strange legal construct and the expansion of the scope of retroactive protection of rights is bound up with the development of technology that enables us to predict the future and explain the past with greater accuracy in the attribution of cause and effect.

Some question the legitimacy of the conditional protection of the rights of the conceived child, arguing that a legal system is inconsistent if liability for damages is recognised for damaging health in the period before a child is born, but neither liability for damages nor criminal liability are recognised for unintentionally depriving a conceived child of its life. One example of this is a car accident involving a pregnant woman. Since the woman is in an advanced state of pregnancy, she is not wearing a seatbelt when the perpetrator of the accident's car runs into her. The accident results in a premature birth and the child is born dead. Polish law fails to recognize the crime of unintentionally causing the death of an unborn child, so the perpetrator of the accident is not held to be criminally liable[3] for this, even if the conceived child was fully developed and was, at the time of the accident, at a stage of development making it possible for it to live outside its mother's body. Insurance companies also refuse in similar situations to accept liability for damages in respect of the death of an unborn child. Another example of this type of controversy could be provided by the case of a doctor who, as the result of carrying out a procedure without due care or a medical error, brings about the death of a foetus. This doctor will not be held criminally liable for unintentionally causing the death of a future child. This was the subject of a judgement by the European Court of Human Rights (*Vo v. France* 2004). It therefore seems paradoxical that a doctor bears additional liability for a child born disabled as the result of a medical error, yet bears no additional liability when, due to a medical error, a foetus is killed (in this case the doctor is only held liable to the child's mother for any harm caused to her health). Any objection of inconsistency can be dismissed by claiming that granting retroactive protection of personal rights extended to the period before birth in exceptional legally defined situations does not amount to conferring legal personality on a conceived child, which is bound up in turn with the conditionality of the legal protection granted to the *nasciturus* (i.e. conditional on the enforcement of the infant's rights at birth).

The retroactive right not to be harmed results in claims extended to everyone who can cause harm, including a child's mother. Sometimes an objection of

---

3   If criminal liability for unintentionally causing the death of the conceived child was also extended to the child's mother, this would cause difficult-to-accept solutions which would punish reckless pregnant mothers for every miscarriage in which it was possible to demonstrate the mother's decisive role. This would favour the emergence of repressive control exercised over pregnant women and the appropriation of the intimate reproductive sphere of life by the state, which would appear to be in complete contradiction to the principles of social coexistence.

inconsistency is raised against a mother being held liable for harm caused to her unborn child, which reverses the objection to the aforementioned medical liability. It is argued that since, in most legal systems, a woman has the right to terminate a pregnancy (the legal grounds for terminating a pregnancy are diversifying), it may seem inconsistent to attribute legal liability to her for harming the foetus when she decides to give birth to the child (Steinbock 1992). However, much like in the case above, these legal solutions do not display any inconsistency. While legal protection does not cover legal entities alone, when it comes to the possession of interests or rights that may be violated, the law is only binding in cases when legal entities possess legal capacity. The notion of preconception and prenatal harm does not therefore presuppose the existence of a right to be born but, assuming the child is born alive, it provides it with the right not to be harmed by anyone.

A mother's liability for harm caused to her child before birth can, however, arouse legitimate controversies for other reasons. First, controversies are provoked by the conflict between the mother's autonomy and the conditional rights of a future child. The following issues have therefore been the subject of disputes in American doctrine: subjecting pregnant woman to forced detoxification, depriving alcohol or drug addicted women of parental rights etc. (Steinbock 1992). There is some debate in Polish legal doctrine over the protection of a pregnant woman's health interests and autonomy within the context of controversies connected with the extension of the legal protection of a child's father's interests to the prenatal period and the controversial notion of appointing a guardian responsible for a conceived child (*curator ventris*) to protect not only the child's future property rights, but personal rights, like its right to life and health (Haberko 2010). Secondly, doubts arise over whether compensation claims are the best protection for a child due to their negative effect on the mother-child relationship, whose protection is also in the child's interest. The rights of a child to be born can neither be treated in isolation from this relationship nor in opposition to parental rights. Much like procreative rights, the rights of a future child are not and cannot be absolute, especially as the child going to be born is biologically dependent on its mother. The mother's role cannot be subordinated to the provision of optimal conditions for the development of a foetus.

The appearance of claims for compensation for prenatal harm to the mother can be understood in American law within the context of American insurance law. The first claim of this kind was recognised by a court in the USA when the focus was placed on both the mother and child obtaining joint compensation from the mother's insurance cover rather than the child seeking compensation from the mother (*Grodin v. Grodin* 1981). The mother and child were therefore not adversaries in this case, and the child's claim against the mother was used solely to obtain additional compensation for the harm to the child from the mother's insurance. When we apply this type of legal construct to continental law, where we have a social insurance system, the question may arise of what type of compensation the child should seek from the mother in a situation when the mother shall continue to act as its legal guardian and bear the costs of looking after it.

4.3.2 Wrongful life actions

A more controversial issue within the reproduction context would appear to be that of harm that could potentially arise through the mere fact of a child being born with a disability that it would be impossible to avoid. In other words, the only option available was for the child in question not to be born at all. This is the case of wrongful life actions. The entity obligated to pay compensation should be liable, according to the construction of this claim, for the child, despite its severe and predictable health impairments, being born and suffering (i.e. living in a state of grievance).

A wrongful life claim *sensu largo* is a claim vested in a child that enters the world in a state of grievance.[4] A wrongful life claim *sensu stricto* is a claim by a child entering the world in a state of grievance pertaining to its health (the sole focus being on issues of a medical, rather than social, economic or any other, nature). The subject of discussion in this chapter is wrongful life action *sensu stricto* (hereinafter referred to as 'wrongful life action'), currently a major focus of legal debate. It surfaced in American jurisprudence in response to the development of modern medical techniques enabling prenatal testing and more control over the reproductive process. Over time, this form of claim also began to appear in other countries (including Great Britain, France, Germany, Holland, Belgium and Poland), provoking fierce controversy.

Wrongful life is type of claim that has given rise to a whole array of new claims in tort law, such as wrongful birth and wrongful conception. Wrongful birth

---

4   A wrongful life claim was first formulated in the case of *Zepeda v. Zepeda* (1963), in which the plaintiff claimed damages for the discomfort felt at being born outside wedlock (so the grievance arose from social, rather than medical, causes). However, claims of this type have been consistently dismissed and the viewpoint has been adopted that only being born with a health impairment could be regarded as a state of grievance that could result in liability for damages.

claims can be pursued on similar grounds to a wrongful life claim, but they are vested in a different group of plaintiffs – in this case, the parents of a disabled child – and only arise in legal systems permitting the termination of pregnancies in cases when a foetus is malformed. They are brought against third parties (e.g. a doctor, medical staff or a clinic) that have prevented parents from taking the decision to abort a foetus in cases when severe foetal damage could conceivably be detected or foreseen (this applies, for example, to the failure to carry out adequate prenatal tests in the event of a high-risk pregnancy, or the giving of incorrect diagnoses). Parents are entitled to pursue a wrongful conception claim for the healthy conception of an unwanted child against third parties (a doctor, pharmacist, medical staff or the facility in which these entities work) that prevented the parents from acting on their own decision on an issue connected with conceiving and the birth of a child (e.g. a faulty sterilisation, faulty contraception or even an improperly performed abortion).

Out of these claims, the greatest controversy is provoked by the claim vested in a child and this is the only one of the claims mentioned here that is usually dismissed in most legal systems. In the next part of this chapter, I will present the main problems relating to both the legal construct and the axiological premises behind the wrongful life claim.

4.3.3 The legal premises of reproductive harm: the causal relationship and the distinguishing features of harm

I shall continue to refer to harm entailing someone being born disabled as 'reproductive harm' to distinguish it from the earlier mentioned prenatal and preconception harm. I understand reproductive harm to be harm caused by the taking of a reproductive decision. The taking of such a decision may arise from both the negligence (undue care) of the mother or parents or their bad motivations.[5] The taking of that decision may also arise from the bad motivations or negligence of third parties (a doctor, medical staff etc.) who have contributed through their actions to the taking of the decision or who have prevented parents from taking

---

5   An example of mother's neglect would be the failure to take appropriate genetic tests or disregarding the advice of a doctor regarding, for example, therapy harmful to the foetus. An example of parents' 'bad intentions' would be their willingness to have a disabled child and using artificial insemination methods to conceive a disabled child. Joel Feinberg considers the example of a mother who decides to give birth to a disabled child out of egotistic motives, because she wants to have a child that will be totally dependent on her and will satisfy her desire to control someone else's life (Feinberg 1992).

the decision. To date, no such claims against a mother or parents have ever been acknowledged, though such subjective restrictions do not arise from the actual construction of the claim. I will also, therefore, be taking into consideration the eventuality of liability for reproductive harm being attributed to a mother (or parents) in the reflections that follow.[6]

A wrongful life claim is usually brought against a doctor, medical staff or a medical facility, when, due to negligence, they have not allowed a mother (or parents) to decide whether or not to give birth to a child (for example, by refusing to carry out appropriate prenatal tests in the event of a high-risk pregnancy, or giving an incorrect diagnosis). As a rule, the reasoning behind a wrongful life claim generally takes one of the following forms: the aggrieved party has a claim for damages against the obligee (a doctor, medical staff or medical facility), because, due to a breach of medical duty, the parents of the aggrieved party were deprived of information regarding threats to the health of the aggrieved party while at the same time being deprived of the opportunity to decide whether to terminate the pregnancy.

Generally, it is accepted that a wrongful life claim is of a tortious nature, because it applies to personal injury caused by a breach of medical duty. Sometimes, it is also proposed that a claim be based on a legal construct pertaining to a violation of contractual rights (Justyński 2003). The advancement of the medical sciences has been accompanied by the appearance of a new trend in law according to which it has begun to be accepted that liability of a doctor or medical staff does not arise from the actual violation of another person's rights, but rather from their breach of the requirements of correct conduct, i.e. negligent conduct. This is bound up with the notion of 'duty of care', whereby medical liability has been extended to protect the interests of all the entities that could reasonably be expected to have had them violated. In this case, the child is not party to a contract as far as prenatal or preconception services are concerned, but given the fact it is covered by the scope of a service, the child's interests should also be taken into account. This is bound up with the extension of the contract's sphere of protection to the child, assuming that this would be in its own interests. It may be assumed that a breach of contractual obligations toward the child has occurred,

---

6   The legal regulations of countries that recognise wrongful life claims generally limit its subjective scope, expressly excluding the possibility of pursuing such claims against a mother or parents. Shaw, among others, acknowledge the possibility of wrongful life claims against the mother (Shaw 1984). Feinberg also argues for civil liability (and even, in some cases, criminal) liability for wrongful life, extended to parents as well (Feinberg 1992).

because the parents' possession of information relating to any threat to the pregnancy would also be in its own interest (regardless of what decision the parents would make). However, a breach of contractual obligations is not in itself tantamount to harm justifying liability for damages being caused to the child. In both cases, for the legitimacy of the claim to be recognised, both tortious and contractual liability would need to be demonstrated before we can conclude that we are dealing with harm caused to the child.

I shall investigate the legal premises for a wrongful life claim by using the example of one of the several cases in which a court granted damages to a child born with a severe genetically conditioned disability, namely *Curlender v. Bio-Science Laboratories* case (1980). Before making the decision to conceive a child, Messrs Curlender underwent genetic testing for the carrier of the recessive gene causing Tay-Sachs disease. The Laboratories carried out the test without due care and the tests failed to detect any threat. If the tests had been carried out correctly, they would have demonstrated the high probability of the disease appearing in Messrs Curlender's offspring and they would have decided against the child's conception and birth. Their child, Shauna Curlender, was born severely disabled and lived in a vegetative state for four years. The parents petitioned on their own behalf and that of their child for damages for the suffering and pain that had been caused and healthcare costs. The plaintiff's attorney also demanded damages for Shauna for being deprived of the possibility of living 72 years and six months longer (the difference between the average life expectancy of women in the United States and the age reached by the child before she died prematurely as a result of the disease). The argument relating to damages for depriving the child of the rest of her life was regarded as inadequate, because the child never had any chance of reaching the average life expectancy of healthy people. If the tests had in fact been carried out correctly, the child would not have been born, while, since they were carried out without due care, the child was born with a serious illness that caused her premature death after just a few years. However, the court recognised the legitimacy of the argument for damages to be granted not only to the parents, but to the child, not for being deprived of the possibility of living longer, but for the very fact of being born in a state of grievance.

The line of reasoning on which the claim was based could be framed as follows:

(1) The obligee (in this case, Bio-Science Laboratories) breached their duties by carrying out tests without due care and incorrectly informing the parent that there was no threat to the health of the future child;

(2) if the aggrieved parties (the parents) had not been deprived of information relating to the threat to their offspring's health, they would have decided against conceiving or giving birth to the disabled child;
(3) the aggrieved party (the child) was born with a severe, irreversible and foreseeable health impairment;

And therefore:

(4) the obligee is liable for damages to the aggrieved parents and aggrieved child (i.e. obligated to provide damages compensating for the impairment suffered by the aggrieved parties for the ensuing harm).

Returning to my previous reflections on causing harm to verify the line of legal reasoning above, it should be clarified whether there is an adequate causal relationship between states mentioned in conditions 1 and 2 and between 1 and 3. It should also be clarified whether conditions 2 and 3 satisfy the worsening test, the counterfactual test or the doubly counterfactual test.

The existence of an adequate causal relationship between states mentioned in conditions 1 and 2 would appear to be obvious. The Laboratories' breach of duty in relation to properly carrying out the genetic testing directly caused the parents to be prevented from making a fully informed reproductive decision. However, demonstrating an adequate causal relationship between the laboratories' actions and the birth of a disabled child is more problematic. The assumption was made in the discussed case that, if the laboratories had fulfilled their duties with due care, the seriously ill child would never have been conceived. As far as the disabled child is concerned, the laboratories' breach of duty can only therefore constitute an *indirect cause of harm*. Both direct and indirect causes are taken into account when assessing liability for damages. As I mentioned above, the adequate cause theory narrows the scope of causal relationships to situations in which we are dealing with causes that *normally* produce particular effects. We are dealing here with an objective relationship among specific causes and specific effects that is always foreseeable. The causality of the cause, in this case the laboratories' breach of duty, is *mediated by the parents' reproductive decision* (Justyński 2003). In other words, if it is to be accepted that the lack of due diligence with which the laboratories carried out the tests did not prevent the conception or birth of a disabled child, it should first be demonstrated that the parents, if they had received adequate information, would have refrained from conceiving a child or, more controversially, would have decided to abort a foetus with genetic defects. It could be argued at this juncture that, in a situation in which causality is dependent on the subjective decision of the entities directly causing the said damage, this could undermine the adequacy of the causal relationship between the action of the entity indirectly contributing to the harm and the harm itself (Safjan 1998; Lang & Safjan 2000). Such argumentation could, however, raise doubts and would not appear to constitute sufficient grounds for rejecting a wrongful life claim. In the discussed situation, in particular, when the future parents underwent genetic testing as a basis for making a decision about whether to conceive a child, it can be assumed that a positive test result would amount, as far as they were concerned, to taking a negative reproductive decision (being an objective, rather than subjective, reason for not giving birth to a child).

Condition 2 bears the hallmarks of harm when it is relatively easy to not only demonstrate that the parents' situation was better (the parents did not have a sick child), but also that it would have been better (the parents would not have conceived a sick child) if the laboratory had carried out the genetic tests properly. The harm to the parents may also be economic (the costs connected with the birth of a sick child) and non-economic (harm entailing the psychological stress of giving birth to and losing a terminally ill child) in nature.

It is much more difficult to demonstrate that Condition 3 (being born with a severe and irreversible health impairment) also bears the hallmarks of harm in a legal sense. The notion of harm presupposes the possibility of comparing current situation with the situation that would occur if a specific action, act of negligence or event did not take place (the worsening test) or with the situation that would occur if a specific action, act of negligence or event occurred in a suitable, foreseeable manner (the counterfactual test). Prior to the genetic test being carried out, the child was not conceived, whereas if the test had been carried out with due diligence, the child would not have been conceived at all. In other words, a comparison is being made between a situation of non-existence or not being born and a situation of being born in a state of grievance. Every birth, not just a birth in a state of grievance, generates costs (both economic and non-economic, e.g. psychological), though this of course does not in itself constitute sufficient grounds for the existence of harm to be confirmed. In this case, for the existence of harm to be confirmed, it should be demonstrated that the birth of a disabled child amounts to a violation of this child's personal rights.

One of the personal rights is the right to health, so I would propose invoking within this context the 'right to be born as a functional being', which was formulated in a ruling of the New York State Court of Appeals in the case of *Park v. Chessin*, during which an American court awarded damages for a child based on a wrongful life claim for the first time (*Park v. Chessin* 1976). Invoking a right of this type can, however, raise many legitimate doubts. First, no consensus could ever be reached on the existence of a positive right that cannot be guaranteed (for the same reasons that the existence of the right of every person to health is questioned). Recognising a right of this type within a reproductive context would lead to the acceptance of strict liability for procreation, i.e. entities deciding to procreate would be liable for the actual effect of this decision, which would be difficult to envisage, especially while natural procreation exists and is permitted.[7] A similar right can only therefore be invoked in a negative sense, i.e. nobody can violate such an individual's personal rights such as their health and bodily integrity, which does not apply to this particular claim. Second, it would be wrong to invoke a right of this type even if its existence were accepted, because the essence of a wrongful life claim is that the aggrieved party should not have even been born. The desirable alternative in this case is therefore not actually being born as a functional being, but rather not to be born at all.

We should therefore examine whether it is possible in this case to invoke the 'right to non-existence' (or the right to not be conceived) or the 'right to not be born'. In other words, the question arises of whether anyone can have a legal protected interest in not existing or not being born. Rights of this type create peculiar controversy when considered within a context in which the right of every person to life is universally recognised. It should, however, be clearly distinguished from the right to die, an issue discussed when there is a need to keep people alive in a terminal state. In both cases, we would be dealing with the issue of a life which causes so much suffering that it is not, in the view of the suffering person, worth living. However, the fundamental difference is that in the case of the right to die, we are speaking about the possibility of someone taking a decision to shorten

---

7   A situation could be imagined in which a society guided by the utilitarian principle of genetic enhancement of the population (see Part II of the book) introduces the obligation to use artificially-assisted methods of procreation applying suitably developed criteria for the genetic selection of embryos. In such a hypothetical 'brave new world', we could be dealing with strict liability in a reproductive context being vested in both parents and medical facilities carrying out fertility treatments. This would be returning to universally discredited authoritarian eugenics. A situation could also be imagined in which parties making use of artificial insemination would enter into an agreement with a clinic performing the procedure stipulating that it is to use genetic testing guaranteeing the birth of a child without genetic defects (assuming that in the future pre-implantation tests would have advanced to such an extent that they could be used to predict all possible genetic defects affecting future offspring). We would then be dealing with a kind of 'child production' situation involving medical entities charged with a sort of peculiar strict liability. This scenario would involve the implementation of a liberal eugenics more in tune with the views of the advocates of wrongful life claims discussed in this chapter.

their life (i.e. the aggrieved party's right to take a decision on the remainder of their life). In the case of the right to not be conceived, taking such a decision is out of the question, because this decision does not and cannot belong to the child that is to be born. What is in fact at issue here is not so much the shortening of a life as its non-beginning. It is justified on the assumption that the suffering in question has accompanied a given person from the moment of their birth, so the best way of minimising the suffering would not to have been conceived or born at all. Therefore, whereas the right to die could be derived from human right to self-determination and freedom, arguments of this type cannot be used to justify the right to not be conceived or not to be born. The implementation of these rights would require the taking of a decision on behalf of the entities holding the rights prior to their appearance. The interested party would therefore be deprived of the right to take any decision at all, assuming this was in their interest. This would be tantamount to *a priori* recognition that, in certain circumstances, people would not want to live. It has been emphasised in numerous court rulings and in the literature that this problem is better discussed by philosophers and theologians than lawyers and doctors (*Becker v. Schwartz* 1978, 411, 416). Nevertheless, before we move on to consider this issue from a philosophical perspective, it is worth taking note of the legal aspects of the above rights.

Rights are correlated with obligations, so the obligations which would be bound up with the recognition of rights of this type should be taken into account. The right to not be conceived would impose on the parents the obligation to refrain from procreating in certain situations (here, the role of the doctor and medical staff would enable the parents to make the correct decisions by providing them with adequate information). The imposition on parents of a *ban on procreation in certain circumstances* would violate their autonomy and lead to dangerous intervention, on the part of the state and health services, in the reproductive sphere of human life. Much the same would apply in the case of recognising the right not to be born, which would be correlated with a parental obligation to abort a foetus following the confirmation of severe damage or negative selection of embryos bearing genetic defects. Thus abortion (or negative selection) would be compulsory in certain situations, which would also constitute an unacceptable violation of reproductive autonomy (Spaemann 2006). Undoubtedly, it is accepted, on the basis of current legal doctrine, that reproductive decisions relating to family planning, both refraining from procreation and abortion in conditions stipulated in the relevant law, are *rights*, and not obligations vested in the mother (Justyński 2003), and are meant to protect both her own interests and those of her offspring (assuming that these interests generally coincide, only entering into conflict in exceptional situations). It would therefore appear that the construction of these rights, rather than protecting certain personal rights, would serve to violate them.

The legal construction of wrongful life claims would therefore appear to be unsound in that it cannot be demonstrated that birth in a state of grievance displays the hallmarks of harm in the traditional understanding of civil law. Furthermore, the existence of these rights presupposes the existence of holders of those rights being able to benefit from them. When discussing the right to non-existence or not be born, we are faced with a paradoxical situation in which an entity would possess a right which, if it were to be implemented, would annihilate the holder of that right (and if this right were not violated, the holder of that right would not exist; cf. Spaemann 2006).

In bioethical discussions, a different understanding of reproductive harm or protected interests has been proposed that, in the view of the authors, could give rise to a moral justification for wrongful life claims and serve as an axiological argument favouring the expansion of legal liability within the domain of reproductive decisions. These proposals attempt to interpret the discussed issue in such a manner as to ensure that the issue of the aggrieved party's subjectivity does not hinder the employment of claims of this type. I shall present these proposals in the next section of this chapter.

4.4 The non-identity problem

Within the context of reproductive harm, we may refer to the distinction between a harmful condition and a harmed condition. In the first case, we are dealing with the harmful situation a person has found themselves in for reasons for which no one is responsible (for example, as the result of natural disaster). In the second case, we are dealing with a situation in which the harm results from being harmed (due to someone's inaction or action). All states of harm are harmful by nature, but not all of them can be characterised as a grievance and, as I mentioned above, both kinds of situation may be subject to liability, albeit on different grounds. Prenatal and preconception harm relate to a situation of being harmed, the harmed (or aggrieved) party in this case being a child born disabled due to someone's action or inaction, as in the situations discussed above relating to rubella or medication harmful to the foetus. In turn, reproductive harm is meant to cover situations in which a child is born disabled due to natural factors, in effect a harmful situation. An example of this would be the situation of a woman who gives birth to a child with Down syndrome even though it would be possible, by carrying out adequate prenatal tests, to avoid the sick child being born by deciding to terminate the pregnancy.

This distinction becomes less helpful, however, when we consider the slightly modified situation of a rubella infection or medication harmful to the foetus. We can imagine a situation in which a woman infected with rubella is informed of the risk the disease presents to a potential pregnancy. In spite of this, she becomes pregnant, not caring about how much her state could affect the health of the future child and as a result, gives birth to a disabled child. We can also imagine a situation in which a woman undergoes pharmacological treatment which has a negative effect on the health of the foetus. She was informed by a doctor that she should not become pregnant for the next three months, while the treatment is still ongoing. Rather than heeding the warning, the women becomes pregnant during the treatment and gives birth to a disabled child (cf. Buchanan et al. 2007). The outcome of this situation is the same as in the situations involving preconception injury discussed above. Furthermore, in both types of situation, the disability has not arisen from natural factors, but rather from action or inaction (in the first case, that of the doctor and drug manufactures, and in the second, that of the mother). The difference is that in the former cases, we assume that if everything had proceeded normally (if the woman had not been infected with rubella or had known how harmful the medication was and could have stopped taking it), the child would have been born healthy. But in the latter cases, if the mother had behaved as we would have been expected (if she had prevented herself from becoming pregnant while she was ill or undergoing harmful treatment), the sick child would not have been born, but another healthy child could have been born in the future. Developing this line of reasoning, advocates of wrongful life claims assume that the availability of medically assisted procreation methods imposes greater liability on parents and doctors (Buchanan et al. 2007; Feinberg 1992). This in effect means that any action or inaction leading to the birth of a disabled child that could have been avoided through the appropriate selection of embryos (using in vitro fertilisation) or making the decision to terminate the pregnancy (using natural procreation) could be classified as harming. For if the parents or doctors had behaved in the way that the creators of this argumentation would expect, the sick child would not have been born, and instead another healthy child could have been born in the future. And if modern biotechnology is enabling us to increase our control over procreation, it can also increase the scope of any liability for damages in respect of actions, inaction or an event resulting in the birth of a child in a state of grievance.

It follows from the foregoing reflections that the distinction made in bioethical discussions between both types of claim essentially comes down to the problem of different identity of a child born in a situation of grievance and that of a child that could have been born if both the parents and the doctors had behaved in a manner that could have been expected from prudent parents and good doctors. In the aforementioned example of prenatal and preconception harm, in which the woman is infected during a hospital stay with rubella, the genetic identity of the conceived child would appear to be preserved. In this case, we can compare the situation of a child that would have been born healthy (due to the pregnancy running its normal course) with that of a child born disabled (due to the pregnant mother being infected with rubella). However, in the situations of reproductive harm, we can only compare the situation of the child with the situation of the *other* child that could have been born healthy if its parents had refrained from procreating for a period of time, if the pregnancy in question was terminated and attempts were made to become pregnant again or if an appropriate selection was made of non-defective embryos.

Derek Parfit has brought attention to what is frequently discussed in the literature as the Non-Identity Problem, illustrating it by employing the example of a girl who becomes a mother at the age of 14 (Parfit 1987). It would have been better if the girl had waited a few years before becoming pregnant, because a teenaged mother is not in a position to guarantee her child as good a start in life as an adult woman. Whereas it is easy to agree that it would be better if the teenager had not become pregnant, it is much harder to agree that this would be better for that child whom she has given birth to at 14 years of age. For if she decided to wait a few years to become a mother, she would give birth to a completely different child.[8] In the example of medication causing the birth of a disabled child, the situation is more serious, because we are dealing with a child's health impairment, yet the same non-identity problem still applies. If the woman had listened to her doctor and waited to complete the treatment, a healthy child would probably have been born instead. Approaching this intuitively, it is easy to agree that the woman did something wrong. However, it is difficult to acknowledge, that she acted wrongly towards the child she gave birth to, for if she had done what her doctor recommended, that disabled child would never have been born. Harm has clearly been caused to a child in cases when a woman fails to provide her child with the medication it needs or refuses to take medication needed by the foetus during her pregnancy (Buchanan et al. 2007). Similarly,

---

8   At another point in time, different gametes would fuse together, resulting in the birth of another genetically different person. This would not therefore be exactly the same person. Furthermore, people are different, even if they there is no variance in their genotype – e.g. identical twins. Each one is a separate being, because each one entered the world separately at a different time (Reiman 2007).

few doubts are raised by the opposite situation, when a woman takes medication causing harm to the foetus during her pregnancy. Although the outcome in all these situations is the same, the problem arises of whether the traditional notion of harm can be extended to accommodate a situation in which the alternative to the reproductive decision is the birth of another child or a child not being born at all. This also applies to genetic reproductive interventions by the parents, for example the selection of a particular sex or particular traits in a child (including handicaps, e.g. a congenital hearing impairment or dwarfism, see Chapters 1 and 3) based on preimplantation genetic testing. As far as these *specific* children are concerned, being brought forth into the world as a result of their parents' negligence or intentional decisions, the parents could not have done anything better. These children, even if they are born in a harmful condition, have not been deprived by anyone of another life they could have led in different circumstances. The children in the foregoing examples had no such alternative.

Parfit claims that the Problem of Non-Identity can be solved by arguing that there is no moral difference between actions that harm certain people and actions that lead to a situation in which the same number of people will find themselves in an equally harmful situation. Parfit calls his stance the No-Difference View (Parfit 1987). He justifies this viewpoint by invoking the utilitarian principle termed the Same Number Quality Claim:

> *The Same Number Quality Claim, Or Q*: If in either of two possible outcomes the same number of people would ever live, it would be worse if those who live are worse off, or have a lower quality of life, than those who would have lived (Parfit 1987, 360).

In Parfit's view, an action can be wrong from a moral point of view even if it has not wronged any specific person. The basis of assessment in this case is a comparison of the quality of life of the same aggregate of people affected by a given decision and not the same people.

A similar argument is proposed by Don Locke in his commentary on Parfit's Problem of Non-Identity (Locke 1987). Locke formulated what he terms the Possible Persons Principle, which states that the rightness or wrongness of an action should be evaluated by taking into account not only those who exist or will exist, but also those who could have existed if another decision had been taken. However, it should be noted that adopting Don Locke's principle is tantamount to acknowledging that abortion is unacceptable.

Parfit's line of reasoning is also followed by the authors of the book *From Chance to Choice*, who formulate a Non-Person Affecting Principle (N):

> N: Individuals are morally required not to let any child or other dependent person for whose welfare they are responsible experience serious suffering or limited opportunity

or serious loss of happiness or good, if they can act so that, without affecting the number of persons who will exist and without imposing substantial burdens or costs or loss of benefits on themselves or others, no child or other dependent person for whose welfare they are responsible will experience serious suffering or limited opportunity or serious loss of happiness or good (Buchanan et al. 2007, 249).

However, according to these authors, the Same-Number Principle will not be applicable to all reproductive decisions relating to the birth of a disabled person. In a situation in which the parents cannot have a healthy child, the alternative to the birth of a disabled person is the birth of no one, so this is a different-number case to which the N principle given above cannot be applied. In such cases, the possession of a disabled child will not always be a morally wrong choice (cf. Kamm 2013). However, in cases in which the number of people that are born agree with each other, the parents have the moral obligation, according to the authors, to decide to give any healthy children the chance of life.

Similar conclusions are reached by R.M. Hare (Hare 2002) and Peter Singer (Singer 2011) by invoking utilitarian argumentation, and also Jeffrey Reiman, who applies deontological argumentation (Reiman 2007). From a utilitarian point of view, it is our moral duty not to bring people into the world who, due to being disabled, will not be able to lead sufficiently happy lives (for more on this, see Chapter 5).[9] For people who are currently alive, whether they are alive as themselves or whether they will be replaced by another person with the same characteristics, is of paramount importance. The interests of future people should, however, be understood, in Reiman's view, differently to those of people who are currently alive. In his view, the decision to conceive a disabled child can be regarded as unfair to future people, even if it cannot be demonstrated that it does not apply to specific people. People possess certain rights and interests that the law should protect, and these include the interest of every person in being born healthy, irrespective of who they will be (or what identity they will have).

---

9   If it is acknowledged that it is our moral duty to not bring people into the world who, due to being disabled, will not be able to lead happy lives, we would then also need to accept the opposite obligation – the duty to bring beings into the world able to lead happy lives. The normative asymmetry between these duties would only appear justified on negative utilitarian grounds guided by the principle of minimising suffering in the world. Negative utilitarianism then naturally leads to the conclusion being drawn that it would be best if humanity stopped reproducing entirely, in effect becoming extinct, thus minimising the suffering of human beings to zero. It would therefore appear that Birnbacher was right when he claimed that utilitarian reasoning can only be applied to maximising the happiness of living people (Birnbacher 1999).

Reiman supports his thesis intuitively by evoking the example of a mother who, on taking a reproductive decision, does not think about the actual person who is to be born, but about the future child, whoever it will be (for a similar line of reasoning, see Steinbock 1992).

Ronald M. Green employs similar argumentation, claiming that human life, when examined before conception, and even before birth, is 'fungible', by which he means that future people are perceived as 'replacements', rather than identifiable, unique entities (Green 1997). He thus draws the conclusion that:

> Parents have a *prima facie* obligation not to bring a child into being deliberately or negligently with a health status likely to result in significant greater disability or suffering, or significantly reduced life options relative to the other children with whom he/she will grow up (Green 1997, 10).

Feinberg, in turn, arrives at similar conclusions to the aforementioned authors, claiming that despite the fact that the parents have not wronged a particular child born in such situations, they have nevertheless acted wrongly, simply by introducing unnecessary suffering into the world that could have been avoided (Feinberg 1992). Feinberg evokes in his reflections what is the objective, in his view, criterion of rationality, claiming that in the case of some very severe disabilities or illnesses, '*it would be rational to prefer nonexistence to that condition*' (Feinberg 1992, 19). Some introduce a distinction here between situations of severe disability (e.g. the earlier mentioned Tay-Sachs disease) falling within the category of wrongful life and all other milder disabilities that are termed wrongful disabilities (Buchanan et al. 2007). The latter relate to the situation of being born with a disability which is not severe enough to consider not being born a more attractive option. However, both cases may be judged as a morally wrong contribution to increasing suffering and disability in the world (see Chapter 5). At this juncture, the important issue arises of establishing universal criteria for quality of life that would enable us to indicate when the birth of a disabled person is morally wrong. The physical suffering criterion pointed out by Singer (Singer 2011) is not in itself enough, because in most of the cases being discussed here, modern medicine is able to either reduce or eliminate physical pain, even in the case of the most severe disabilities. Philip Kitcher proposes that the criterion for leading a valuable life should be the possibility of formulating one's own conception of life plan (Kitcher 1997). The list of such criteria is set to grow, since each criterion is arbitrary in nature, evoking a subjective understanding of happiness, something we shall return to in the next chapter. The objective of this chapter is to apply these philosophical proposals to the legal notion of reproductive harm being analysed here. I shall move on to this in the next section.

4.5 Harming and legally protected interest detached from a legal entity

Let's consider Feinberg's stance first, which states that in the discussed examples, we would be dealing with wrongdoing. The wrong being done is directed against an abstractly conceived society that includes past, current and future generations. Taking this approach, it would be possible, for example, to justify legal regulations banning human cloning, the creation of animal-human chimeras and hybrids etc. The legally protected good in this case would be social security. However, within the context of the reproductive decisions being discussed here, which result in the birth of a disabled child, it is difficult to speak of any threat to social security. What is at issue here are the increased costs that parents or society bear associated with caring for disabled people and their social activation. In these cases, therefore the priority of reproductive autonomy over social interest or well-being would appear to be without question if we wish to avoid universally discredited eugenics policies (Art. 2 of the European Convention on Bioethics).

The Same Number Principle discussed above can only be applied to the notion of harm by modifying the notion of harm presented in the introduction to incorporate not only a situation affecting a person (person-affecting harm), but also a situation of harm affecting the same number of people regardless of their identity (number-affecting harm). In the first case, the prevention of harm is applied to decisions affecting the same person, while in the second, the prevention of harm would be applied to a certain class of people, rather than a specific person. Treating the notion of harm in isolation from the harmed person is, however, counterintuitive and is at odds with the legal construction of this notion.

The issue being discussed here can be resolved on legal grounds by employing at least two solutions in which there is absolutely no need to apply the notion of reproductive harm. The first method would involve subsuming some of the examples discussed above under the notion of preconception harm without changing the actual notion of harm or getting embroiled in philosophical cul-desacs relating to human identity. Law is not designed to settle philosophical and theological issues relating to human nature. This is not a requirement on legal grounds, because 'inhabitants of the legal world are legal entities rather than people', as Tomasz Gizbert-Studnicki observes, going on to add that 'A subject of law is not an actual person, that is, a bundle of individualised characteristics', but rather a bundle of certain rights that can also be granted to 'creations not possessing a human substrate (e.g. a foundation)' (Gizbert-Studnicki 1992, 154).

Law is tasked with attributing rights which can be enforced in respect of others or the state. From a legal perspective, it could therefore be argued that a situation in which a woman becomes pregnant during a medical treatment harmful to her foetus is no different from one in which medication harmful to the foetus is taken during pregnancy. In both cases, according to this line of reasoning, she is harming a future child which will be able to claim damages from her if it is born alive. For the child is being born worse off than it could have been if everything had progressed in line with the normal course of events, i.e. a course of events in which the mother behaved prudently by neither becoming pregnant during the treatment nor taking harmful medication during pregnancy. In other words, a 'sensible motherhood' standard of some kind should be used here. It is possible to get around the Non-Identity Problem by arguing that what is at issue here in every case is a legal entity, i.e. a specific bundle of rights, rather than individualised characteristics. This will therefore be a specific woman's child defined in terms of the order in which it appeared (e.g. her first child). This argumentation would appear to at least partially accord with Reiman's notion of every person's interest in being born healthy irrespective of who they will be (or what identity they will have).[10] The applicable comparison here would be between a state of disability, and a state of non-disability, if everything had proceeded normally. In such cases, the law neither applies the utilitarian same-number principle nor compares the quality of life of a person currently alive with one that could have lived instead. From a legal point of view, the most pertinent factor is the actual mother-child relationship, and any harm arising from this relationship may result from a mother's negligence in respect to a child that has entered the world disabled, or a child that could have entered the world disabled. This argumentation cannot be applied to cases where the alternative to a child being born is terminating the pregnancy, because in such cases there is no negligence involving the conception of a disabled person and the right not to be born does not belong to anyone and cannot form the basis of the claims for damages mentioned before.

The above argumentation has limited application and can also provoke controversy. This construction is based on the evident legal fiction of an aggrieved entity, which may appear to be too far removed from the common sense notion of an aggrieved person (people think of themselves as concrete individual beings

---

10 Only partially, because Reiman argues that it may also be in future people's interest not to be born, which is untenable from a legal perspective, as was made clear before. Further critical analysis of Reiman's stance can be found in Chapter 5.

rather than bundles of rights). Doubts may also be raised, as mentioned above, by the actual construction of preconception injuries, particularly the granting of claims for damages to a child against its mother in respect of what happened before its birth.

State interference in the delicate sphere of human procreation should always be perceived as a last resort. For this reason, there would appear to be a more sensible second solution to the issues being discussed in this article. This solution would involve abandoning the notion of harm in the discussed situations relating to the reproductive decisions of parents. This would result in legislative interference being limited to indirect actions, such as various kinds of social and education programme promoting responsible procreation (for example, social programmes tackling teenage pregnancies, suitable educational programmes and genetic counselling should make future parents aware of the kinds of threat posed by particular genetic diseases, while abiding by the principle of non-directiveness applied to genetic counselling which was discussed in Chapter 1). Some restrictions on access to medically assisted reproductive techniques could also be legally justified (e.g. age restrictions, restrictions to embryo selection etc.), or restrictions governing the use of prenatal and pre-implantation genetic testing (e.g. restricting tests exclusively to traits relevant to health and the most severe genetic defects or those requiring therapeutic action). While everyone has the right to be protected from state interference or third parties in procreation, it does not necessarily follow that everyone would have the right to unlimited access to resources aiding procreation, including medically assisted reproduction methods. As Onora O'Neill rightly observes, there is no reason why people using medically assisted reproduction should not undergo the same verification procedures as people trying to adopt a child (O'Neill 2007). Legal regulations of this type, like legal restrictions on the trade of gametes or embryos, do not violate reproductive autonomy in its negative sense, and restricting reproductive autonomy in its positive sense would seem to be justified when we appeal to the interests of society.

The liability of a doctor, medical staff or health facility for damages to a child in respect of prenatal and preconception harm is much less controversial. It is therefore worth asking whether extending this liability to cases subsumed under a wrongful life claim would be advisable. Excessively extending the liability of doctors whose role in procreation, especially medically assisted procreation, is constantly being expanded, can be problematic. Doctors' fear of being sued by a child on the grounds of being born disabled could lead to them promoting pro-abortion and pro-eugenic stances among parents. It would be essential to establish a new standard for medical services being offered in the field of procreation, yet it would be extremely difficult to define their exact scope, i.e. what information and prenatal diagnoses would be within a scope of medical obligations (Botkin 2002). This would depend on what we would consider to be a desirable standard of living of an adequate quality, as mentioned above.

4.6 Reproductive responsibility – legally protecting not only the parties, but the parental relationship

Advocates of wrongful life claims often allude to the words of John Stuart Mill, who wrote:

> The fact itself, of causing the existence of a human being, is one of the most responsible actions in the range of human life. To undertake this responsibility – to bestow a life which may be either a curse or a blessing – unless the being on whom it is to be bestowed will have at least the ordinary chances of a desirable existence, is a crime against this being (Mill 2003, 174–175).

In the above quotation, Mill is not focusing on medical issues, but on the most pressing economic problems of his era, which included overpopulation and lacking the material resources to support offspring. This is not, however, the main cause of misunderstanding surrounding the philosopher's words. First and foremost, it must be stressed that the 'most responsible actions' mentioned in the above passage are of a moral nature, so cannot be directly translated into legal language and certainly cannot be investigated within the context of liability for damages. Parental responsibility for causing the existence of a human that is dependent on them entails the provision of appropriate care, love and concern over its well-being. It could therefore be claimed that the most obvious 'crime' against a born being would be rejecting responsibility for it, rather than the fact of causing the existence of a disabled, less intelligent or deformed person. This is the central problem associated with procreation, which will be reappearing within the context of our reflections in the following chapters.

If the issue of disabled people is considered within a socioeconomic context, it could also be said, after Mill, that it is not a 'crime' against every such person to cause their existence, but it is a 'crime' if a society does not provide them with the care affording them the opportunity to lead a satisfactory existence. The main reason for the appearance of legal discussions on harm within a reproductive context, including wrongful-life-type harm, is the issue of the immense hardships that parents of disabled children are faced with, including the substantial costs associated with supporting and treating them. The parents or caregivers of severely disabled children whose birth could have been avoided have usually acted on their own behalf and that of their children when seeking compensation to guarantee their sick offspring the appropriate medical care and support. Nevertheless, as has been rightly observed in the literature, private law should not get involved with social security issues which should be resolved with the assistance of an appropriate social insurance model (Safjan 1998, Justyński 2003). Furthermore, if we are to remain consistent with the ideal of solidarity on which our societies are based, there would appear to be a need to create a suitable system of assistance for disabled people rather than guaranteeing maintenance costs using claims that presuppose that they should not even be born.

Parental moral responsibility is much broader than parental legal responsibility, since it relies on parents' decisions being guided by their offspring's best interests and the building of a parental bond based on love, trust and respect towards their progeny. I do not think that this responsibility should be interpreted as responsibility for the result of procreation (cf. Steinbock 1992).[11] One interpretation that would appear to be more consistent with intuitions about procreation as a social practice accepts that what is at issue here is responsibility for a parental relationship and our role in this. A mother who disregards medical advice to refrain from becoming pregnant during therapy harmful to a foetus is behaving irresponsibly from a moral standpoint. What is at issue here is not her behaviour towards a specific child, but her behaviour as a future mother who should regard her offspring's health as important. Her behaviour fills us with fear that she will be very unlikely to provide the child with adequate care after its birth. This is not the case, however, when we examine the example of a woman who discovers that it is very likely for genetic reasons that she will give birth to a child that is sick (e.g. a haemophiliac) or disabled (e.g. with Down Syndrome), but even so decides to take the risk of becoming pregnant or giving birth to a child (after discovering the foetal defect during the course of her pregnancy).

---

11 Bonnie Steinbock formulates a principal of parental responsibility that differs somewhat from the one proposed in this chapter as a criterion for the evaluation of parental reproductive decisions. According to her, a reproductive decision cannot be the mere effect of parents wanting to pursue their own interests, but must, above all, take into the account the well-being of the future child and what its parents are able to guarantee it regardless of how the child will turn out (regardless of its identity, for what is at issue here is not the well-being of a specific child, but the well-being of a child that parents can bring into the world under certain circumstances). By focusing on the child's welfare, understood as a sphere of life opportunities, the author concludes that in certain circumstances (like severe disability), the responsible behaviour would be to terminate the pregnancy. Julian Savulescu's similar claim that reproduction should involve the possession of children with the best prospects will be discussed in the next chapters (Savulescu 2009).

In this case, we have no reason to believe that this woman is an example of an irresponsible mother who disregards health issues relating to her offspring and could also neglect her child after its birth. Quite the contrary, we would rather amire her for being heroic mother who is not afraid of having a disabled child and providing it with further necessary assistance.

Of course, the problem of reproductive irresponsibility not only applies to the issues being discussed here relating to the influence of parental decisions on the health of their future offspring. It likewise applies to social issues. This is exemplified by dysfunctional families in which one child after another is born even though the parents do not want them and are unable to provide them with love or care. It cannot be assumed that procreation in any circumstances and at any cost is right from a moral standpoint, because procreation should not only be regarded as a means to achieving egoistic ends, and nor should it be regarded as an end in itself. The aim of procreation should in fact be to create bonds between parents and children based on love, respect and trust accompanied by a readiness to accept moral responsibility for the well-being of any child that is born, irrespective of how it will turn out. As Michael Sandel underlines, it is actually this parental relationship based on love and acceptance that exerts the greatest influence when it comes to guaranteeing a child's full development and shaping its identity (Sandel 2007, Walzer 1985).

4.7 Summary

In conclusion, I believe that the notion of reproductive harm is not well-founded and should not be introduced to legal regulations following the example of prenatal and preconception harm, which also raise certain doubts with regard to claims directed against mothers. The new genetic knowledge with which parents may be equipped today does not justify legal interference in the sphere of reproductive decisions, but can justify legal restrictions to access to medically assisted reproductive techniques. Greater knowledge of procreation and its effects imposes greater moral responsibility on future parents, forcing them to be more aware of the risk posed by genetically transmitted diseases when making reproductive decisions. However, the legal language of claims, which sets children in conflict with their parents, appears to be ill-equipped to deal with the parental relationship within the context of taking reproductive decisions. It should not permeate, or even worse, act as a determining factor in discussions on procreation and obligations between parents and their children where it is more appropriate to apply the moral notion of responsibility. Borrowing the notion of harm from legal language has nothing to contribute, only serving to corrupt ethical debate on reproductive decisions.

Acknowledgements

This text was originally prepared in Polish and published in a modified version in chapter 2 in: Soniewicka M (2018). Selekcja genetyczna w prokreacji medycznie wspomaganej. Etyczne i prawne kryteria. Wolters Kluwer, Warszawa. Translated from Polish into English by Philip Palmer.

References

Birnbacher D (1999) Odpowiedzialność za przyszłe pokolenia [Verantwortung für zukunftige Generationen]. Oficyna Naukowa University, Warszawa.

Botkin JR (2002) Prenatal Diagnosis and the Selection of Children. HeinOline, Florida, State University Law Review.

Buchanan A, Brock DW, Daniels N, Wikler D (2007) From Chance to Choice: Genetics and Justice. Cambridge University Press, Cambridge & New York.

Feinberg J (1992) Wrongful Life and the Counterfactual Element in Harming. In: Feinberg J (auth) Freedom and Fulfillment. Philosophical Essays. Princeton University Press, New Jersey, pp. 3–36.

Gizbert-Studnicki T (1992) Język prawny a obraz świata. In: Skąpska G (ed) Prawo w zmieniającym się społeczeństwie. Wydawnictwo Adam Marszałek, Kraków, pp. 149–160.

Green RM (1997) Parental Autonomy and the Obligation Not to Harm One's Child Genetically. Journal of Law, Medicine & Ethics 25:5–15.

Haberko J (2010) Cywilnoprawna ochrona dziecka poczętego a stosowanie procedur medycznych. Oficyna, Łódź.

Hare RM (2002) Essays on Bioethics. Clarendon Press, Oxford.

Ito T, Ando H, Suzuki T, Ogaura T, Hotta K, Imamura Y, Yamaguchi Y, Handa H (2010) Identification of a Primary Target of Thalidomide Teratogenicity. Science 327(5971):1345–1350.

Justyński T (2003) Poczęcie i urodzenie się dziecka jako źródło odpowiedzialności cywilnej. Zakamycze, Kraków.

Kamm FM (2013) Bioethical Prescriptions to Create, End, Choose, and Improve Lives. Oxford University Press, Oxford & New York.

Kitcher P (1997) The Lives to Come. The Genetic Revolution and Human Possibilities. Touchstone, New York.

Lang W, Safjan M (2000) Odpowiedzialność prawna za szkody prenatalne i prekoncepcyjne. In: Lang W (ed) Prawne problemy ludzkiej prokreacji. Wydanictwo Adam Marszałek, Toruń, pp. 384–411.

Locke D (1987) The Parfit Population Problem. Philosophy 62:131–157.

Mill JS (2003) Utilitarianism and On Liberty. Including Mill's 'Essay on Bentham' and selections from the writings of Jeremy Bentham and John Austin, 2nd ed. Warnock M (ed). Blackwell Publishing, Oxford.

O'Neill O (2007) Autonomy and Trust in Bioethics. Cambridge University Press, Cambridge.

Parfit D (1987) Reasons and Persons. Clarendon Press, Oxford.

Reiman J (2007) Being Fair to Future People: The Non-Identity Problem in the Original Position. Philosophy & Public Affairs 35(1):69–92.

Safjan M (1998) Prawo i Medycyna. Ochrona praw jednostki a dylematy współczesnej medycyny. Oficyna Naukowa, Warszawa.

Sandel M (2007) The Case against Perfection. Ethics in the Age of Genetic Engineering. The Belknap Press of Harvard University Press, Cambridge, MA & London.

Savulescu J (2009) Genetic Interventions and the Ethics of Enhancement of Human Beings. In: Steinbock B (ed) The Oxford Handbook of Bioethics. Oxford University Press, Oxford, pp. 516–535.

Shaw M (1984) Conditional Prospective Rights of the Fetus. Journal of Legal Medicine 5(1):63–116.

Singer P (2011) Practical Ethics. Cambridge University Press, Cambridge & New York.

Spaemann R (2006) Granice. O etycznym wymiarze działania. Oficyna Naukowa, Warszawa.

Steinbock B (1992) Life Before Birth. The Moral and Legal Status of Embryos and Fetuses. Oxford University Press, Oxford.

Walzer M (1985) Spheres of Justice. A Defence of Pluralism and Equality. Oxford University Press, Oxford.

Case law references

Becker v. Schwartz 46 NY2d 401 (1978)

Curlender v. Bio-Science Laboratories case, 106 Cal. App. 3d 811, 165 Cal. Rptr. 477 (1980)

Grodin v. Grodin, Mich. App., 301 N. W. 2d869 (1981)

Park v. Chessin 387, N.Y.S. Zd 204 (1976)

Vo v. France, App. No. 53924/00 (ECtHR, July 8, 2004)

Zepeda v. Zepeda (190 N.E. Zd 849, Illinois (1963)

Marta Soniewicka

5 Selective procreation and disability

5.1 Introduction

The idea of the enhancement of reproductive choices rests on the assumption that increased genetic knowledge about one's progeny is always an asset for prospective parents. Yet having more reproductive choices does not necessarily mean that the choices will be better. The use of genetic knowledge for selective reproduction gives rise to moral concerns, such as those expressed by Adrienne Asch:

> The tests do nothing to promote the health of the developing fetus or the health of the pregnant woman. Rather, they are offered so that people may decide against becoming a parent of a child with a particular characteristic that clinicians and policy makers understand to be detrimental to a satisfying life for the child or the family, or that may require outlays of societal resources (Asch 2003, 336–337).

To elucidate the problem, let me invoke the distinction between phenotypic and genotypic preventive techniques in medicine emphasized by Eric T. Juengst (Juengst 2009). By phenotypic prevention one means avoiding the manifestation of a particular phenotype (a disease) and rests on the following assumptions: there is a living individual who may benefit from it; diseases are best defined at the level of their actual symptoms; disease is distinct from a person it burdens. Genotypic prevention, on the other hand, is aimed at avoiding the birth of people with particular genotypes and rests on such assumptions as: there are societal benefits (e.g. reducing healthcare costs) from the prevention of the birth of a person with a disease (individuals whose births are avoided cannot be beneficiaries – see Chapter 4); diseases are best understood at the level of genotype; diseases and their burdens are not fully distinct from their bearers. The conceptual difference between these two kinds of genetic prevention in medicine should be recognized, irrespective of the assumed normative status of a foetus or an embryo. Phenotypic prevention is one of the major goals of medicine, yet genotypic prevention remains highly controversial since it requires an external value judgment about somebody's life:

> Genes are not, like germs, external infectious agents that can be kept (or cleaned) out of a living person's body. (...) That means that to justify geno-prevention, someone (parents or society) must make the judgment that the burden of coping with cases of a disease outweighs any other value that individuals with a given genotype might bring to a family or community (Juengst 2009, 482–483).

5.2 Some major ethical arguments concerning genetic selection and disability

5.2.1 Utilitarianism

'Modern utilitarianism, despite its radical heritage, no longer defines a distinctive political position' as Will Kymlicka puts it (Kymlicka 2002, 48). Since it is too broad and too diversified a doctrine to present its common results in the discussed matter, I shall concentrate on one of the most radical views presented by Peter Singer and Richard Hare and applied to reproduction.

According to Singer and Hare, prospective parents should 'maximize the chances of bringing into the world a human being with a high prospect of happiness' (Hare 2002, 188–189). By giving birth to an abnormal child (disabled, impaired, chronically ill etc.), they do not harm the particular child since bringing into existence cannot be considered as harmful (see Chapters 4 and 12). But such a decision, if it were possible to avoid, is considered a moral wrong according to the so-called *non-person-affecting-principle* and *the-same-number-principle* (Buchanan et al. 2007), since it introduces disability, weakness, dependence, suffering and unhappiness into the world. Thus, if the specific genomic knowledge about the potential child is available, parents are morally obliged to prevent the birth of a disabled child. It is assumed that such parents could have a healthy child instead which rests on the assumption that children are 'replaceable' (Singer 2011, see Chapter 4).[1]

The utilitarian account rests upon two tightly connected arguments: (1) the quality of life; (2) costs and benefits analysis. The former one assumes the separation between two domains of human life: biological and social, where the former has an instrumental value – it should enable the pursuit of human values that transcend biological existence (Walter 2003, Singer 2011). The latter one assumes that one may calculate according to one universal standard (a common moral value such as utilities) all of the costs and benefits of a reproductive choice, including the preferences of prospective parents, future children, taxpayers and everybody affected by such a decision, which all require equal consideration (Hare 2002). The utilitarian ethics is a consequential one, concerned with the outcomes. Thus, considering genetic selection, one has to calculate the costs of

---

1 I.e. one can substitute one child with another one of exactly the same nature and value. Some argue that when the parents could not have a healthy child instead, giving birth to a disabled child would be permissible (Buchanan et al. 2007), while others claim that it would be still considered as morally wrong (Kamm 2013).

the loss of life (of an aborted foetus, or destroyed embryo) against the benefits of 'the gain of a better life of life for the normal child that will be conceived only if the disabled one dies.' (Singer 2011, 164). As Singer argues:

> [W]e have to take account of the probability that when the death of a disabled infant will lead to the birth of another infant with better prospects of a happy life, the total amount of happiness will be greater if the disabled infant is killed. The loss of happy life for the first infant is outweighed by the gain of a happier life for the second (Singer 2011, 163).

Hare constructs a thought experiment of 'a pre-natal dialogue in some noumenal world' carried out by an abnormal child who already exists in a form of a foetus with his possible normal brother, who is the potential child 'who would not have been contemplated if they [the parents] had a paralyzed child in the family.' (Hare 2002, 187) Assuming that the parents are planning to have only one child, and that all the probabilities are right, the future normal child has more reasonable arguments, claims Hare, to be born than the abnormal one since it has higher 'prospect of having a normal, happy life' and of making 'a reasonable contribution to the happiness of others' (Hare 2002, 187). *Withholding* life from a normal child ('the next in the queue') is, as Hare argues, a greater loss than *depriving* of life the abnormal child (Hare 2002, 190). Singer takes this argumentation one step further, claiming that there is 'no logical basis for restricting parents' choice to these particular disabilities' that are available for the identification before the birth of a child. This brings him to the *repulsive*[2] conclusion that 'killing a disabled infant is not morally equivalent to killing a person. Very often it is not wrong at all' (Singer 2011, 167).

What is more, it is morally irrelevant from the utilitarian perspective whether the parents let the disabled or chronically ill child to be born, or if they intentionally created a disabled child to have a child which would share their own disability (see Chapter 1). In both cases, selecting for disability and not selecting against disability would be considered as equally wrong if the birth of the disabled child could have been prevented. In utilitarian ethics one may use the same arguments to claim for avoiding disability and to claim for not choosing to give birth to a disabled child when one could have chosen assisted reproductive technology (ART) to guarantee that a healthy child would be born instead.

To gainsay these arguments let me invoke a moral dilemma invented by Cora Diamond (Diamond 1990). Two people are drowning and we have to make a

---

2   The debate over the 'repulsive consequences of utilitarianism has focused on cases in which utilitarianism allows or requires us to do something which other moral theories hold that we are not allowed to do at all...' (Diamond 1990).

choice of whom to save, assuming that only one can be saved. Both drowning people are the same in every aspect known to us, except their number of legs – one of them has one, while the other has two. Utilitarian reasoning provides us with rational arguments to save the life of an able-bodied person instead of a disabled one. If you choose to save the one-legged person over the two-legged, it would be equally wrong as if you caused the loss of a leg of a person since: 'the number of legs in the world (or, better, legs attached to people) is down by one in comparison to what it would have been had you chosen differently' (Diamond 1990, 150). The wrongness of our choice depends on the *final effects for the world* and the conclusions would be the same no matter whether we are considering life-saving decision concerning actual persons or life-giving decision concerning potential persons. Since everybody agrees that one would be happier having two legs than only one, it is argued that there will be less happiness and more suffering in the world than it would be if we have instead rescued a two-legged person. 'You are not causing any person to have a disability; but that is irrelevant to the utilitarian. What matters is that you are causing there to be a disabled person when there need not have been', as Diamond summarizes (Diamond 1990, 155).

Although its striking simplicity, such utilitarian reasoning remains deeply counterintuitive. It disregards 'all significant moral differences between actions and omissions, between doing and allowing-to-happen' (Scheffler 2008, 37–39). In our common moral reasoning we do distinguish between what we *do* to other people, what we *fail to do*, and what *happens* to them.

Moreover, utilitarianism does not differentiate between people but only utilities, treating people instrumentally as the locations of utilities (Diamond 1990; Kymlicka 2002). Yet it does matter for most of us, whether a particular decision advances *our* opportunities for life or whether it maximizes someone else's preferences (e.g. the next baby in the queue). If we agree on the utilitarian claim of making existing people happy, it does not follow that we would agree on the conclusion to *produce* people who could be the happiest in the future.[3] Assuming that we are morally obliged to make only those happy who already exist, the maximization of the prospects of happiness of a future child should be translated into the maximization of *parental or societal preferences* based on their expectations. Taking such a line of argumentation one step further, one could claim that the prevention of the birth of a person with a certain sex (see Chapter 3) or

---

3   The obligation to refrain from producing people with limited prospects for a happy life is just as justified on utilitarian grounds as an *obligation to produce* people with the best prospects for happy lives; yet the latter seems deeply counterintuitive (Birnbacher 1999; Stein 2002).

pigmentation is fully justified on the grounds of the social obstacles that such persons may meet. The idea of having 'successful children' strongly depends on what particular societies value the most. As discussed in the context of sex selection, selective reproduction within a stereotyped structure of a society may confirm stereotypes that should be challenged (Kamm 2013). One cannot discriminate against those who were never born, but one can discriminate against those who already live with disabilities by arguing that their disabilities justify the decision of preventing the birth of a person. This is the so-called *expressivist argument*, according to which the genetic selection against disability sends a negative message to people with disabilities (Parens & Asch 2003).[4] From the assumption that disability reduces welfare, some authors conclude that disabled lives are less worth preserving than are the lives of nondisabled (Singer et al. 1995). This is the so-called double jeopardy policy which can be rejected on utilitarian grounds, arguing that it would bring more harm to existing disabled people (causing resentment, fear, anger and diminished sense of self-worth) than the benefits to the nondisabled whose lives would be preserved (Stein 2002).[5] It seems also arbitrary to consider disability as the only quality-of-life-factor relevant to the distribution of life, leaving other qualities such as intelligence, beauty and wealth aside.

Yet one may also object to the very assumption of this utilitarian reasoning concerned with the relation of disability to happiness. Contemporary liberal societies promote the idea of the social inclusion of disabled people, claiming that they can be as happy and productive as most nondisabled people whilst simultaneously promoting the idea of selective reproduction against disability on the grounds that disabled people are in general less happy than nondisabled people, thus undermining the former claim (Stein 2002).[6] This paradox is rooted in an ignorance of the variability of human life and the complexity of human happiness which simply escapes calculation and cannot be easily grasped in the terms of being worse or better off. The intrinsic value of life cannot be reduced to

---

4   Kamm argues that the only message sent by selective reproduction would be that some properties, not people, are less worthy (Kamm 2013). But the problem is that in these reproductive decisions one cannot detach properties from their carriers as mentioned in the Introduction to this chapter.
5   Even if there is no such intention, the aggregative impact of such individual decisions made within the social structure which puts pressure on prospective parents to forgo genetic testing, can be understood as harmful for the community of disabled people.
6   The author notices that many psychologists prove that 'people have a great capability for hedonic adaptation to adverse situations, including disability' (Stein 2002, 223–224).

the number of our legs or to the other abilities we have. As Diamond accurately notices, *the disabled person gains no less than the healthy one by gaining her life*, and loses exactly the same as the healthy one in losing her life (Diamond 1990). Prospects for happiness are a matter of our own participation in life and which should be enabled by our families and societies so as to permit people with different genetic endowments to flourish. Disability does not possess a medical meaning alone but also a social one (Parens & Asch 2003; Asch 2003), which means that significantly limited prospects for the happy life of the disabled child are rooted in the *social arrangements* that can be challenged and improved.

Finally, the outcome-oriented utilitarianism disregards the moral significance of our relationships (Scheffler 2008; Kymlicka 2002), the intrinsic value of goods and meanings of social practices (such as reproduction). Our meaningful relationships not only shape our identity, but also produce special moral obligations that have to be taken into account in our moral choices. The parent-child relationship belongs to one of the most significant and produces the most far-reaching moral obligations. Prospective parents are in a different position than an abstract impartial observer in a thought experiment who has to choose between healthy and unhealthy life of a stranger. In making both reproductive and moral choices we make comparisons, but something else counts in them than just outcomes. What is good or wrong is tightly connected with how we define ourselves and with the significances (such as birth, sexuality, death) which shape our moral personality (Diamond 1990).

A full-fledged moral theory should provide us with 'an imaginative understanding of the kind of beings we are' (Diamond 1990, 174). Utilitarianism fails to give us an 'imaginative understanding' of ourselves and of the connection between who we are and how we live. It constitutes the *failure of imagination* which means, as Diamond points out, that we see life and death as mere facts only, failing to see the significance of its mysteriousness, and such a failure has profound impact on 'our capacity to live [and to choose] well' (Diamond 1990, 173).

5.2.2 The principle of procreative beneficence

Utilitarian claims are partly shared by Julian Savulescu who has formulated the so-called Principle of Procreative Beneficence (PB) which has raised heated debate (Savulescu & Kahane 2009; Savulescu 2001; Stoller 2008; Bennet 1999; Bennet 2014; Hotke 2014; see Chapter 12). According to PB:

[C]ouples (or single reproducers) should select the child, of the possible children they could have, who is expected to have the best life, or at least as good a life as the others, based on the relevant, available information (Savulescu 2001).

The principle is applied to the situations where selection is possible and does not imply selection against disability, if prospective parents can only have disabled children. PB excludes by definition dysgenic decisions, providing no morally significant difference between negative enhancement and the failure of positive enhancement. PB is a positive claim – if you choose an embryo without a predisposition towards asthma instead of one with such a predisposition, having no other information at hand, you are not selecting against 'a potential Mozart,' but in favor of 'a potential Mozart but without asthma,' so the argument goes (Savulescu 2001, 418). The claim that prospective parents are morally obliged to test for genetic predispositions and conditions to both disease states and non-disease states (like intelligence, temper) rests upon the assumption of rationality (see Chapter 2). Savulescu applies the metaphor of the Wheel of Fortune to procreative decisions, claiming that one 'should use all the available information and choose the option most likely to bring the best outcome.' (Savulescu 2001, 414).

One may pose two fundamental questions: what is the best outcome and for whom? By 'best outcome' Savulescu means selecting for 'the life with the most wellbeing' and invokes some theories of wellbeing, such as hedonistic, desire-fulfillment, objective list theories (Savulescu 2001, 419). Savulescu agrees that defining wellbeing is the most intricate and controversial task in his approach, even though he believes it is possible but does not specify how. 'The best outcome' argued by Savulescu cannot be the best to a potential child which has not been selected. It seems that, just like within the utilitarian approach, it is supposed to be the best outcome for the population at large (which is an eugenic claim) or for prospective parents. Assuming that there is no moral duty to maximize social/parental welfare, prospective parents cannot be morally obliged to have the best possible children (Hotke 2014). From the statement that parents are morally obliged *to guarantee the best life possible* for their future children it does not follow, as Savulescu claims, that they are also morally obliged to aim *to have the best possible children* (Savulescu & Kahane 2009; cf. Bennet 1999). The parental obligation of care for their children means that they owe their children the best possible protection, which may include providing the best conditions for their wellbeing. Yet it cannot include a parental obligation to guarantee the best possible genetic conditions of future children since one cannot be obliged to anybody that he or she will become somebody else. To avoid the trap of the afore-mentioned non-identity problem, one has to claim that PB constitutes an obligation towards a society or towards some abstract future generations. The former claim implies that future children are treated instrumentally as a mere means to an end which is highly questionable and which Savulescu rejected (Savulescu & Kahane 2009). The latter claim needs a justification which is not provided by Savulescu and which will be discussed in the following section.

5.2.3 The rights-based approach

The idea of avoiding the non-identity problem by invoking the rights and interests of future people was introduced by Jeffrey Reiman and based on the famous Rawlsian thought experiment, in which people are equally situated in the 'original position' and placed behind a 'veil of ignorance,' being deprived of any particular knowledge about themselves – they do not know their sex, social status, genetic endowments, or to which generation they belong etc. (Reiman 2007). According to Reiman, the thought experiment enables us to justify principles of inter-generational justice, including obligations of prospective parents towards their future progeny. The original position is supposed to prevent an asymmetry in the rights and obligations between actual and potential persons. The properties of the world (social condition) are treated here on a par with the properties of a person (disability). Future people have, according to Reiman, an interest in being born with particular properties, but not in being a particular person. Reiman admits that no one has the claim to be someone else since it would mean that one wants to not exist and for somebody else to exist instead (Reiman 2007; Williams 1973). Yet he argues that one may violate some 'individuals' rights even though the alternative is that they would not have been born' (Reiman 2007, 78) since:

> [E]ach future person has a right to the reasonable efforts of present people to ensure that they are capable of normal functioning and that they face normal life expectancies and morbidity rates (Reiman 2007, 89).

He claims that such a principle is a deontological rather than a utilitarian one since it does not require any comparison of the quality of life between actual and potential people who could have been born instead, nor does it aim at maximizing social welfare. What is more, one may claim that the deontological approach to reproduction distinguishes between the cases in which the prospective parents let the disabled or chronically ill child be born and the case in which the parents *intentionally create* a disabled child. Bringing a child who is intentionally disabled into the world may be considered to be morally worse since the efforts of the parents to have the disabled child seem to be less reasonable than the absence of effort on the part of parents to prevent the birth of a disabled child.

According to this approach, intentions and motivations, not consequences, do matter in the moral evaluation of our actions and omissions.

There are many controversial points in this line of argumentation. Firstly, according to such a principle there is no difference in violating the rights of a living person and violating the rights of a future person who could be born hundreds of years later, which seems counterintuitive. Secondly, the relational character of our rights and obligations towards each other is morally significant – actual people may owe something to future generations since the latter depend on their decisions but not the other way round (the existence of actual people does not depend on future generations). The asymmetry in relations between living and future people, just as the relational asymmetry between parents and children, is not only unpreventable but it is also an essential part of the understanding of these relations. Moreover, the concept of *non-person-generated rights* is just as troubling (see Chapter 12) as the afore-mentioned concept of a non-person-affecting harm (see Chapter 4). Finally, genetic properties are not external to human beings and thus cannot be treated on a par with the social properties of the world. Both have a significant impact on who we are, yet one may to a certain degree distance oneself from the latter (e.g. social class), but not, or almost not, from the former (e.g. sex, disability).

The Rawlsian thought experiment was invented to consider how self-interested rational persons who want to protect themselves would impartially think about treating the least of their fellows.[7] The point is that egalitarian principles do not cover the problem of how reasonable and rational persons should *create* their children. Our natural properties, even limiting ones such as disability, do not count as injustice but rather as misfortune (see Chapter 8).[8] Rawls points it by saying that natural allocation is neither just, nor unjust: 'These are simply natural facts. What is just and unjust is the way that institutions deal with these facts' (Rawls 2003, 87). The Rawlsian approach transfers our moral attention from people's natural endowments incorporated in our genomes, to *the fair construction of social institutions that should guarantee equal opportunities for*

---

7   It was criticized as so-called 'blind liberalism' (Taylor 1994). The capability approach is a modified version of the egalitarianism which was developed by Sen and Nussbaum to avoid egalitarian failures in recognizing special social needs (Nussbaum 2006; Sen 2009).

8   Injustice, by contrast to misfortune, depends on what people may reasonably expect in a given society (Shklar 1990). Assuming that reproduction should not be understood as a visit to a 'genetic supermarket' (Nozick 1974; cf. Sandel 2007), one may claim that genetic properties are not a matter of social expectations.

unequally endowed people. The rights-based approach, based on the assumption of equality and impartiality, excludes justification of the priority of one life over another. Neither able-bodied nor disabled people have a stronger right to live; in such situations as a rescue-choice or a reproductive choice, it simply seems inadequate to talk about rights. The 'Just Creation Question' (i.e. *what a creator owes to its creature*) posed by Kamm (Kamm 2013) seems misleading when considered in terms of social fairness and entitlements.

5.2.4 Recognition-based and virtue-based approach

Now I turn to the recognition-based approach complemented by the virtue-based approach which offer some insights worthy of consideration in the discussed matter. To elucidate the already posed question concerning the impact of genetic selection against disability on the life of disabled people, let me ponder the concept of recognition first.

Human beings have moral worth – human dignity (Andorno 2014), irrespective of their differences. Limitations (physical, cognitive etc.) are certainly not good and should not be claimed as such. Disability is not just a variation, it is a *limiting* variation which is usually neglected or questioned by the proponents of dysgenic decisions. One owes equal respect to every human being which means that one should be *sensitive*, but not affirmative, to different expressions of the uniqueness of individual or collective identities (Taylor 1994). It is worth emphasizing that one's own identity depends to a certain degree on its *recognition*, the absence of the recognition or misrecognition by the others. As Charles Taylor aptly notes, 'Due recognition is not just a courtesy we owe people. It is a vital human need' (Taylor 1994, 26). Although our true identity should be inwardly generated, and not socially derived (Taylor 1994), we cannot fully understand ourselves without the others who significantly shape our own image and self-esteem. By learning our roles in a society we are 'able to understand how other respond to us and how our responses to them are apt to be construed' as Alasdair MacIntyre claims (MacIntyre 2007, 216). 'Withholding of recognition can be a form of oppression' (Taylor 1994, 36), arguably one of the worst. The claim that disabled children should not be born since disability limits social welfare and defines the worth of life is a form of withholding of recognition to the existing disabled people. It is based on the reductionist view of human nature and identity which reduces persons to their genetic characteristics (e.g. disabilities) constituting the common mistake of treating a *part as a whole*. Although the genome exerts a significant impact on our life and identity, neither could be understood by the analysis of the genome, just as one cannot know what a movie is about by putting a DVD under a microscope (Pinker 2009).

Asch emphasizes that most selective decisions against disability are based on misinterpretation of what disability is (on stereotypes of burdens and suffering), and she argues for improving education about lives with disabilities in order to guarantee truly informed reproductive choices.[9] But whatever we learn about disabilities, we would never be able to fully understand people with most disabilities. Being born blind or with Down syndrome is simply beyond our imagination. But these limitations to our imagination do not have to constitute *failures of imaginations*. The failure of imagination consists in the rejection of the recognition of significance of somebody's life. Our attitude to disability is usually determined by such aspects as: (a) fear of difference (deeply rooted atavism) which results in rejection, exclusion and ignorance; (b) superiority (asymmetry of natural powers) which may result in either domination and abuse, or in benevolence and pity. The approach of the full recognition of human dignity suggested here is determined by *respect* (love, especially in parents-children relationship) and openness to vulnerability as the part of human condition which cannot be challenged by the current 'vital politics.' We have to assume that the perspectives of disabled people are worthy of recognition and care. We are *not allowed to assume that a society would be better off if they were never born*.

Moreover, rational moral reasoning not only fails to understand disability, but it also fails to fully address such key concepts as reproduction. Reproductive choices are rarely based on abstract principles (utility, rights), but rather on experience on how the agents understand themselves and their roles, and on significant relationships which shape the interpretation of principles and duties and determine their application. To take reproductive decisions one needs to first answer the question of how one understands reproduction and parenthood, what does the good life mean and in most of the cases the answer to this question would be much more complex than the answer based on the quality of life measure offered by the utilitarian thinking (Sandel 2007). Thus, I claim that rational moral reasoning may be significantly enhanced by virtue-based approach (see Chapter 1). This combined approach would pay attention

---

9 Parents who face such problem should have the opportunity to not only get a medical description of the disability, but also to meet people with such disabilities and their families; should be provided with all the information on the legal rights and social capabilities of people with disabilities etc. (Parens & Asch 2003).

to the meaning of our practices and relationships, as well as intentions and motivations, capturing the moral difference between dysgenic decisions and the decisions 'to let nature decide' which is more consistent with our basic moral intuitions.

The meaning of such social practices as reproduction can be defined on the grounds of our shared intuitions and moral insights, which are open to the permanent interpretation of those who are involved in this practice and those who participate in a society (Walzer 1985; Sandel 2010). In defining the meaning of reproduction, the distinction made by MacIntyre between goods which are external and internal to a practice may be of help (MacIntyre 2007). External goods are 'contingently attached' to a practice by 'the accidents of social circumstance' (MacIntyre 2007, 188). Since external goods are not specific to that particular activity, a person interested in them may find other ways to achieve them. Internal goods, on the other hand, can be only specified in terms of a particular practice and 'can only be identified and recognized by the experience of participating in the practice in question.' (MacIntyre 2007, 188). The internal good of reproduction can be identified with the creation of a unique relationship between the parents and the child based on love and care, while among external goods one may name: self-satisfaction, fulfilling one's own desires, preventing loneliness etc.

Virtues are the necessary means to attain the goods internal to communal practices, according to the interpretation of Aquinas, which means that 'the end cannot be adequately characterized independently of a characterization of the means.' (MacIntyre 2007, 184). Virtue, as defined by Aristotle is a settled and purposive disposition to act and feel (to respond to our feelings) in particular ways which enables achievement of the *telos* of a man (Aristotle 2011). In other words, virtue is a habitual disposition to act well; it encompasses both feeling what is good and the capacity to act according to it; it is not an automatic reflex, but rather a habit guided by reason. Virtuous parents would be able to unconditional love and care towards their progeny irrespective of the particular qualities of the child. The special relationship between parent and child implies a unique responsibility built upon it.

Invoking Michael Sandel, one may argue that the idea of parenthood should be based on the balance between accepting and transforming love which remains at odds with any kind of 'selective mentality' (including both positive and negative selection of disability) in reproduction (Sandel 2007). Andrew Solomon addresses the challenge for parenthood brought by the children who are the most unlike their parents (considering the case of dwarfism, deafness, Down syndrome etc.). Loving our own children for who they are and not for who we want them to be, is 'an exercise for the imagination,'[10] which is easier to fail, the more different our children are from us. The author invokes his own experience in order to elucidate the matter:

> My mother didn't want me to be gay because she thought it wouldn't be the happiest course for me, but equally, she didn't like the image of herself as the mother of a gay son. (…) The problem was that she wanted to control *her* life, and it was her life as the mother of a homosexual that she wished to alter. Unfortunately, there was no way for her to fix her problem without involving me (Solomon 2012, 18).

Following this claim in a social dimension, we should aim at challenging the social properties which create difficulties for disabled people, instead of selecting against human beings with 'burdensome' genetic properties. Even though some people are naturally limited in their abilities (e.g. a paralyzed person will never be able to climb Mount Everest), the aim of society is to transform their disabilities into capabilities – guaranteeing the conditions in which they are able to make use of their freedom and are able to find their own fulfillment by having their contribution to the lives of others and society. To realize this aim one should consider the ethical importance of recognition and virtues which lead to a more nuanced and morally preferable view as compared to the afore-mentioned alternatives.

5.3 Concluding remarks

Utilitarianism and egalitarianism provide principles for the fair distribution of welfare or resources, but they both fail to provide any intuitive principles for reproductive decisions. It is very hard to maintain that in such an intimate sphere, parental decisions should be governed by any universal, purely rational ideals. Reproductive decisions are not a matter of the fair distribution of life, at least as long as reproduction is not in charge of a state, but rather a private endeavor resulting from meaningful relationships. The question of whether one should be engaged in reproduction in certain ways and at certain risks can be separated from the question about fairness and the outcomes produced by these decisions for a society since the former depends on how we understand ourselves and our relationships.

---

10 This kind of 'exercise of imagination' is called 'attention' and is analysed by Iris Murdoch. The notion was borrowed from Simone Weil and understood as a special reflective and imaginative activity, directed by love, directed away from self 'towards the great surprising variety of the world,' which has a transformative and unifying power (Murdoch 2014, 54).

Christina's World – one of the iconic works of American modern art, painted by Andrew Wyeth shows a crippled woman who was the artist's neighbor in Maine. He caught her in the moment of crawling through the field in the direction of her house, which seems incredibly far away for a person in such a condition as hers. As the painter explained, Christina inspired him since she 'was limited physically but by no means spiritually' and the greatest challenge to him 'was to do justice to her extraordinary conquest of a life which most people would consider hopeless.' (Hoptman 2012, 23). Addressing the problem of genetic selection against disability, we face the same question as the one posed by the artist, of 'how to do justice to extraordinary conquest of life considered commonly as hopeless.' The way in which we answer the question will shape our societies and our identity, just as it does the identity of people with disabilities who struggle for our recognition and care.

Acknowledgements

This is a slightly revised version of the article which has been previously published in: M. Soniewicka, Failures of Imagination: Disability and the Ethics of Selective Reproduction, Bioethics, 29 (8), 2015: 557–563, © John Wiley & Sons Ltd.

References

Andorno R (2014) Human Dignity and Human Rights. In: ten Have HAMJ, Gordijn B (eds) Handbook of Global Bioethics. Springer, Dodrecht, pp. 45–57.

Aristotle (2011) Nicomachean Ethics (trans: BartlettRC, CollinsSD). Chicago University Press, Chicago, IL & London.

Asch A (2003) Disability, Equality, and Prenatal Testing: Contradictory or Compatible? Florida State Univeristy Law Review 30:315–342.

Bennett R (1999) The Fallacy of the Principle of Procreative Beneficence. Bioethics 23:265–273.

Bennett R (2014) When Intuition Is not Enough. Why the Principle of Procreative Beneficence Must Work Much Harder to Justify its Eugenic Vision. Bioethics 28:447–455.

Birnbacher D (1999) Odpowiedzialność za przyszłe pokolenia [Verantwortung für zukunftige Generationen]. Oficyna Naukowa University, Warszawa.

Buchanan A, Brock DW, Daniels N, Wikler D (2007) From Chance to Choice: Genetics and Justice. Cambridge University Press, Cambridge & New York.

Diamond C (1990) How Many Legs. In: Gaita R (ed) Value and Understanding: Essays for Peter Winch. Routledge, New York & London, pp. 149–178.

Hare R (2002) The Abnormal Child. Moral Dilemmas of Doctors and Parents. In: Hare R (auth) Essays on Bioethics. Clarendon Press, Oxford, pp. 188–189.

Hoptman L (2012) Wyeth Christina's World. The Museum of Modern Art, New York.

Hotke A (2014) The Principle of Procreative Beneficence: Old Arguments and a New Challenge. Bioethics 28:255–262.

Juengst ET (2009) Population Genetic Research and Screening: Conceptual and Ethical Issues. In: Steinbock B (ed) The Oxford Handbook of Bioethics. Oxford University Press, Oxford, pp. 482–485.

Kamm FM (2013) Bioethical Prescriptions To Create, End, Choose, and Improve Lives. Oxford University Press, Oxford & New York.

Kymlicka W (2002) Contemporary Political Philosophy. An Introduction. Oxford University Press, Oxford.

MacIntyre A (2007) After Virtue, 2nd ed. Notre Dame University Press, Notre Dame, IN.

Murdoch I (2014) The Sovereignty of Good. Routledge, New York.

Nozick R (1974) Anarchy, State and Utopia. Basic Books, New York.

Nussbaum M (2006) Frontiers of Justice: Disability, Nationality, Species Membership. Harvard University Press, Cambridge.

Parens E, Asch A (2003) Disability Rights Critique of Prenatal Genetic testing: Reflections and Recommendations. Mental Retardation and Developmental Disabilities Research Reviews 9:40–47.

Pinker S (2009) My Genome, My Self. The New York Times 11 January. https://www.nytimes.com/2009/01/11/magazine/11Genome-t.html (accessed: 30 July 30 2018).

Rawls J (2003) A Theory of Justice. Harvard University Press, Cambridge.

Reiman J (2007) Being Fair to Future People: The Non-Identity Problem in the Original Position. Philosophy & Public Affairs 35:69–92.

Sandel M (2007) The Case against Perfection. Ethics in the Age of Genetic Engineering. The Belknap Press of Harvard University Press, Cambridge, MA & London.

Sandel M (2010) Justice: What's the Right Thing to Do? Farrar, Straus and Giroux, New York.

Savulescu J (2001) Procreative Beneficence: Why We Should Select the Best Children. Bioethics 15:413–426.

Savulescu J, Kahane G (2009) The moral obligation to create children with the best chance of the best life. Bioethics 23:274–290.

Scheffler S (2008) Boundaries and Allegiances. Problems of Justice and Responsibility in Liberal Thought. Oxford University Press, Oxford.

Sen A (2009) The Idea of Justice. Harvard University Press, Cambridge.

Shklar JN (1990) The Faces of Injustice. Yale University Press, New Haven, CT & London.

Singer P (2011) Practical Ethics. Cambridge University Press, Cambridge & New York.

Singer P, McKie J, Kuhse H, Richardson J (1995) Double jeopardy and the use of QUALYs in health care allocation. Journal of Medical Ethics 21:144–150.

Solomon A (2012) Far from the Tree. Parents, Children, and the Search for Identity. Scribner, New York.

Stein MS (2002) Distributive Justice and Disability. Utilitarianism Against Egalitarianism. Yale University Press, New Haven, CT & London.

Stoller SE (2008) Why We Are Not Morally Required To Select the Best Children: a Response to Savulescu. Bioethics 22:364–369.

Taylor C (1994) The Politics of Recognition. In: Gutmann A (ed) Multiculturalism and the Politics of Recognition. Princeton University Press, Princeton, NJ, pp. 25–73.

Walter JJ (2003) Quality of Life. In: Post SG (ed) Encyclopedia of Bioethics, vol. 3. MacMillan Reference Books, pp. 1388–1393.

Walzer M (1985) Spheres of Justice. A Defence of Pluralism and Equality. Basic Books, Oxford.

Williams B (1973) Problems of the Self. Cambridge University Press, Cambridge.

Wojciech Lewandowski

6 Parent-God analogy in procreative decisions

Making reference to parental responsibilities is one of the ways of justifying moral judgements of genetic selection. This approach is used to solve the non-identity problem and indicate the scope of reproductive autonomy. The second approach to evaluating reproductive decisions is to refer to arguments that impose conditions whose fulfilment allows to consider these decisions right. The 'playing God' argument is one of these. It states that currently human limitations cause certain biomedical interventions to not meet these conditions or – in a more absolute version – to never meet them. The 'playing God' argument is most often addressed to scientists and medical personnel involved in actions that result in bringing new humans into existence. David Heyd expanded the scope of this argument to all people whose decisions affect the creation of a new child (Heyd 1992), and at the same time used the parent-God analogy to reject moral obligations towards potential children. Thus, the prospect of parents striving to have a baby is present in both of these approaches, although it holds a distinguished position only in the first case. In this chapter, I will present the implications of the parent-God analogy in judging procreative decisions with regard to the problem of acceptable arbitrariness in choosing or accepting to bring a child affected by a medical condition into the world.

6.1 Parental perspective and the problem of the limits of arbitrariness

Most positions in the discussion on the moral evaluation of assisted procreation are based on attempts to solve the problem of judging the actions that result in an ill child being born. The non-identity problem remains at the centre of the discussion. The problem is that, on the one hand, the low general quality of the child's life could serve as a foundation for recognizing a reproductive decision as morally wrong, but on the other – alternative versions of this decision would preclude any chances of this child's existence. Here, the inability to apply the traditional category of harm forms a basis for attempts to modify it or give it up within the discussion on the moral justification of procreation. These two dominant approaches bring certain difficulties. Positions that forgo the categories of harm and judge procreation only in terms of an action that makes the world, in a certain way, a better or worse place seem too demanding. They subject procreative decisions to the imperative of maximising happiness, and constitute too significant a burden on the broadly understood right to reproductive autonomy. On the other hand, positions that refer to harm must cope with the challenge of providing justification to the moral status of potential children and the resulting claims. Giving future children a moral status similar to the one enjoyed by those already existing once again brings about the problem of imposing excessive restrictions on reproductive autonomy (see Chapter 12).

The aforementioned difficulties are the main argument for resorting to the perspective of the parents. Analysing the reasons and motives present when making reproductive decisions is an increasingly frequent way of describing the moral nature of procreation. According to David Wasserman, arguments that have appeared in the discussion thus far can be successfully translated into the language of parental responsibilities (Wasserman 2005, 135). The imperative to maximise the value of the world by bringing happy children into it would seem all the more convincing if it were formulated more or less as follows: 'the existence of my child should be good for me, for the child, and for the entire world'. The awareness that the existence of our child adds value to the world, and that the value of the world is significantly dependent on the child's welfare, or at least on limiting suffering in its life, forms a backdrop for the argument brought up by positions based on the category of harm. From the parental perspective, the suffering of a child caused by our action or neglect constitutes obvious harm – without the need for referring to complex models of justice or comparing alternative states of affairs. On the other hand, a child's suffering that has not been intended in any way and which could not have been avoided would not seem to constitute a sufficient basis for ascertaining harm in this approach if the child's life was still worth living.

The ability to solve the non-identity problem is not the only argument for resorting to the reasons and motives that potential parents have. The second argument is that these reasons may be important for formulating and justifying policy and legal decisions concerning medically assisted procreation. Steven Lecce and Erik Magnusson analyse the possibilities of referencing parents' motives in evaluating the birth of savioursiblings. These motives may be relevant to moral judgement in three ways: as a basis for predicting future care for their child, as a basis for justifying procreative decisions, and as a form of expressing their attitudes and moral beliefs about procreation in front of the community (Lecce & Magnusson 2015). The aspect of predictability is important for evaluations made in light of both consequentialism and non-consequentialism. In line with a consequentialist judgment, natively selfish reasons for bringing a child into existence may be deemed wrong due to the likelihood of all other future actions towards the child being subjected to the same reasons, which would lead to worse consequences than if it were conceived because of its expected good. According to a non-consequentialist judgement, selfish reasons may serve as a basis for suspecting that parents are not aware of their role towards the child, the resulting duties, and principles of justice that govern it. These pessimistic scenarios do not have to prove true if one takes into account that becoming a parent is a process that also includes moral development – which could lead to some changes in the value hierarchy (Lotz 2009, 2011). It seems, however, that despite the limited possibility of predicting the future attitude of parents based on their current motivations and desires, they may constitute one of the most important foundations for moral evaluation at a time when the child does not yet exist and other criteria allowing to predict their future attitude towards the child are unavailable[1]. The second aspect of the judgement, i.e. the aspect of justification, is based on the fact that the child comes into the world without its own consent and without control over the conditions of its life (Overall 2012). The dramatic asymmetry between the respective positions of the parents and the child causes that only referencing the conditions imposed on parents' reasons and motivations may form a basis for a retrospective assessment of whether the child has reasonable grounds to complain. Answers such as: 'at least you exist and have a moderately good life' or 'you wouldn't have existed in different conditions and with a different genetic endowment' are less compelling to a child that makes a claim than answers that would allow to understand why parents opted for procreation. The third aspect of the judgement, concerning the expression of parents' moral attitudes, seems to be important in the context of social debates on the value of life. The decision to give birth to a disabled child may express not only acceptance towards the child, regardless of its appearance or health, but also a public plea to respect the less-favoured and observe their rights (see Chapter 5). This argument has limited scope. To many people, it would be difficult to accept as a rationale for selecting disability, although it could be used as a justification for the total rejection of genetic selection. It seems, however, that in itself the argument cannot serve as a factor that decides the problem of judging reproductive decisions, and its strength depends on the power of other arguments. Expressing respect for the value of human life is convincing only if the parents of a disabled child are trying to show their experience of its value, which they gained while

---

1   According to Lecce and Magnusson, predictiveness is the only aspect that can be relevant for evaluating procreative decisions from the point of view of justice-based entitlements (Lecce & Magnusson 2015, 164).

developing their relationship with it. The message to society is significant only if it remains reasonable and voices some moral truth, which is sometimes difficult to discern from the outside.

Aside from arguments solving the non-identity problem and the social judgement of procreation, the third set of arguments for referencing the parents' perspective is based on the premise that parents are the best guardians of the child's interests, and the possible conflicts between the interests of the parents and of the child are so rare, that going beyond this perspective would be justified only in rare cases. Parental love is a source of both motivation for providing the child with the best possible life, as well as of reasons limiting or imposing admissibility conditions on reproductive decisions. The judgement of bringing a disabled child or a saviour sibling into the world has to, in line with this approach, ultimately depend on whether the parents – under given circumstances – make the decision out of their love for the child and whether they will be able to love it after it comes into existence. The categorical nature of parental love and the necessary sacrifices associated with childcare are blurring the boundaries between obligatory and supererogatory acts, which is the basis for believing that moral judgements and standards resulting from this role should be formulated primarily from the first-person perspective. In turn, social requirements of being a parent would pertain to the minimum acceptable level of involvement in the relationship and care for the child, as well as to conditions for justifying the failure to meet these requirements in situations where the parent is unable to meet them.

Reducing external evaluation criteria for reproductive decisions, such as the predicted quality of the child's life or justice-based entitlements, to the role of auxiliary criteria poses a significant problem to the approach based on the parents' perspective: we have to look for the ultimate criterion in the inner world of the parent, and try to arrive at an experience of duty towards the child that's convincing and possible to be universalized. The question about the extent of my right to natural or assisted procreation, genetic selection, or foregoing it, choosing an ill or healthy child, boils down to a question about the extents of arbitrariness in my decisions. The relationship between love and arbitrariness is a traditional subject of philosophical considerations.

The term 'arbitrary' refers to 1) decisions made without justification, 2) decisions based on self-interest, and 3) decisions based on subjective criteria. All types of arbitrariness can result in positive or negative judgements. Decisions made without justification are subject to criticism in the context of political and legal decisions, but seem acceptable in other areas, as long as any justification is not required, such as when choosing a tie, or impossible to give, e.g. in case of a conflict of reasons based on symmetrical options. Random methods of decision making are one of the main competitors of arbitrariness as a method for resolving symmetric conflicts. In the debate over a situation in which only one of two persons can be saved, making a choice through a coin toss is a better way than relying on instinct. A random method is supported by more objectivity and certainty that the decision will not be made by anyone who relies on unconscious biases, e.g. concerning race or gender. The argument for allowing this kind of arbitrariness is that depending entirely on chance would equal to resigning one's role as a moral agent facing a choice. Relying on one's instinct indeed seems to include a random element, as one's behaviour depends on the context of the situation – what details one will pay attention to in a given situation, and how will they affect the process of taking action. Arbitrariness in such situations, however, would be the product of a random situational context and the subject's psychological endowment. The admissibility of this kind of arbitrariness is limited to those rare situations involving symmetrical moral conflicts. Expanding it onto other situations would result in the inability to predict the decision, or changing it in the future by those potentially affected by them or – if the decision has a legal and political dimension – it could form a precedent from which others will benefit (Cook 1942, 163). From the citizens' point of view, eliminating arbitrariness gives a sense of security and guarantees that the adopted law is rational and stable. In the context of genetic selection, this type of arbitrariness is problematic. On the one hand, it seems that procreation does not require justification, as it applies to a private area of activity and does not always involve an informed decision about having a child. On this backdrop, arbitrariness may seem acceptable as a conscious use of the right to procreative autonomy, emphasizing moral subjectivity in making reproductive decisions – similarly to settling symmetrical conflicts. However, on the other hand, procreative decisions with no justification may be considered undesirable, as they collide with the idea that having a baby, due to the importance and consequences related to bringing a new person with a specific identity and genetic endowment to this world, should be carefully thought out in all of its aspects.

The second type of arbitrariness relates to decisions justified by referencing the self-interest. In this sense, a decision would be arbitrary if one hired a less competent but more sympathetic employee. As before, arbitrariness is found in the context of conflicting options, although in this case they can be compared quite easily. Unlike the previous type of arbitrariness, here the decision maker is consciously relying on the criterion of their own interests. It should be added that this criterion may be treated entirely objectively by them, i.e. they will only select the option which objectively gives them more benefits than the alternatives. The admissibility of this kind of arbitrariness appears less controversial than that of arbitrariness understood in the first sense – when deciding to have a child, parents always consider their own desires. The primary limitation of this kind of arbitrariness is the condition of non-collision with parental love, based on – among others – the readiness to accept responsibility for the child regardless of whether it meets parents' expectations. As before, distinguishing these motivations is difficult and requires a phenomenological description of the world of the parents' internal experiences.

The third type of arbitrariness is seen in decisions based on subjective criteria. Compared to the previous type, this one would be evident – for example – in hiring an employee who, due to objective criteria, should be considered less competent, but the agent has subjective reasons to think that they will be better suited to the proposed job. An attempt to justify this type of arbitrariness can be found in the assumption that objective criteria do not take into account the entire complexity of circumstances under which a decision is taken. On the one hand, the margin of freedom in individual assessment left within the decision-making process brings with it the aforementioned risk of the decision which incorporates subjective criteria being based on prejudice, while on the other – a conscious combination of objective and subjective criteria seems inevitable when it comes to an individual person's judgement. While this kind of arbitrariness is debatable in the public domain, it seems quite commonly accepted in the area of close relationships. Dietrich von Hildebrand takes note of the precedence of subjective criteria over objective ones when describing the phenomenon of love. According to him, when it comes to loving another person this distinctive feature can be expressed as 'Perhaps they are better but you are good' (von Hildebrand 2009, 65). At the same time, he strongly rejects the possibility of considering this attitude arbitrary, reducing arbitrariness to the second type mentioned above – based on one's own self-interest. What justifies relying on subjective criteria is that love entails giving oneself to another person, which means that the lover has no obligation to choose a loved one, the beloved person cannot have any claim to be chosen, and there is no third party that can have any claims to the fact of choosing a loved one or not. Thus, the situation of parents deciding to have a child has something in common with the situation of a person who sacrifices their own life to save another. The willingness to perform such an act of heroism seems to give complete freedom when it comes to choosing the person to be saved.

The problem in justifying this type of arbitrariness in procreative decisions is the difficulty of finding out whether the parents' arbitrary choice is motivated by love, or does it originate in moral flaws (Wasserman 2005, 146). The examples of such parental defects include lack of sensitivity, indolence, and weakness of will.

Lack of sensitivity is expressed in the indifference towards potential suffering or difficulties the child will be faced with. Indolence is understood as a lack of any effort to estimate how both their and their child's life will look. Indolence can have its source in the fact that the future seems too distant to be estimated. Finally, weakness of will would consist in the fact that a parent knows they should make a rational assessment, but is unable to do so, leaving responsibility in the hands of fate.[2] Since parents can claim credit for nobler intentions than they actually have, once again it seems necessary to search for proper motivations and reasons to have a child in what makes up the gist of the parental perspective. A promising way of discovering this essence is to compare the parent's perspective with the perspective of God.

6.2 God's perspective and motives of procreation

The aforementioned arguments for referencing the perspective of parents when solving moral problems concerning procreation are similar to the argument of David Heyd – to put these problems in the 'genesis context' (Heyd 1992, 3), which is the situation of a Creator faced with a deserted universe and having the power to fill it with people (pure *genesis* context)[3], or a situation in which people already exist in the world – and the question is whether to create more of them (impure *genesis* context). The premise of this comparison is that there is an analogy between the perspective of people participating in procreation and the perspective of God.

> Parent – God analogy assumption: 'divine creation and human procreation are guided by the same principle and motive' (Heyd 1992, 3).

The obvious similarity between these perspectives is that in both cases we are dealing with rational entities capable of love and decisions that may result in a new person coming to existence. Heyd sees this similarity in control over the existence and number of future people and in being a source of value for the world (Heyd 1992, 7). The advantages of limiting context in such a way are found in using the theistic image of God creating man as a thought experiment

---

2   This problem is due to the limited capacity of foreseeing and controlling the child's future quality of life in the case of natural procreation.
3   The term 'genesis context' refers to the 'genesis problem' formulated by Partha Dasgupta in relation to population ethics. The problem is whether a situation in which the population is 0 can be considered a starting point in determining the optimal population (Dasgupta 1987, 640; Dasgupta 1988, 110).

that allows to settle the problems related with the obligation or admissibility of procreation, determining the optimum population size, and the criteria of acceptable well-being of people brought into the world. Purifying the context of procreation would also allow to discover the ultimate reasons behind procreative decisions. Revealing these reasons may open the way to determining whether any of the above types of arbitrariness is acceptable in procreative decisions, and what are the limitations of such arbitrariness. At first glance, the primary limitation of this analogy is that the parents' situation is considered to be the impure genesis context, which means that they must take into account the interests and rights of already existing people (Dasgupta 2007, 222; Heyd 1992, 5). However, the parent-God analogy could retain its strength if one considered that God's possible motives may be the same when creating both the first and each subsequent person. In addition, one may say that in the case of parents who are planning their first child, the nature of the situation remains at least partially similar to that of the pure genesis context.

In the context of genesis, God might have three motives for creating mankind. These are: improving the world, creating people that have their own intrinsic value, and spreading one's own image in the world. The first motive is based on an unbiased calculation that the world would be better with humans (or with a larger number of them) than without them. The decision to create man would have to be based on an indication of the extent to which their life increases the value of the world. This approach assumes that a new person has an objective value, but makes it dependent on the impact on the overall value of the world. On the one hand, there is no room for arbitrariness, at least in the first two meanings mentioned above. On the other, assuming the existence of non-confrontational criteria of rationality in formulating the criterion of the value of the world based on population size and the quality of life of potential people, God could arbitrarily choose one of these criteria. It would depend on God, and whether He adopts a criterion that leads to maximising population or the quality of people's lives. Recognizing the right to such arbitrariness would also allow granting it to parents who are planning out the size of their family. The main problem with recognizing this nature of the parent-God analogy is that this approach is difficult to reconcile with individual care for the created being[4]. It would not only require modifying the image of God, but would also omit the arguments cited earlier in

---

4   Here I am omitting the most often cited problems of this approach related to non-intuitive conclusions resulting from each of the possible criteria in the context of creating a new person, whose life is subject to significant suffering or who has a minimal, although positive, quality of life. The most famous of these problems is the 'repugnant

favour of adopting the perspective of parents in ethical debates – a perspective according to which the concept of care has a key role and causes only the criteria compatible with this category to be intuitively acceptable. The main argument in favour of the impartial concept of God would be its potential to enhance the parental perspective with a morally significant aspect of considering the concern for others. Parents are naturally guided towards promoting and protecting the interests of their children, which bears the risk of them overly favouring their own children – even in situations that require impartiality[5]. The perspective of an impartial God, the Creator of all people and one caring for the interests of everyone, both existing people and generations set apart in time, would allow to reduce parental partiality by showing them a broader context and how their procreative decisions are cumulative with the decisions of other people, and what impact do they have on the future.

The second motive concerns creating people who have their own intrinsic value. It seems to combine an impartial recognition of the value of a new person equal to the value of all other people with the ability to discern the individual nature of this value. Impartiality is based on the recognition that every human life has an objective value that increases the value of the world, but at the same time it cannot be reduced solely to this function. Discovering the close link between the inner value and individuality of a person would only be possible by establishing a relationship with them. This juxtaposition of impartiality and individual approach would take into account the fact that – despite the same intrinsic value of all people – we care more about people close to us[6]. God entering into such an individual relation may be used as a model for judging the previously mentioned types of arbitrariness. Establishing a relationship by God without any justification would be arbitrary in the first sense. In the second – His self-interest would be the ultimate reason for entering into a relationship. According to the third one – the divine plan set up for man could be the reason for establishing the relationship. Each of these three interpretations allows great freedom in reproductive decision-making. Thanks to them, one may refer examples of God's apparent arbitrariness as a model for parental arbitrariness. God's decision to accept Abel's sacrifice instead of Cain's one or to choose Isaac

---

conclusion' related to the imperative to maximize population, even at the cost of significantly reducing their quality of life (Parfit 1984).

5   Creating and strengthening social inequalities is one of the examples how parental partiality negatively impacts the future (Douglas 2015).
6   Simon Keller explains this fact, stating that features of the close relationship enable the value of beloved person to generate reasons for caring about her (Keller 2013).

instead of Ishmael, and Jacob instead of Esau as ancestors of the chosen people could only form a basis for justifying genetic selection. It seems, however, that the motive of creating man due to their intrinsic value can be reconciled only with the third kind of arbitrariness. This motive assumes that an individual relationship based on love is established with everyone, that is, also with Cain, Ishmael, and Esau. Justifying the prohibition of neglecting the 'unchosen' ones is possible only when the concept of 'choosing' is relativized to the divine plan for each individual person. Choosing Abel, Isaac, or Jacob would mean that the creator has a plan for them as leading figures in their individual lives. This does not necessarily mean the rejection of other created persons (although some biblical texts may point to this), but may refer to a plan that assumes establishing a different kind of relationship with them and as part of other stories. Bringing a new person into the world, both from the perspective of God and of the parents, would therefore draw its justification from the category of love. It seems to fit the parent-God analogy perfectly and delineates the framework for permissible arbitrariness. Referring to objective value places the parent-God analogy on the objectivist side of the Euthyphro dilemma. The reason for bringing a new person into the world lies in its value, and the value depends neither on the will of the creator, nor on the desire to bring it into the world. The main challenge this concept is facing – aside from the need to clarify the notion of love – is that, in the genesis context, it is difficult to invoke the intrinsic and objective value of a person before it comes into existence. According to Heyd, this difficulty is the basis for referring to the third possible motive for creating man in the genesis context.

The desire to reproduce one's likeness as the third motive of creation is strongly rooted in the following passage from the Bible:

> Let us make mankind in our image, in our likeness, so that they may rule over the fish in the sea and the birds in the sky, over the livestock and all the wild animals, and over all the creatures that move along the ground (Genesis 1,26).

In Heyd's interpretation, mankind's existence is valuable to God. His ability to make valuations is a source of value in the world. Under this interpretation, creating mankind introduces further sources of value to the world. The relationship between mankind and the world is analogous to the relationship between God and mankind. Justifying this motive in the pure genesis context would be difficult. It would require referring to theological interpretations of the passage cited above and reflecting on why does God need, or want, to recreate His likeness in the world. In relation to the parents' perspective, this motive can be understood fairly easily. According to Heyd, people want to have children to realize self-transcendence and achieve a certain kind of immortality by populating the world with people who are similar to them in terms of biology and shared ideals (Heyd 1992, 213). This kind of justification refers to the second and third meaning of arbitrariness. What procreative decisions are based on is the desire for self-transcendence and the dependence of future value on the will of the creator. Compared to the previous motive, here we are dealing with the second element of the Euthyphro dilemma. It is the will of the creators (God or parents) that gives value to a new person – whose existence depends on them. The advantage of this approach is that it avoids the paradox of referencing the individual value of a person before it comes into existence. The primary flaw, however, lies in relativizing the created person's moral status to the decision of the creator. Even if we assume that the motive of reproducing one's image offers plenty of potential for arbitrariness in relation to people who do not yet exist and depend on our decisions, the problem remains of explaining how a new person coming into being might form a basis for limiting one's arbitrariness towards it. The existence of a new human being, especially in its first stages, continues to be dependent on the will of the creator (Singer 1998, 394).

Of the motives stated above, the second one seems the most promising to the parent-God analogy when it comes to judging procreative decisions. Referring the category of love based on readiness for accepting, caring, and establishing a relationship with a new being that has its intrinsic value seems compatible both with the traditional image of God and common-sense expectations towards the parents' role. To answer whether God creating man due to this motive may form a model for judging the attitudes of future parents requires an analysis of the limitations of this analogy.

6.3 Limits of analogy, limits of arbitrariness

There are four groups of possible solutions to the problem of the parent-God analogy in relation to justifying arbitrariness in procreative decisions:

A. God and parents cannot be arbitrary.
B. God can be arbitrary, but parents cannot.
C. Parents can be arbitrary, but God cannot.
D. God and parents can be arbitrary.

The problems with using the parent-God analogy to point out the appropriate motives for reproductive decisions follow two directions. Firstly, the assumption behind the analogy can be easily doubted by stating that it is difficult to apply God's principles and motivations to the situation of the parents, and the parents' principles and motives to the situation of God (B and C). Secondly, even if the analogy can be defended, it is necessary to properly apply it to reproductive decisions (A and D).

Arguments behind A consist in shifting the problem of evil from philosophy of religion to the area of reproductive ethics. For David Benatar, the existence of suffering makes human procreation morally problematic. The justification is based on a conjunction of four conditions: 1) the presence of pain is bad, 2) the presence of pleasure is good, 3) the absence of pain is impersonally good – regardless of whether the one who avoids pain actually exists, while 4) the absence of pleasure is not impersonally bad – its lack can be felt only in relation to the person who has been deprived of said pleasure (Benatar 2006, 30). This argument excludes arbitrariness in the first and second sense, or at least limits it. The fact that pain exists causes that procreative decisions cannot disregard how the child's life will look. Omitting or attaching less importance to it than to own self-interest would constitute proof of indifference towards the child. Empathy is one of the basic requirements of being a good parent. Its absence before the child comes into existence results in arbitrariness in procreative decisions to be improper. Interestingly, empathy seems compatible with arbitrariness understood as reliance on subjective criteria. The fact that parents are beings who have also experienced suffering throughout their lives allows to diminish Benatar's criticism. Its strength primarily refers to the pure genesis context – devoid of people and suffering. Procreative decisions are already present in the context of suffering. Parents and children form a relationship aimed at sharing a common fate, which may sometimes bring suffering. The readiness to minimise opportunities for suffering and eliminating it when it appears, being ready to accompany the child and supporting it in situations when suffering cannot be avoided is an objective moral requirement for parents. Limited ability to eliminate suffering causes the problem of evil in procreative decisions to differ from the problem of evil in philosophy of religion, which mainly concerns the relationship between suffering and the ability to provide people with free will.

If the parents' individual life story and their sensitivity to suffering is the determinant of parental arbitrariness, then parents who are more sensitive or those who have experienced significant suffering will probably attach more importance to Benatar's argument, while the reasons and motives of less sensitive parents, or those who have not experienced substantial suffering throughout their lives, will probably deem it less relevant. Such subjective estimation of the degree of suffering in a child's life seems to remain within an acceptable level of arbitrariness, since – regardless of individual differences in experiencing suffering – it would still be limited to a typical scope of human sensitivity to this experience. That recognition allows to justify the motives of procreation based on both love and the desire for self-transcendence. In the first case, procreation is creating new, uncountable value of the child's existence and the relationship between it and its parents, while the potential difficulties the child encounters in its life do not overshadow that value, but – if they cannot be avoided – provide an opportunity to strengthen the relationship. In the second case, the parents, having their own experiences of both good and bad aspects of life, bring into existence a being similar to themselves, who will first face the world together with them, and afterwards – on its own.[7]

The above argument seems to point towards accepting argument C, however, there is a certain problem that forces us to analyse option B, which eliminates the parent-God analogy, and gives priority to God's perspective. This problem lies in the following question – to what extent can parents allow a child's severe suffering, if it is greater than the one experienced by them. The premise behind this problem is this: if the difference between the experience of suffering on part of the parents and the potential suffering of the child is significant, they may not comprehend the burden to which it may be exposed. In this situation, parents are in a less privileged position than God. An obvious spot where the analogy seems to fall apart is the parents' lack of divine attributes of omniscience, omnipotence, and perfect goodness. If one accepts that God is not only an impartial observer, but He may also establish an individual relationship with anyone, His empathy is much greater than that of the parents', who – due to their limitations – have no such possibility. At the same time, God's omniscience allows to objectively determine the burdens the child will be subject to and, thanks to omnipotence, He may ultimately derive good from any suffering[8]. Parents are left only with making attempts at estimating the future quality of the child's life and only from the perspective of a purely impartial observer, one not involved in a relation with anyone. Alternatively, they could assume a partial perspective which makes their child the most important, but potentially also impairs an objective estimation of its quality of life. The inability to unify these two moral perspectives could

---

7   In itself, the argument concerning parents' suffering is insufficient – it ultimately refers to the parents' competence and willingness to care for the child in all possible circumstances. When the child comes into existence, the parents' experiences cease to have meaning – responsibility for the child becomes independent from one's own life story.
8   This advantage God has over parents is well reflected in the following passage: 'Can a mother forget the baby at her breast and have no compassion on the child she has borne? Though she may forget, I will not forget you!' (Is 49:15)

constitute an argument for prohibiting parents from playing God. It is most often cited by conservative authors in support of the prohibition of biomedical intervention in human procreation[9]. In the discussed context, this argument would be even more fundamental, supporting scepticism towards the moral justification of human procreation, or at least undermining the right to broad parental arbitrariness understood as using subjective criteria. The limited capacity of predicting the future quality of the child's life makes procreation a risky bet with high stakes, to which child is exposed without its consent (Velleman 2008, 251). Jason Marsh points out, however, that the difference between the attributes of parents and God might also work to the detriment of the latter, provided we adopt a rule that allows to create men only if they experience less suffering than their creator (Marsh 2015, 73n). The absence of suffering on God's part would eliminate the permissibility of creating a world where suffering exists, leaving limited acceptability of human procreation[10]. This argument again seems to lead to accepting claim C.

The general premise of claim C is that greater powers of creating human beings attributable to God would impose more responsibility on him. Here, parents' limitations act to their benefit, and God's privileged status constitutes a problem to positions that defend His perfection. While bringing a child into this world by its parents may be acceptable due to their inability to prevent evil, this argument does not work in relation to an almighty God. According to authors who formulate arguments against the parent-God analogy in the context of philosophy of religion, even assuming that God could have reasons for allowing evil into the life of a created human, it is the duty of a loving parent to try and avoid prolonged and intense suffering, or at least attempt to explain its meaning (Dougherty 2012, 21).

Providing company in suffering is another important moral requirement of parental love:

---

9 Nils Holtug presents four possible versions of the argument, that refer to: 1) assigning divine prerogatives to oneself, 2) acting against nature, 3) making decisions due to wrong criteria, and 4) making decisions despite the inability to predict their consequences (Holtug 1997, 15).
10 The way to remain at claim C is to justify the possibility of God experiencing suffering. Perfect compassion in relation to every human being would create such a large sum of experiences that would allow to create a man with any quality of life possible. This argument is limited to the impure genesis context. In the pure genesis context, a God who has never suffered would not be able to create beings exposed to suffering.

A loving parent would never permit her children to experience prolonged, intense and apparently gratuitous suffering together with a sense she has abandoned them or never existed in the first place if she could avoid doing so (Wielenberg 2015, 307).

The fact that this assumption is intuitively acceptable would point to the parental perspective's natural precedence over the divine one. It would seem that an even stronger argument would be intuitive – one that demands attempts at avoiding any suffering, or at least instructing to accompany the child in this experience, regardless of its intensity and longevity. In philosophy of religion, the existence of an incomprehensible evil may lead to stating that God does not exist, or that the relationship between God and man is of different nature than the parent-child relationship (DePoe 2014, 40). The argument that God, by allowing evil, respects the freedom of every man seems incompatible with the perspective of a parent, to whom protecting their own child is more important than providing freedom of choice to potential evildoers. From the point of view of ethics, regardless of whether one can solve the problem of evil, the radical dissimilarity of God's perspective eliminates the possibility of using the parent-God analogy when justifying the permissible arbitrariness in procreative decisions.

The consequence of adopting thesis C is the recognition that a reference to God's perspective is not useful in settling moral problems related to procreation, because it does not provide an answer to the question on acceptable motives of procreation, nor to the one on the nature of parental arbitrariness. The answers to these questions seem to lie in the nature of the parent-child relationship, which forms the basis of the obligation to prevent suffering and accompany the child. The only way of upholding argument D is to find an aspect, in which the parent's perspective is consistent with the perspective of God. Even if the aspect is not key in settling procreative problems, it may shine some additional light on the role of parents making a decision that leads to bringing a child into existence. According to Wasserman, unlike God, parents cannot love a future child as they would love an existing child, love it as 'infinitely dear despite its tribulations' (Wasserman 2005, 148). However, it seems that their love can, as in the case of God, be expressed by providing a chance to exist, and it may be reconciled with predicting difficulties the child will inevitably face in life, but only if treated as a necessary condition of larger goods it will be able to experience. This time, the argument taken from philosophy of religion and concerning the possible reasons why God allows evil is used to refer to the parents' situation, where the child has no other chance of existing other than living a life burdened by illness or disability. According to Robert Adams, the rationality condition for creating the world does not require it to be the best possible one. It is enough for it to be a good world (Adams 1972, 317). It is important for God to have a plan when creating the world and mankind, and for the plan to assume man's well-being and give hope for a stable relationship if there are difficulties in its implementation.

The ability to formulate a plan seems to refer to the essence of parental arbitrariness. It boils down to creating a child on the basis of a subjective vision of living together with it and – in the long run – its independent life. This subjective vision can serve as a starting point for establishing a relationship. However, it must be flexible and possible to be reconciled with obligations arising from that relation. The parental relation, which is one of the key reasons for creating a child, must be durable regardless of possible future changes to the life of the parent or to the child's quality of life. Arbitrariness based on the subjective vision of living together with the child may not restrict the future prospects of the child's life and, after it comes into existence, it must give way to the adaptation of the parents' activities to its condition and needs. Thus, the parents' motives and reasons must be flexible enough to not allow images of a perfect life with the child take precedent over reality, and persistent enough so that potential changes and difficult events this relationship may be exposed to would not serve as a basis for challenging it. The biblical vows that God swears to man seem to illustrate the sense of responsibility for the created men that is present in the parental perspective. The phenomenon of this vow – sworn even before the child exists, but already covering its entire existence – on the one hand, sets the scope of arbitrariness, and on the other – of the possible application of the parent-God analogy. To potential parents, the image of an almighty God making this kind of an oath to man may constitute a reference point and a source of motivation when deciding to have a child and carrying out the obligations arising from the role of a parent.

6.4 Conclusions

The primary limitation of the parent-God analogy is the asymmetry of attributes and the resulting differences in judging responsibility for suffering a created person may be exposed to. Arbitrariness in procreative decisions may be considered acceptable if it involved forming a relationship with them, assumed the willingness to take responsibility for the child, minimised its suffering, and accompanied it in enduring difficult events they encounter in life. Arbitrariness based on a subjective vision of living together with the child and assuming its intrinsic value seems most compatible with these conditions. The possibility of discovering these terms without referencing God's perspective allows one to grant priority to the perspective of parents when judging procreative decisions.

The primary function of this analogy would be to highlight the phenomenon of being a parent by emphasizing the existential degree and responsibility related to bringing a new human being into existence.

Acknowledgements

Translated from Polish into English by Aeddan Shaw.

References

Adams R (1972) Must God Create the Best? Philosophical Review 81:317–32.

Benatar D (2006) Better never to have been. Clarendon Press, Oxford.

Cook TI (1942) Law, arbitrariness and ethics. California Law Review 30(2):151–171.

Dasgupta P (1987) The ethical foundations of population policies. In: Johnson DG, Lee RD (eds) Population growth and economic development. University of Wisconsin Press, Madison, pp. 631–659.

Dasgupta P (1988) Lives and well-being. Social choice and welfare 5:103–126.

Dasgupta P (2007) Human well-being and the natural environment. Oxford University Press, New York.

DePoe JM (2014) On the epistemological framework for skeptical theism. In: Dougherty T, McBrayer JM (eds) Skeptical theism: new essays. Oxford University Press, Oxford, pp. 32–44.

Dougherty T (2012) Reconsidering the parent analogy: further work for skeptical theists. International Journal for Philosophy of Religion 72(1):17–25.

Douglas T (2015) Parental partiality and the intergenerational transmission of advantage. Philosophical Studies 172(10):2735–2756.

Heyd D (1992) Genethics: moral issues in the creation of people. University of California Press, Berkeley, London.

Holtug N (1997) Altering humans: the case for and against human gene therapy. Monash Bioethics Review 16(4):14–26.

Keller S (2013) Partiality. Princeton University Press, Princeton.

Lecce S, Magnusson E (2015) Do motives matter? On the political relevance of procreative reasons. In: Hannan S, Brennan S, Vernon R (eds) Permissible Progeny? The morality of procreation and parenting. Oxford University Press, New York, pp. 150–169.

Lotz M (2009) Procreative reasons-relevance: on the moral significance of why we have children. Bioethics 23(5):291–299.

Lotz M (2011) Rethinking procreation: why it matters why we have children. Journal of Applied Philosophy 28(2):105–121.

Marsh J (2015) Procreative ethics and the problem of evil. In: Hannan S, Brennan S, Vernon R (eds) Permissible Progeny? The morality of procreation and parenting. Oxford University Press, New York, pp. 65–86.

Overall C (2012) Why Have Children? MIT Press, Cambridge, MA.

Parfit D (1984) Reasons and persons. Oxford University Press, Oxford.

Singer P (1998) Possible preferences. In: Fehige C, Wessels U (eds) Preferences. Walter de Gruyter, Berlin, New York, pp. 383–398.

Velleman D (2008) The gift of life. Philosophy & Public Affairs36(3):245–266.

von Hildebrand D (2009) The nature of love (trans: Crosby JF, Crosby JH). St. Augustine's Press, South Bend, IN.

Wasserman D (2005) The nonidentity problem, disability, and the role morality of prospective parents. Ethics 116(1):132–152.

Wielenberg EJ (2015) The parent–child analogy and the limits of skeptical theism. International Journal for Philosophy of Religion 78(3):301–314.

Wojciech Lewandowski

7 Spare embryos and parental obligations

During the *in vitro* process, anything from a couple to more than ten embryos are created. Following diagnosis, a number of these are chosen for implantation into the woman whilst the fate of the remainder lies in the hands of a number of other factors. Embryos which have been diagnosed as having morphological or genetic faults are not considered for implantation. The healthy remainder may be frozen in order to be used by the parents in order to ensure the pregnancy is a successful one or – in the long term- for further attempts to have children. If the parents do not plan to have any more children, the embryos may be frozen, given away for adoption or given over for research purposes.

In discussions on the moral permissibility of genetic selection, arguments concerning the embryos to be implanted tend to dominate the discussion. The arguments range from, on the one hand, impartial reasoning such as do the embryos have a moral status which requires them to be treated with respect by all rational agents to – on the other – the parental obligation to show unconditional love and to guarantee their right to an open future. The majority of these arguments make some reference to the number of embryos. Impartially recognising their moral status rules out actions which may lead to their death or prevent their development. In the instructions to be found in *Dignitas Personae*, the fate of excess embryos is defined as a grave injustice which, in terms of the lack of morally accepted means, may not be given redress (Congregation for the Doctrine of the Faith 2008). Activities such as utilising the embryos for research purposes, giving them up for adoption or permitting them to die are regarded as not being in accordance with their moral status. In turn, for positions which hold that embryos do not have moral status, the situation of the excess of embryos leads or permits all kinds of treatment of them or may lead to an impartial imperative for them to be utilized for research.

In discussions over excess embryos, the perspective of the parents often arises in the context of the right to dispose of them. It seems that appealing to the perspective of the parents also in the context of moral obligations towards the embryos can complement and indicate the limitations of the arguments regarding the moral status of embryos. The text below presents an analysis of argument against the selection of embryos based on the premise that the existence of an excess of embryos presents parents in a situation of a moral dilemma.

The reasoning is as follows: 1. Embryo is an actual part of parent-child relationship; 2. This relationship is a basis for parental obligation; 3. Genetic selection between embryos leads to conflict of parental obligations which constitute a moral dilemma; 4. We should avoid decisions leading to moral dilemmas. Hence: We should avoid interventions which include genetic selection.

7.1 The embryo as a part of the parent-child relationship

Research conducted amongst potential parents in fertility clinics with regard to embryos shows that some regarded them as forming a family bond with them immediately (Blythetal. 2011; de Lacey 2005, 2007; Goedeke & Daniels 2017; Kirkman 2003; Melamed et al. 2009; Nachtigall et al. 2005; Parry 2006; Provoostetal.2009; Stieletal. 2010). There are two main ways of normative justification of this attitude. The first lies in showing that it is possible for a parent-embryo relationship to generate a moral obligation in terms of the moral status of an embryo. The second consists of showing that the moral status of both parties is not always a condition for entry into the moral responsibilities of the relationship generated by one side to the other. An argument for choosing the first strategy is that it is impossible to define moral relations without making reference to the moral status of the entities which form that relationship. This argument is also supported by the intuitive reaction to examples like: R1: a man and his stone or R2: a man and his collection of model aeroplanes. In both cases, the fundamental doubt we have to consider with regard to their moral relations is the fact that in each of them the correlate is not a sentient being. Examples of the type R3: a man and his dog or R4: a parent and baby allow us not to intuitively place greater emphasis and weight on the latter examples but also to show the moral obligation which stems from them. Regardless of the discussion on this basis, the decision on the moral status of acorrelative relationship would determine its moral character and the obligations arising from it. In accordance with the first strategy, an embryo might be regarded as forming a parent-child relationship under the condition that one may defend the thesis that in terms of the relations of the R1 or the R2 type, one may talk about the moral status of entities that do not have the capacity to feel or display the kind of relation (e.g. a parent and their child who has permanently lost consciousness) which would allow us to intuitively regard them as moral despite one side not being capable of feeling.

The second strategy relies upon proving that one may defend the moral character of the parent-embryo relationship without considering the question of moral status.Among the many possible moments at which women begin to see themselves as mothers are when they find out about the pregnancy, see an ultrasound image, experience the first movements of the child, the moment of birth or at any time thereafter. Equally broad is the scope for the possible moments at which one may regard oneself as being a father. On the other hand, regarding oneself as a parent need not coincide with the beginning of parental obligations. One of the fundamental decisions regarding abortion is the recognition that one is not yet a parent or that one does not wish to be. According to Heather Draper, the acceptance that one may enter into a parent-child relationship is independent of the consideration of the problem of the moral status of an embryo:

> But it seems to me that if we can take it for granted that a baby at birth can be considered to have parents whose views about how it should be treated and so on are to be awarded considerable respect *because* they are the parents, and if we grant that a newborn baby has the same status as an embryo or fetus, then there is reason to suppose that both embryo and fetus can have parents too. In other words, whether or not one has parents does not seem to be related to whether or not one is a person (Draper 2014, 13).

Draper's argumentation rests on the assumptions of respect for the procreational autonomy of the parents and the equal moral status of the newborn and the embryo. The justification of the first implies asymmetry between the rights and obligations of parents. If it is possible to have parental rights with regard to the infant or embryo without referring to his moral status, it is not unreasonable to also adopt the notion of having parental duties without reference to this status. Possessing the right to decide the fate of newborns or embryos would be accompanied by having certain duties towards them. The main challenge for this argument is to show that the laws relating to embryos have the same nature as those relating to the child and are not, for example, the same as the right to decide about the fate of their genetic material. A key argument for Draper is, therefore, the second thesis concerning the equal moral status of the embryo and newborn.

Any justification of the possibility of the parent-embryo relationship requires one to distinguish between the impartial and the parental point of view. When we want to determine whether the embryo has the same rights as the infant or an adult, we refer to arguments which justify the status held. The success of these decisions depends on questions such as the problem of personal identity, the ability to feel pain, human dignity or the possibility of the universalization of judgments about moral status. It does not depend directly, however, on the basis of the recognition or non-recognition of the embryo by the parents as something forming a part of their parent-child relationship. It seems that the direction of recognition of the objective value of the child from the perspective of the parents is different. In the case of natural procreation we do not begin to perceive the child from the perspective of objective knowledge about personal identity and the development of the embryo or fetus, but rather the experience of the father or the mother in their new role having learnt of the possible beginning of a pregnancy. Within the parental perspective, recognition of the embryo does not have to be the primary moral experience, but may be mediated in terms of the relationship which develops between us and the child. The recognition of parent-child relationship thus becomes typical – although not one which excludes others – a way to discover and recognize the moral status of the child. To recognize oneself as an actual parent is enough to formulate a judgment about the existence of a child, without the necessity of determining the identity, number or moral status of the correlates in the relationship.

This allows for parent-child relationships to be classified as relations which don't require any reference to equality, utility or any other agent-neutral reasons for its justification. What distinguishes an R1–R3 relationship from a parental relationship would be the fact that it is directed at the discovery of the objective dignity of the child in a primary and independent manner that supports the justification of its moral status. This position allows one to account for the natural growth in the parent-child relationship which stems from the state where the child does not exist, but the potential parents decide or undertake to have a child, through the state in embryo begins to exist with the embryo up until the point when the moral status of both sides does not arouse controversy.

The fundamental counterargument against acknowledging the parent-embryo relationship would be the argument from the death of embryos, which research suggests are at rates of 45–75% within the first two weeks of fertilization under natural circumstances (Ord 2008, 16). Recognition of a possible parent-embryo relationship would be at too great a psychological cost for many parents. The awareness that 45% of our children die within the first 2 weeks would be unacceptable hard to square with both the naturalistic and religious worldviews.

Furthermore, the recognition of this relationship in conjunction with the fact of the natural loss of embryos would lead to the same difficult to accept consequences as the recognition of the moral status of the embryo, namely, that there is parental and social responsibility to use as many resources as possible to reduce the mortality of embryos (Ord 2008). A possible, though difficult, answer could be based on the fact that the fragility of human life from its very beginning means that parents must always bear the unbearable weight of the possible loss of a child. Until we reach a biomedical level at which procreation is not indelibly linked with such high rates of loss, natural procreation protects in this sense as parents are often unaware of the loss of an embryo. This 'blissful ignorance' does not feature, however, in assisted procreation where decisions regarding the number of created, implanted and excess embryos is unavoidable.

Another answer to the charge based on the death of embryos would be to maintain the symmetry of the embryo-newborn with the justification that the parent-child relationship would retain its character even in the most adverse circumstances of human procreation. I will call this argument 'the argument from risky procreation': consider a scenario in which the Earth is inhabited by a generation of people who have been decimated by a widespread, incurable disease that means that every fertilized egg survives, developing into an embryo and foetus, but only one in ten pregnancies ends in the birth of a child. In other cases, the pregnancies end in the painless death of the child immediately after birth. In such circumstances, the only chance of being a parent for most people is solely the experience of the relationship they have with the child during the nine months of pregnancy. It seems that even in the case of risky procreation, there would still exist reasons to be a parent. What is more, the infant mortality rate would not constitute an argument against their moral status.

It would seem that the power of the argument of risky procreation depends entirely on adding the assumption to this scenario that the survival of the human species depends on each successfully completed gestation period. The moral status of the newborn would not just be based on its intrinsic value, but the value that it adds to the existence of the entire human population. Such a situation does not occur, however, in the creation and destruction of embryos in the current conditions of human procreation. In addition, assisted procreation in the above-mentioned conditions would have the goal of increasing the probability of the survival of the embryo until the moment of birth by making as many pregnancies, and then selecting and supporting the development of the embryos that have the best chance of coming to term and surviving. It should be noted, however, that regardless of the purpose of assisted procreation, the parental right linked to the creation and formation of relations still holds and continues to retain its power.

A stronger objection to the thesis about the existence of a relationship between the parent-embryo is the appeal to the observation that becoming a parent is a process that develops, grows and changes over 9 months. In the case of embryos, the time is too short and parents may not even be aware that fertilization has occurred. The best answer from defenders of the parent-embryo relation consists firstly on the claim that, even if it is true that interpersonal relationships need time to develop, this assumption with regard to the time required is not a condition of entry into the relationship. In all interpersonal relationships, the time in which they develop is independent of both parties. What determines them is the decision to enter into a relationship itself.¹ The second element of the response is to question the knowledge of the existence of the other person as a condition of the existence of the relationship. With a slightly weaker formulation, willingness to enter into a relationship could replace the condition of knowledge in a list of these conditions.

The above observations show the kind of challenges faced by the conception of the very existence of the potential to justify the possibility of the parent-embryo relationship. This justification alone is, however, insufficient for this to show that moral obligations stem from this relationship.

7.2 The parent-embryo relationship as the basis of obligation

The discussion as to whether – and if so, how – the relationship could give rise to moral obligations is mainly centered around showing agent-relative reasons that justify having duties towards the person with whom agent shares a relationship, without also having these responsibilities to others. Traditionally this position claims that

> It is impermissible for human beings voluntarily to become parents of a child, and yet to refuse to rear it to a stage of development at which it can independently take part in social life (Donagan 1977, 101).

The above principle cannot be applied to situations in which embryos would arise without parental consent. Although these situations are extremely rare in the context of assisted procreation, the basic problem with the recognition of this principle is to determine whether the intention of being a parent is the factual basis of possible obligations towards the embryos. An affirmative answer could be justified from the voluntarist perspective which claims that the only basis for special duties are voluntary acts or omissions which cause formulation of certain expectations rational from an impartial point of view. Voluntarism assumes that the special relationship does not constitute an independent basis for moral obligations, and that the latter can be justified only by putting them into an

---

1   An example supporting this argument would be recognizing that it is perfectly rational and acceptable to marry someone who has but one day left to live. It is fairly easy to find a counter-example to this situation, with a couple who have decided to have a child and know that after the birth they will have very little time left in the world. This decision seems to be more controversial, although not impossible to justify on the assumption that the child could not exist in other circumstances, and assuming additional conditions have been met to provide the child with care and to leave them everything they will need.

impartial perspective. The main argument for voluntarism is the claim that it would be unjust if people bore the cost of fulfilling particular obligations which they had not previously agreed to either *implicite* or *explicite* (Scheffler 1997, 191). The agreement to participate in assisted procreation which assumes the creation of embryos could be interpreted as a voluntary undertaking of responsibility for the fate of the excess embryos. Critics of this position, however, have drawn attention to the difficulties in establishing a criterion of rational expectations (Scheffler 1997, Kolodny 2010). Not all of the actions that we undertake on a voluntary basis are associated with the creation of relationships and obligations to care for them. Without justification, this criterion cannot explain why the voluntary entry in relationships of the R3 and R4 type is on the basis of obligations while those in R1 and R2 relationships are not.

The consequentialist approach adopts a similar kind of argumentation based on reduction of parental responsibilities to impartial reasons. The condition of agreeing to undertake parental responsibilities would not be necessary in this case because their existence would be determined by the reasons to choose the action which brings the best results from impartial point of view. The consequentialist justification of parental responsibilities towards embryos would be possible even if it failed to justify that the parent-embryo relationship is one of the most effective ways of maximizing happiness. It would be difficult, however, to accept this thesis due to the fact that embryos are not capable of feeling and therefore the loss of the embryo can always be offset by the creation of a new baby in the future or any other act of maximizing overall benefits.

A non-reductionist justification of parental responsibilities presupposes the existence of non-derivative agent-relative reasons. The most frequently defended reasons of this kind appeal to the significance of biological ties or responsibility for being the cause of the existence of the new person. An example of the first kind of justification is the position of Leon Kass who holds that every child has a right to natural ties, bonds, roots and that which constitutes their identity (Kass 2002, 98–100). The thesis of the close relations between biological ties and self-identity may, however, be questioned. In the opinion of Bernard Prusak, the parent-child relationship based on genetic ties does not contain any value which would not feature in a relationship that began with adoption (Prusak 2013, 39). Furthermore, the potential preferences of the parents to have their own genetic offspring (sharing asimilar genotype or physical similarity) seems insufficient as a reason to rule out adoption as an obligation (Rulli 2014), and even more as a reason to justify such an obligation. In accordance with this notion, even though we accept that biological ties are important as they provide the right to know about one's genetic origins, parental care is such a strong and enduring obligation that it requires a stronger justification.

An example of the second type of argumentation is the position which states that the source of parental obligation is to be the cause of the existence of the child (Nelson 1991; Bigelow et al. 1988; Blustein 1997; Archard 2010, Prusak 2013). This position allows one to avoid problems associated with the former claim and attempt at justification. On the one hand, moving away from the intentions and the biological bond between parent and child allows for an explanation of a wide range of situations in which this relationship finds its beginning (e.g. planned/unplanned parenthood, natural/assisted procreation), on the other hand emphasizing the responsibility of parents as a consequence of their actions does not impose on them the obligation to maximize positive effects. According to Bernard Prusak, since procreation encumbers the child with demands and risks which have arisen without his consent, his creators are obliged to minimize the risk and scale of these charges where possible and accompany the child in overcoming them. This means that these duties involve both protecting the child from possible damage or danger, as well as supporting and developing a parent-child relationship based on love (Prusak 2013, 33–35). Applying this concept to the problem of the parent-embryo relationship allows the justification of responsibility towards all embryos: sick and healthy, those destined for implantation and surplus ones.

The argument stemming from obligations arising from being the cause of existence may be challenged by a counterargument which bestows upon parents the right to decide about the reduced quality life for children or even its end, as their creators, as long as their existence to date is deemed to be beneficial for them in comparison with not existing at all (Sidgwick 1907, 347). One possible answer is to appeal to their possession of moral status from the moment of them coming into being, which restricts the rights arising from the procreative autonomy of parents, reinforcing the importance of the duties they possess. Another possibility is to say that whatever rights and obligations which lead to a causal relation of creator-created depend on the objective purpose which can develop this relationship. It should be noted that the reference to the objective goal of the parent-child relationship can also support some of the previous positions: genetic (biological constraints can only provide a basis for the development of the interpersonal relationship based on love) and voluntaristic (deriving from the decision to enter into a relationship, the objective purpose of this relationship provides the normative basis for this decision). Furthermore, this objective purpose is what allows one to distinguish between the different types of R1–R4 relationships. So why not consider that the intrinsic value of the relationship itself which stems from its objective goal, defining at the same time the manner of its implementation by building a strong relationship based on love, would not form the basis of moral obligations? The problem with the recognition of this as the basis of responsibility would be the first objection, since not every objective purpose imposes an obligation in a relationship. Secondly, if an objective approach to relationships might be possible from an impartial point of view, then even if there are obligations arising from the parent-embryo then reference to the perspective of the parents would not be necessary. In addition, this objective goal can be expressed in consequentialist terms (maximizing everything that makes life worth living among the different parties in the relationship) or voluntarist ones (the fulfilment of mutual expectations arising from this relationship), and thus this leads the entire justification into a vicious circle. A possible answer to these problems is to try to justify the claim that only from the perspective of the parent is it possible to tackle the unique nature and goals of the relationship between parents and their children (see Chapter 6).

7.3 Genetic selection and moral dilemmas

When discussing situations that may be considered a moral dilemma, two aspects are often mentioned: objective and subjective. Authors proposing an objective approach characterize moral dilemmas as a conflict of symmetrical or non-comparable moral requirements, which can be described without referring to the perspective of the agent: their feelings and moral beliefs. Proponents of accentuating the subjective aspect of a dilemma stress the perspective of the agent facing a given situation as being key for defining moral dilemmas. The tragic nature of this situation associated with the necessity to choose evil and the inability to find an exit from the conflict between duties one recognises is demonstrated by a distinctive class of feelings experienced by the agent, known as moral residue. These are feelings of guilt or remorse. A moral dilemma, according to this approach, is a situation in which, regardless of the decision, the agent experiences these feelings and in each case experiencing them can be considered appropriate (McConnell 1996, 37–38).

The situation of parents having spare embryos can be described as a moral dilemma only when considering these two aspects. A moral dilemma would be an objective conflict of responsibilities, of which at least some are ultimately justified in the parent-child relationship recognised from the perspective of a parent. In objective terms, the need for genetic selection of embryos can be described as a choice between symmetric values. From the consequentialist perspective, the symmetry may be broken by considering the probability of a successful pregnancy and giving birth to a child in good medical fitness that allows for high quality of life as a selection criterion. From the parents' perspective, however, such a criterion cannot be applied, since health or lack thereof may not constitute grounds for differentiating engagement in the parent-child relationship. Another way of describing the situation of parents as a moral dilemma is by referring to the category of incomparability of options. Recognizing pluralism and incomparability of reasons maintains the dilemma, which consists in the fact that it is not possible to carry out all parental responsibilities. Regardless of the decision, certain obligations will remain unrealized, and the attempt to fulfil all of them leads to even more conflict.

The structure of a moral dilemma that takes into account parental responsibilities toward spare embryos would be multi-level in nature. The first level of the moral dilemma concerns the need to decide about the fate of spare embryos. Some studies concerning such a decision show that many parents are either not interested or delay making it (see Goedeke et al. 2017, 3). Some authors believe this attitude as avoiding responsibility for the fate of spare embryos or an attempt to shift the responsibility to the clinic (Cattoli et al., 2004; Svanberg et al., 2001). The justification for this assessment seems independent from the recognition of the moral status of embryos, but it seems to assume that the right to enjoy discretion over embryos must be accompanied by the obligation to decide as to their fate. Since they were created on the initiative and at the request of the parents, this responsibility can be justified voluntaristically, as well as by using Prusak's criterion of causal responsibility or by the intrinsic value of the relationship. The lack of a decision can be justified by a statement about the lack of embryos' moral status (Blyth et al 2011). In this respect, the decision would not constitute a moral obligation, and any negligence as to disposing of embryos would not be serious enough to generate rational moral residue. However, this justification cannot be formulated on the basis of a position assuming parental responsibilities arising from the special parent-embryo relationship. In this case, the lack of a decision may be regarded as unequal treatment of spare embryos and embryos to be implanted. Recognition of the inadmissibility of unequal treatment does not require a solution to the problem of the moral status of embryos and it can be justified by the obligation to place the same responsibility on all parties connected with the parent by the same normative relationship. The above answer would eliminate the parental dilemma, leaving only an impartial duty to treat embryos equally, and this, in turn – assuming the other parental responsibilities – would lead to recognizing the obligation to implant all created embryos. It seems, however, that the basis for recognising the need to make the decision lies elsewhere, namely in the nature of the parent-child relationship. Some relations, such as friendship, can be spontaneously broken up by mutual neglect of persons involved in them. It seems that the parent-child relationship cannot be broken up in this way. Parents who, in certain circumstances, decide to disclaim responsibility for their child should regulate his legal position giving him a chance for adoption. Irrespective of the criticism of such a decision, the lack of giving the chance appears to have negative moral value[2].

Making a decision concerning spare embryos constitutes the second level of the moral dilemma associated with the conflict between moral requirements requiring the choice of one of two groups of options. The first one includes actions leading to the death of embryos or refraining from actions that result in avoiding death, the second – actions aimed at implanting the embryos and allowing them to develop. Describing decisions taken at this level as a moral dilemma assumes that each option belonging to one of these groups is violating parental responsibilities. In the case of options from the first group, evading the dilemma would be possible only if impartial reasons were to be regarded as having priority over parental reasons. Donating spare embryos to stem-cell research could be justified by the hope of discovering new therapies. Giving priority to impartial reasons, however, does not eliminate the dilemma, but the entire perspective of parental responsibilities. An easier, but more tragic attempt to solve the dilemma could be found in justifying the embryos' natural death by refraining from their cryopreservation. If the death of the embryos is not intended by their parents, but only foreseen, and mortality of embryos in the *in vitro* procedure is comparable with the mortality of embryos in case of natural procreation, then this option would consist in accepting the loss of a child together with the social obligation to bring about the emergence of effective techniques of assisted procreation that minimizes the loss of spare embryos. The main argument against this possibility refers to the fact that creating spare embryos is embedded in the structure of the entire procedure and aims to increase the probability of giving birth to a healthy child. Creating a large number of embryos only to increase the possibility that one or few of them survive subjects parental reasons to instrumental reasons, which again is incompatible with the status of moral obligations formulated from the parental perspective.

---

2   The problem with supporting this argument consists in whether they can be reduced to reasons referring to the best interests of the child. If so, then this assessment would not have to be negative in a society that ensures excellent living conditions to children with a legal position unregulated by their parents. According to the position recognizing the intrinsic value of the parent-child relationship, the requirement to provide a substitute relationship cannot be reduced to the requirement of meeting the child's needs.

The group of options leading to implanting and giving birth to embryos includes becoming pregnant again using spare embryos or donating them to embryo adoption programs. In the first case, after giving birth to the child, parents would be required to bring about the implantation of the remaining embryos, even provided the low probability of success (Watt 2016, 73). Since parental responsibilities towards each of the embryos result in asymmetry of options, they preclude selection. On the other hand, the lack of selection would lead to exposing the child to the risk of being born with serious malformations. According to the opponents of genetic selection, the essence of the moral dilemma stems from the fact of creating embryos in a controlled procedure, which strengthens the obligation to do everything to provide the created embryo with a chance for a happy life.[3]

Is a similar conflict of responsibilities present in the case of embryos' adoption? The main difference between adopting embryos and implanting them in the body of their genetic mother is that potential parents applying to embryo adoption programmes do not have any moral obligations towards them yet. Their decision to accept parental responsibility is – similarly to ordinary adoption – supererogatory. Selecting embryos for implantation does not breach this responsibility, similarly to choosing a child that has already been born. Therefore, solving the parental dilemma would consist in transferring responsibility to people, to whom this choice does not constitute a conflict of duties. There are at least two problems with this solution, both referring to agent-relative reasons.[4] The first assumes that embryo adoption is contrary to the procreative integrity of the adoptive mother (Geach 1999) and constitutes an ambiguous beginning of the mother-child relationship by simultaneously assuming the roles of biological and adoptive mother (Watt 2016, 112–113). Both these arguments can

---

3   The only solution possible in the future to this kind of dilemmas could consist in utilising technology allowing for embryo treatment and their safety during the pregnancy. Such technology would eliminate not only the moral dilemma, but also the need for genetic selection, which causes the dilemma.
4   Objections based on impartial reasons point to difficulties in selecting embryos to be saved. Assuming that it is not possible to save them all, and the personal value of each of them is identical, the selection would have to be made either through a draw or basing on empirical characteristics. Both solutions carry their own problems. Drawing seems to be a method that is irrational and risky both for them, and for the woman opting for adoption. In turn, selecting embryos on the basis of genetic endowment could give rise to allegations of discrimination, since the preference for having a healthy child reduces the chance of saving embryos with defects.

be resolved by stating that saving lives can justify the violation of procreative integrity, whereas the ambiguity of relationships when adopting embryos can be regarded as one of the many challenges the adoptive family must successfully face when forming a genuine parental relationship. The second argument against donating embryos for adoption states that it would eliminate the dilemma only in respect of agent-neutral reasons. In line with this perspective, if there is an impartial obligation to perform an action, it does not matter who performs it. In terms of parental reasons, the fulfilling of parental responsibilities by adoptive parents does not eliminate the normative strength of these duties and considering as appropriate the moral residue resulting from waiving responsibilities towards embryos with less favourable genetic endowment, which did not become the first choice as a result of selection.

7.4 The obligation to avoid moral conflicts

If genetic selection leads to a situation where, regardless of the selected option, one of the parental responsibilities is violated, then the argument against genetic selection must be based on a moral imperative to avoid these situations. In itself, this dictate is not controversial, however the problem with this part of the argument consists in the difficulty of determining whether it is agent-neutral or agent-relative. In other words, whether parents are required to avoid moral dilemmas, since each rational agent has such an obligation, or does parental perspective bring something important to this principle.

The principle of avoiding moral conflicts is, according to Ruth Marcus, a second-order regulative principle, which states that

> [A]s rational agents with some control of our lives and institutions, we ought to conduct our lives and arrange our institutions so as to minimize predicaments of moral conflicts (Marcus 1980, 122).

Although due to the complexity of circumstances in which we operate, we are not able to predict whether our decisions put us in a situation of moral conflict, recognizing the close relationship between genetic selection and the situation of a moral dilemma would allow to apply this principle by all potential parents. This principle would require choosing such a way of reproduction, which does not include genetic selection, i.e. natural procreation or assisted procreation based on technology that allows the creation of a desired number of embryos, all of which would be healthy and implanted into the woman's body. The lack of spare embryos eliminates moral conflicts associated with the need to dispose of these embryos.

Aside from other reasons for and against genetic selection, recognizing the principle of minimizing conflicts as a universal obligation implies that genetic selection is not an intrinsic evil, but rather a violation of the rationality requirement, analogous to making a promise while knowing that fulfilling it in the future may, for objective reasons, come into conflict with the performance of other duties. Recognising this principle as a second-order obligation raises the question of the possibility of comparing it with basic reasons justifying selection based on a valid requirement of increasing the probability of giving birth to a healthy child. On the one hand, its universal and neutral nature reinforces reasons based on parental relationships, and on the other – if, from a consequentialist perspective, reasons of impartial maximization of happiness precede over agent-relative reasons, then the potential conflicts of parental responsibilities that may appear as a result of genetic selection constitute merely the cost that can be justified, if one takes into account that violating these obligations does not cause suffering for anyone. The easiest position would be to recognize the second-order principle as having precedence over any first-order rules. This allows one to avoid difficulties of comparing agent-relative and agent-neutral reasons, at least in the present context.

Aside from agent-neutral reasons, one may indicate parental reasons supporting the principles of minimizing conflicts. Establishing the parent-child relationship is a unique and long-term process, during which a new human being begins to exist, having rights that will ultimately go beyond the moral requirements resulting from this relationship. Although the decision to have a child and how to bring it to this world, at its outset, takes place within a wide range of acceptability, and is guaranteed by the right to procreative autonomy, the principle of minimizing future conflicts would constitute one of the basic moral principles in cases when the procedure of creating embryos has not started yet. In addition, the modern discussion on moral dilemmas shows that examples concerning the necessity to choose one of one's children constitutes one of the most common examples of moral conflicts.

7.5 Conclusion

In this article, I have analysed the conditions for recognizing the situation of parents opting for assisted procreation involving genetic selection and creating spare embryos. A reference to the parental perspective is one of the possibilities of justifying the actuality of moral dilemmas arising from genetic selection. Settling the problem of the moral status of human embryos is not necessary when adopting the position concerning the parent-child relationship, proclaiming that parental responsibilities derive directly from recognizing oneself as being involved in this relationship and recognizing the intrinsic value of this relationship. Recognizing genetic selection as the cause of moral conflicts does not necessarily result from accepting the pluralism of agent-relative or agent-neutral reasons. The moral dilemma presented in this article consists of the lack of the ability to meet all obligations resulting from the procedures of creating spare embryos and genetic selection. Elimination of the dilemma is possible by reducing parental responsibilities to agent-neutral reasons or reducing the rank of these responsibilities in comparison to agent-neutral ones. Recognizing the legitimacy of the principle of minimizing conflicts leads to the conclusion that reconciling competing criteria of rationality cannot be limited only to the matter of genetic selection, but it must take into account consistency with the reasons applicable when deciding on having a child.

Acknowledgements

Translated from Polish into English by Aeddan Shaw.

References

Archard D (2010) The obligations and responsibilities of parenthood. In: Archard D, Benatar D (eds) Procreation and Parenthood. Oxford University Press, Oxford, pp.103–127.

Bigelow J, Campbell J, Dodds S, Pargetter R, Prior E, Young R (1988) Parental autonomy. Journal of Applied Philosophy 5:3–16.

Blustein J (1997) Procreation and parental responsibility. Journal of Social Philosophy 28(2):79–86.

Blyth E, Frith L, Paul MS, Berger R (2011) Embryo relinquishment for family building. How it should be conceptualized? International Journal of Law, Policy and the Family 25:260–285.

Cattoli M, Borini A, Bonu M (2004) Fate of stored embryos: our 10 years experience. European Journal of Obstetrics & Gynecology and Reproductive Biology 115 (Suppl. 1):S16–S18.

Congregation for the Doctrine of the Faith. Instruction Dignitas Personae on certain bioethical questions. The Holy. See 8 Sept 2008, n. 19. http://www.vatican.va/roman_curia/congregations/cfaith/documents/rc_con_cfaith_doc_20081208_dignitas-personae_en.html (accessed 28 Jan 2017).

de Lacey S (2005) Parent identity and 'virtual' children: Why patients discard rather than donate unused embryos. Human Reproduction 20:1661–1669.

de Lacey S (2007) Decisions for the fate of frozen embryos: Fresh insights into patients'thinking and their rationales for donating or discarding embryos. Human Reproduction 22:1751-1758.

Donagan A (1977) The theory of morality. University of Chicago Press, Chicago, IL.

Draper H (2014) Martha as a mother. Parents, parental choices, and preimplantation selection. Cambridge Quarterly of Healthcare Ethics 23:8-16.

Geach M (1999) Are there any circumstances in which it would be morally admirable for a woman to seek to have an orphan embryo implanted in her womb? In:Gormally L (ed) Issues for a Catholic Bioethics. The Linacre Centre, London, pp. 341-346.

Goedeke S, Daniels K (2017) The discourse of gifting in embryo donation: The understandings of donors, recipients and counselors. Qualitative Health Research 27(9):1402-1411.

Goedeke S, Daniels K, Thorpe M, du Preez E (2017) The fate of unused embryos: discourses, action possibilities, and subject positions. Qualitative Health Research 27(10):1529-1540.

Kass L (2002) Life, Liberty and the Defence of Dignity. Encounter, San Fransisco, CA.

Kirkman M (2003) Egg and embryo donation and the meaning of motherhood. Women and Health 38(2):1-18.

Kolodny N (2010) Which relationships justify partiality? The case of parents and children. Philosophy and Public Affairs 38(1):37-75.

Marcus RB (1980) Moral dilemmas and consistency. The Journal of Philosophy 77(3):121-136.

McConnell TC (1996) Moral residue and moral dilemmas. In: Mason HE (ed) Moral Dilemmas and Moral Theory. Oxford University Press, Oxford, New York, pp. 36-47.

Melamed RM, de Sousa Bonetti TC, Braga DP, Madaschi C, Iaconelli A, Borges E (2009) Deciding the fate of supernumerary frozen embryos: Parents' choices. Human Fertility 12:185-190.

Nachtigall RD, Becker G, Friese C, Butler A, MacDougall K (2005) Parents' conceptualization of their frozen embryos complicates the disposition decision. Fertility and Sterility 84:431-434.

Nelson JL (1991) Parental obligations and the ethics of surrogacy: a causal perspective. Public Affairs Quarterly 5:49-61.

Ord T (2008) The Scourge: moral implications of natural embryo loss. The American Journal of Bioethics 8(7):12–19.

Parry S (2006) (Re)constructing embryos in stem cell research: Exploring the meaning of embryos for people involved in fertility treatments. Social Science & Medicine 62:2349–2359.

Provoost V, Pennings G, de Sutter P, Gerris J, van de Velde A, de Lissnyder E, Dhont M (2009) Infertility patients' beliefs about their embryos and their disposition preferences. Human Reproduction 24:896–905.

Prusak B (2013) Parental Obligations and Bioethics: The Duties of a Creator. Routledge, New York.

Rulli T (2014) Preferring a genetically-related child. Journal of Moral Philosophy 13(6):669–698.

Sidgwick H (1907) Methods of Ethics. MacMillan, New York.

Scheffler S (1997) Relatonships and responsibilities. Philosophy and Public Affairs 26(3):189–209.

Stiel M, McMahon CA, Elwyn G, Boivin J (2010) Pre-birth characteristics and 5-year follow-up of women with cryopreserved embryos after successful in vitro fertilisation treatment. Journal of Psychosomatic Obstetrics and Gynecology 31:32–39.

Svanberg AS, Boivin J, Bergh T (2001) Factors influencing the decision to use or discard cryopreserved embryos. Acta Obstetrica et Gynecologica Scandinavia 80:849–855.

Watt H (2016) The Ethics of Pregnancy, Abortion and Childbirth: Exploring Moral Choices in Childbearing. Routledge, New York.

Part II: Genetic Enhancement

Marta Soniewicka

8 The question of justice in the debate over human enhancement

8.1 Introduction

Transhumanism can be defined as a movement composed of those advocating the use of all available technologies, including neuro-, bio- and nanotechnology, to enhance the human species (Birnbacher 2008). The form of human existence arising from the application of radical technological transformation termed 'posthumanism' is advocated by, among others, Nick Bostrom, Nicholas Agar, Ingmar Persson and Julian Savulescu (Bostrom 2008; Agar 1998; Persson & Savulescu 2012).[1] It is pointed out that medical and genetic interventions could in the future enable the following forms of enhancement: enhanced cognitive abilities (including memory and learning skills), increased growth, improved hearing, improved musculature, increased immunity to diseases, enhanced predispositions toward experiencing moods (or emotional states), a reduced need for sleep, delaying the ageing process, etc. (DeGrazia 2012). Posthumanism aims to transcend the limitations built into the human condition we currently know of. Bostrom understands 'posthumans' to be individuals who possess at least one 'posthuman' ability, that is, an ability surpassing the normal abilities of the human species that may be health-related (e.g. a life expectancy of over 100 years), cognitive (e.g. a superior intelligence quotient) or emotional (e.g. superior empathy) (Bostrom 2008).

As Dietrich Birnbacher notes, 'transhumanism' and 'posthumanism' are internally paradoxical notions, because they suggest that the aforementioned interventions could lead to the creation of a new biological species or change human nature (Birnbacher 2008). However, the actual ability to transcend the limitations built into the human condition is a distinctive human trait, so the idea of transhumanism would actually appear to confirm what is human rather than transcending humanity (see Chapter 9). The notion of humanity, as Birnbacher writes, is dynamic, so that all that can be discussed in this case is transcending what, for us, is typically human at our current state of development rather than what is human in a general sense.

---

[1] There is no consensus among transhumanists as to the aims and boundaries of human enhancement.

The dispute over the boundaries of human nature enhancement is primarily a dispute over values – relating to a normative, rather than purely biological, conception of humanity. Bioconservatives, such as Leon Kass, C.S. Lewis, Jürgen Habermas and Francis Fukuyama (Kass 2002; Lewis 2000; Habermas 2003; Fukuyama 2002), generally, when writing about the 'dehumanising' effects of heritable genetic interventions directed at the enhancement of human nature, invoke the moral aspects of what is human (see Chapter 9).

8.2 The new liberal eugenics

In this chapter, I shall mainly be focusing on the idea of enhancement by means of genetic interventions in human reproduction. It is hardly coincidental that this idea can be readily associated with the eugenics that appeared in the form of socio-political programmes at the beginning of the 20th century in many countries, including the USA, Sweden, Denmark, Norway and Germany.[2] Many modern bioethicists accept that it was not so much the actual idea of eugenics that was morally questionable, but rather the methods used to implement it (Buchanan et al. 2007). First, these methods were often based on state coercion, which stands in opposition to the ideal of individual freedom adopted in liberal democratic societies, as discussed in the first chapter in the guise of the notion of reproductive autonomy. Second, those methods often based on pseudoscientific assumptions were ineffective, since they were unable to achieve the intended

---

2 In the United States, around 60,000 people were subjected to forced or 'voluntary' sterilisation (often children were sterilised, raising major concerns over whether conscious consent had been granted in these cases), and this continued right up to the 1960s. The eugenic programme that lasted longest, at over 40 years, was implemented in Sweden. It was not discontinued until 1975, by which point 63,000 people had been sterilised. The greatest efficiency in this area was achieved by the Germans, who forcibly sterilised ca. 350,000 of their own citizens over only three years during the Third Reich. When war broke out, sterilisation was replaced by the euthanasia (or 'mercy killing') of the mentally retarded (euthanasia was carried out on 70,723 sick people, including deaf-mutes). Proponents of eugenics attempted to justify these sterilisations on fallacious assumptions grounded in biology, mainly 'medical necessity' (state of health, gene quality), race (based on pseudoscientific anthropological theories of a fallacious social evolutionism) or social factors, where dangerous simplifications were employed, leading to the adoption of the false claim that a low intelligence quotient in children from the lower classes, rather than being caused by poverty, actually causes it – in fact, low IQ is caused by malnutrition and certain conditions of development not being met. For more on eugenics, see Glover 2008; Kevles 2008; Müller-Hill 2006; Gould 2008.

objective. What we know about genetics today, when combined with technology, seems to provide us with much more precise tools for realising that objective, leading the authors of *From Chance to Choice* to postulate the replacement of the old authoritarian eugenics with a new liberal eugenics implemented while respecting the will of parents (Buchanan et al. 2007). In their view, in the liberal societies of today, the main threat to reproductive freedoms is no longer state interference, but rather social and market pressures bound up with the commercialisation and privatisation of assisted reproductive techniques and medical services. The authors believe that, if we are to mitigate against the threats associated with a 'genetic supermarket' (Nozick 1974) where wealthy parents will be choosing their offspring's traits and reproduction will be absorbed by consumption practices, access to genetic advancement technologies should be regulated by the state. Genetic interventions, due to them being heritable in nature, need to take the social perspective into account, rather than being left to the devices of individual choices grounded in the free market. Restrictions on reproductive autonomy can, in their view, only be justified when unnecessary harm (see Chapter 4) and injustice are prevented.

It can be argued that reproductive decisions made by parents with a view to having the best possible children are not *sensu stricto* eugenic in nature, because the parents are taking these decisions without special concern for the species. Their only wish is to possess the best possible children. Much the same applies to the interventions humans could use in their wish to enhance themselves – they need not assume that their individual decisions should conform to the idea of improving the species. However, the legal regulations and social institutions that enable individuals to take decisions on the enhancement of their offspring and define the scope of these are eugenic in nature if they are motivated by an aim to improve a population (Buchanan et al. 2007). This is particularly evident in the argumentation of advocates of genetic enhancement who assume that the goal is to enhance the qualities of an abstract conception of offspring rather than concrete individuals (Kamm 2013; Harris 2013). The main purpose of applying these techniques is in fact the birth of individuals 'superior' to those who would be born without such intervention (see Chapters 4, 5, 12).

The argument that injustice may be committed, which can be generated in various ways from access to reprogenetics, occurs among both advocates and opponents of genetic enhancement. For the former, this is often the only serious charge, apart from the issue of the safety of genetic interventions, that should be addressed when investigating the problem of regulating access to genetic enhancement (Kamm 2013; DeGrazia 2012; Buchanan et al. 2007). However, for the latter, this is often an insufficient argument, because it fails to question the actual idea of enhancement through genetic interventions and only draws attention to the problem of making access to the discussed techniques generally available, which is a politico-economic issue falling within the scope of wide-ranging aspects of social justice that have long existed (Sandel 2007). In this chapter, I shall be drawing attention to the two main issues in which the idea of genetic human enhancement could conceivably completely change our previous understanding of justice or move reflections on justice on to a different level. The first issue relates to the threat of new social divisions in which enhanced individuals would dominate unenhanced individuals. The second issue relates to the influence a genetic offspring enhancement programme could exert on a just social structure. But before I go on to reflect on these issues, I shall discuss the issue of the difference between offering treatment and enhancement, an issue that could be of great concern when reflecting on distributive justice.

8.3 Treatment versus enhancement

A crucial issue affecting both moral judgement and potential legal regulation of access to enhancement techniques is the difficulty of establishing a clear boundary between treatment and enhancement of the human condition (Buchanan et al. 2007). This distinction between treatment and enhancement need not coincide with a division into genetic interventions that are permissible and those that are not. However, this distinction may be of crucial functional importance when determining those treatments that should or should not be carried out within the framework of a social insurance system. This problem of making a distinction is bound up with the difficult-to-define notion of health. The definition of health the World Health Organisation (WHO) given in the preamble to its Constitution says that health should be understood as 'a state of complete physical, mental and social well-being.' Based on this definition, so-called reproductive health also incorporates the right to abortion, irrespective of any health causes and the course of the pregnancy, because possessing a (sick or healthy) child can be incompatible with someone's well-being, subjectively conceived. When we adopt such a broad definition of health, almost every action is possibly justifiable by promoting one's own well-being, including all manner of enhancements, like, for example, wrinkle correction or nose reshaping. For these reasons, Norman Daniels proposes that health should be defined as normal species functioning or species-typical functioning (Buchanan et al. 2007). Based on this definition, abortion is not, except in cases where the mother's life or health is threatened, a therapeutic activity. However, this does not pose any obstacle, in the author's view, to acknowledging that certain treatments fall within the scope of medical treatments whose cost should be reimbursed for social reasons.

However, even this definition of health is not watertight, for it is based on two premises: one descriptive and the other, normative. The former describes normal body function by invoking the frequency of occurrence of a given function or dysfunction in representatives of the species at a specific stage of the body's development. However, the latter relates to the establishment of which departures from a 'norm' are to be regarded as desirable or tolerable, and which, as undesirable or destined for removal (treatment). Furthermore, the second premise does not follow from the first and may lead to disputes.

Apart from that, further controversy may be provoked over the issues of whether certain departures from a norm may arise from bodily dysfunction or whether the fact that there is a departure from a norm, whatever the cause, is enough. The most common example given in such a case is stunted growth (Buchanan et al. 2007). Assuming that in a specific population, e.g. Europeans, a male height of 160 cm or less is a clear departure from the norm, the question arises of whether a case in which a man is 160 cm tall due to his body not producing growth hormones should be differentiated from a case in which a man is exactly the same height even though his body is functioning normally, and the causes are genetic (short parents). Administering pharmacological growth hormone substitutes to the man in the first case would be a treatment complying with the definition of normal body function, while in the second case, we are already dealing with enhancement, even though the outcome of using or not using pharmacology would be exactly the same. For these reasons, some bioethicists believe that the cause of a given human condition is irrelevant, and any evaluation of the availability of certain treatments should focus on their effects alone (Harris 2013).

Such a consequential approach is not free of controversy, because it obscures the principal aim of medicine, i.e. to eradicate the causes of dysfunction rather than just eliminating its symptoms. Distinguishing between treatment and enhancement, even if this is a largely intuitive process with a fuzzy boundary, is of paramount socio-medical importance and it would be difficult to totally abandon it. The main purpose of this distinction between treatment and enhancement is to prioritise medical tasks and help us to understand ourselves. I think that, for most of us, it is important to know if our mood changes are the outcome of persistent body dysfunction requiring treatment or a temporary side effect of environmental factors (changes in the weather, stress, etc.), which can be changed in various ways without any absolute need to apply pharmacological measures.

Harris provides the examples of labour pains and natural effects of ageing, like, for example, visual deterioration, to question the division between treatment and enhancement based on normal body function. It would appear, however there is no need to totally reject that division for the examples he mentions to be covered by therapy. However, the fact should be taken into account that, along with medical advances, the notion of 'norm', in its descriptive sense, is changing in step with increasingly accessible technological possibilities. Modern medical advances enable older people's sight or hearing to be corrected, which is affecting our perception of what normal functioning at a given age entails – the use of hearing aids, like that of spectacles, is becoming the norm, while operations can provide an alternative option to such everyday conveniences. Once it was the norm (in a descriptive, non-normative sense) for prematurely born children to die, but today we are able to preserve their lives outside their mother's bodies in incubators, significantly increasing the survival rates of newborns. Pain, including labour pains, fulfils a specific biological function, yet is of no value in itself and can also be excessive. If reducing pain does not impede its functioning while also not having any negative effects, for example, on a child being born, then the doctor may decide to reduce it. Advocates of transhumanism will argue that is this evolving notion of 'norm' that is in fact facilitating the incorporation of all manner of forms of enhancement into medical practices. For if we believe today that mentally retarded people are sick because their cognitive abilities are lower than a certain level, in the future, if genetic interventions increasing IQ were to exist, causing average intelligence levels to rise significantly, it would be people we today regard as being less mentally agile (not so bright) who would be classified as disabled. It would appear, however, that such reasoning is too much of a simplification. We intuitively differentiate people who run slowly because they do not get enough exercise or have no predisposition toward running from people whose mobility limitations are caused by health complications or their advanced age. The difference lies in the fact that, in the case of worsening mobility among older people, we are still dealing with bodily dysfunction that may be 'natural' in the sense that it is a typical sign of ageing. However, it does not cease to be an example of dysfunction, much like labour pains do not cease to be pains despite their specific assistive role in childbirth. Medical advances are enabling the elimination or reduction of these dysfunctions or effects, evoking an *optimal state* for bodily functioning (a kind of standard) entailing accurate vision and hearing, normal mobility and no oversensitivity to pain, while, in the case of prematurely born children, they are making it possible to keep vital functions working as efficiently as they would in the mother's body if the birth had not occurred prematurely. In cases where

IQ-type qualities, height or strength are average or even less than average, we are not alwyas dealing with dysfunction. The distinction between disease ('an objectively discernible abnormal state anatomically, physiologically, biochemically, or psychosocially') and illness or sickness (subjective states of feeling unwell) could be of help here (Mitchel et al. 2007, 115). The former is determined by experts, the latter by the patient herself. Extending the notion of disease or dysfunction to all states in which one feels dissatisfied with one's body, mind or spirit, would bring about 'medicalisation' of every aspect of our life and would have an adverse effect on our self-understanding and self-esteem.

If we maintain the proposal to make a distinction between treatment and enhancement by evoking normal bodily functioning, it should be noted that the same application of the same measures will be therapeutic in nature for some, and enhancing for others. Many examples exist of medical interventions currently applied that illustrate this issue. Medicines devised as a form of treatment for the symptoms of some disease or disorder, e.g. Ritalin, usually prescribed for difficulties with concentration (ADHD), or Prozac, prescribed for depression, can also be administered to healthy people as a means of stimulating brain activity or mood. Much the same applies to plastic surgery, which can be used to reconstruct parts of the body damaged by disease or accidents (e.g. breast reconstruction after a mastectomy) or to improve appearance. Administering the aforementioned growth hormone to a person of average height can make them taller than average.

Due to this fluid, though intuitively graspable, distinction between treatment and enhancement, it would be difficult to find a single bioconservative opposed to all enhancements as such. Even if many people are justifiably sceptical about healthy people using mood-enhancing medication or their obsession with going under the scalpel to enhance their appearance, no one is calling for similar practices by adult people to be prohibited, since that would constitute an unjustifiable form of paternalism. The charges bioconservatives level at enhancement focus on the idea, promoted by transhumanists, of offspring enhancement. The main line of objection therefore concerns the idea of enhancement using heritable genetic interventions, an idea defined at the population, rather than individual, level.

If methods such as gene therapy or CRISPR/Cas9 were totally safe (for that to be the case, we would need to be able to predict the possible long-term outcomes of such interventions, quite a demanding premise) and made it possible to realise therapeutic goals such as immunising people against the HIV virus or eliminating genetic defects (rather than eliminating embryos possessing defective genes) resulting in, for example, such diseases as Huntington's, many bioconservatives would enthusiastically embrace such interventions, just as the possibility of using vaccines is embraced with relief today. If, however, these same methods were used to increase cognitive abilities or strength, serious reservations would appear as to whether we have the right to determine what qualities will be beneficial for future generations (see Chapter 9). As the authors of *From Chance to Choice* rightly point out, if we are to speak of natural assets, it should be borne in mind that what is of concern here is not so much a neutral conception of human traits, but rather traits incorporating evaluative judgements. This requires the invoking of certain values that are differentiated in liberal societies:

> [T]he fact of value pluralism and the fact that the value of traits is relevant to social conditions call for caution about any commitment to genetic equality (Buchanan et al. 2007, 81).

We are dealing here with one of the oldest philosophical questions – what makes human life flourish. In liberal democratic societies, the principle has been adopted that decisions about ideals of living should be left to the personal choice of individuals rather than being programmed at the population level. Defining the goals of enhancement at the population level requires the advance assumption of the existence of a certain ideal, one of the primary axes of dispute in this debate. The problem relates to whether we should adopt the perspective of the good of the individual, as opponents of genetic enhancement argue, or the greater good (that of the population), as advocates of genetic enhancement call for. The individual perspective is much more akin to the traditional ideal of liberalism and it is precisely the undermining of this ideal, rather than the ineffectiveness of the means that are to be employed or the actual use of coercion, that constitutes the main charge levelled at the eugenic idea.

8.4 The domination of the enhanced over the unenhanced

In the genetic enhancement debate, the charge has appeared that technology employed to this end is so costly that access to it will be restricted, so heritable genetic interventions could, with time, lead to social divisions between enhanced super-individuals and ordinary unenhanced people. The former could dominate the latter, subordinating their needs to their own interests. A scenario featuring such new divisions has been presented by the biologist, Lee Silver, who opines that heritable cognitive enhancement of parts of a population could lead to the gene-enriched considering themselves to be members of a separate species from which further distinct sub-groups would develop, creating an infinite number of new species (Silver 1985). There is no clear biological definition, as

Dietrich Birnbacher notes, of the human species, so biologists continue to debate whether the criterion for species affiliation should be based on genotype, phenotype or the capacity between specimen to possess common offspring, and each of these criteria can provoke separate doubts in marginal cases (Birnbacher 2008; Daniels 2013). It is also possible to invoke the genealogical criterion mentioned by Birnbacher, which would treat those sharing the same origin as representatives of one species, a concept of shared species affiliation that would also incorporate human-animal creations (chimeras and hybrids, see Taupitz, Weschka 2009) that could come into being in the future if their creation was not prohibited. The genealogical criterion is too broad, because it fails to take into account significant differences between organisms sharing a common origin. Although many scientists accept that humans possess a common ancestor with apes, this does not mean in the least that they constitute one species. Silver's scenario takes these controversies into account by indicating that species affiliation would be discretionary in nature. The gene-enriched would regard themselves to be representative of a new species due to their cognitive abilities giving them a marked advantage over the remaining, unenhanced, representatives of *homo sapiens*. So, what is of concern here is an understanding of species that incorporates both an empirical (the possession of specific traits and abilities) and normative (the adoption of specific traits and abilities as a criterion for the recognition of higher species affiliation) element.

As Daniels notes, enhancements that would result in wholesale species change rather than the mere creation of individual freaks possessing atypical properties are quite unlikely (Daniels 2013). For Silver's scenario to be realised, certain additional conditions would in fact need to be fulfilled: the change would need to be drastic; the change would need to go far beyond the level of typical human abilities; this change would need to affect a significant proportion of some population isolated from others (enhanced individuals could only procreate with other enhanced individuals). David DeGrazia finds a solution to this last condition by introducing to this scenario the assumption that mixed couples would be infertile (DeGrazia 2012). Even if the realisation of such an improbable scenario were possible, these authors do not believe that changing human nature (traits currently typical of *homo sapiens*) would, in itself, be inherently wrong. For, since our abilities are adaptive in nature and a product of evolution, this means that they are dynamic in nature rather than being fixed forever. As constantly occurring changes continue to affect the environment in which we live, our abilities should continue to evolve, enabling further adaptation. As Birnbacher notes, biological evolution is an extremely slow process, while our current biological makeup evolved during the Palaeolithic era and may not be quite adequate enough for the conditions in which we function (Birnbacher 2008). This is why human social evolution (including technology and medicine) is attempting to make up for biological evolution's shortcomings.

Rejecting the idea of preserving human nature as something possessing value in itself (cf. Annas et al. 2002), DeGrazia reflects on the consequential arguments relating to the risk of drastically changing human nature on account of its social consequences, such as power advantage and the dominance of the enhanced over the unenhanced. However, he claims that such a risk certainly provides no justification for the Precautionary Prohibition of all enhancements, or even the precautionary prohibition of heritable enhancements (Precautionary Noninheritability). In his view, genetic enhancements bring more benefits than risks, and may even turn out to be necessary to cope with the negative effects of civilisational development, for example, environmental pollution (Buchanan 2011). DeGrazia also claims that introducing Precautionary Prohibition is impossible, since, for it to be effective, there would need to be a unanimous consensus on this issue and effective regulation on a global level, which would appear to be unlikely (DeGrazia 2012; Singer 2013). Only introducing prohibition in some states fails to solve the problem, even enabling the creation of a superpopulation who would be able to attain an advantage over the remaining unenhanced populations. In DeGrazia's view, this kind of prohibitions would also result in the appearance of a black market for enhancements, which could lead to a situation of greater threat than would be the case with enhancements carried out under sensible regulation. He therefore proposes that, rather than a prohibition on enhancements being introduced, the law and institutions protecting individuals from domination and discrimination should be strengthened, government control over access to genetic technologies should be guaranteed, and, in exceptional cases, such as when there is too great a disparity between the enhanced and unenhanced, precautionary measures (Contingent Future Noninheritability) should be applied, like, for example, restricting certain people's access to certain enhancements. In other words, the author proposes that enhancements should be restricted rather than prohibited outright.

The problem, however, lies in the fact that if enhancements would indeed lead to the appearance of a new variety of living beings with a significant advantage, in terms of cognitive abilities, strength and immunity, over unenhanced human beings, there would be no question of justice between them. Aristotle was one of the first to underline that justice can only be applied toward such subjects that are equal (Aristotle 2011). In a relationship of submission and domination, it is impossible to speak of justice in the full sense of this word, because one of the parties is dependent on the other, causing a situation in which the outcome of any exchange, shared obligations or distribution of goods will never be objectively just, because it will never be possible to speak of equilibrium between the profits and losses of both parties. Justice, as modern philosophers also emphasise, is based on the assumption of relative equality and the vulnerability of human nature (Hume 2010; Rawls 1999; Hart 1994). Of course, natural inequalities exist between people who differ in terms of physical strength and mental and intellectual predispositions, as well as talents or health. However, it is accepted that an approximate equality of natural strengths arising from species affiliation exists between people, and, thanks to this, no individual is capable of permanently dominating others without their cooperation. Assuming that people are not only approximately equal with regard to their strengths, but also their vulnerabilities, anyone can attack anyone else, and their plans can be blocked by others (especially, when others join forces). The vulnerability of human nature is also an assumption that indicates that people are not self-sufficient and need to cooperate with each other to survive.

If genetic enhancement would lead to certain traits of human nature being transcended in a certain part of a population, as Silver and DeGrazia suggest in their fictional scenarios, this would undermine the equality assumption and thus the idea of justness would be made impossible. Referencing these scenarios to make an analogy with the current relationship between able-bodied and disabled people (Wikler 2013) is ill-advised. The solidarity healthy people feel toward people disabled from birth or as the result of illness or chance events takes into account and does not question the assumption of equality between people. Although a power asymmetry exists between able-bodied and handicapped people, all people nevertheless still remain in a symmetrical relationship toward disability arising from the genetic lottery or chance events. For, even if we are able-bodied, we can never be sure that some chance event won't completely deprive us of our mental or physical powers, and we are even less sure of whether some disability will happen to our offspring or loved ones. This kind of symmetry forms the basis of an interpersonal solidarity which would disappear in a relationship between an enhanced and unenhanced population. For, as the above scenarios suggest, a population coming into being as an outcome of enhancements would be free of certain kinds of physical and cognitive limitation, giving it a permanent advantage over a population of unenhanced individuals and undermining the idea of justice being applied to relations between such different populations. For these reasons, we should concur with Habermas' view that, in such a case, heritable genetic enhancement undermining the idea of symmetrical equality between people is inherently wrong (Habermas 2003) rather than just being consequentially doubtful on account of the potential risk.

It should, however, be acknowledged that it is very unlikely that a new species of beings could be created without central planning. For, if a genetic enhancement programme were not implemented as state policy introduced on a broad scale within a certain population, it is difficult to envisage that cumulative parental decisions would lead to the creation of such a new genetic breed among people. It would seem to be more realistic to assume that such enhancement would deepen the already existing problem of social inequalities and the privileged population's domination over the non-privileged. For these reasons, it is argued that enhancement, rather than being left to the actions of the free market, should be subject to the regulation and supervision of state institutions that would guarantee universal access to basic forms of enhancement, on the same principles that apply to the guaranteeing of basic medical services (Buchanan et al. 2007). Advocates even take things a step further, arguing that enhancement should be introduced to a certain extent to guarantee that the idea of equality of opportunity would be better realised, which I shall move on to now.

8.5 Justice as fairness (fair equality of opportunity)

Justice as fairness is an egalitarian concept promoted by John Rawls aimed at guaranteeing equality of opportunity when accessing basic social goods, such as education, healthcare and employment. Two interpretations of the idea of equality of opportunity can be distinguished. The first one aims to guarantee equality of opportunity by eliminating legal and social barriers to accessing basic goods. John Roemer calls this approach the non-discrimination conception of equal opportunity (Roemer 1996). The second one, which is adopted by Rawls, who regards the first one as insufficient, not only realises this aim by eliminating barriers to accessing basic social goods, but also by envisaging a need for 'levelling the playing field' (Rawls 1999). I shall briefly present the possibility of applying these conceptions to the development of genetics and biotechnology.

8.5.1 The prohibition of genetic discrimination

Unequal access to assisted reproduction technologies, including genetic selection and offspring enhancement, could lead to the offspring of rich people holding a greater advantage over the offspring of less affluent people in terms of their health condition (including susceptibility to genetically conditioned diseases) and innate abilities than is the case in today's world, where the factors that differentiate opportunities are often the environmental conditions of development. Genetic information could then become a dangerous discrimination tool potentially restricting access to professions, education and health insurance. Genetic discrimination is most frequently understood to be the negative treatment of people on the grounds of their genotype (Soniewicka 2011). Genetic discrimination relies on the fact that in certain situations heritable genetic traits are not an adequate criterion for the diversified treatment of people or are unjustifiably embedded in certain aims of social institutions.

The phenomenon of genetic discrimination, which could, according to some authors, replace racial and class discrimination or discrimination on the grounds of gender is based on the faulty premise of genetic determinism (Annas 2009, 2010). Genetic determinism (essentialism or reductionism) presupposes that genes completely determine identity and human life. Although genetic determinism is scientifically unjustifed, many people (especially advocates of genetic enhancement) share a kind of belief in deterministic or quasi-deterministic role of genes (Ramsey 1970). The following frequently quoted words of James Watson appear to express this type of stance:

> We used to think that our fate was in our stars. Now we know, in large measure, our fate is in our genes (Watson in Buchanan et al. 2007 1989, 91).

The fundamental problem with this type of approach is that it fails to sufficiently take other important information about humans and their development into account, such as external (social, environmental, etc.) determinants, or the personal decisions of individuals (arising from their abilities to reflect and feel). Genetic information, however strong its predictive value, is not the sole determinant of our condition. Besides this, genetic determinism is often based on a naïve belief in the existence of a gene X responsible for a specific human predisposition. Meanwhile the genetic backgrounds to most of our diseases, as well as our predispositions or character traits, are much more complex, involving a whole complex of interconnected genes as well as interaction between our genes and the environment (Buchanan et al. 2007). An attempt should always therefore be made to distinguish a disease from predisposition or susceptibility to disease, and existing symptoms from those that may occur. No one should be reduced to the genetic traits they possess. As James Sherley correctly noted: 'We're more than our genes. We're the expression of our genes'[3] (Sherley in Angrist 2010,

---

3   This is exemplified by identical twins, who develop distinct personalities despite their identical genetic profile. Even when they are raised in the same environment and an identical model for behaviour has been instilled in them, their characters may differ markedly from each other and they certainly continue to be separate persons.

131). It is therefore difficult not to concur with Murray that 'We should give genes their due, but no more than that' (Murray 1997, 70).

There are various models for legal regulation directed against genetic discrimination (Soniewicka 2011). Two stances on this issue should first be distinguished. The first treats genetic information as an instance of legally protected sensitive information and also includes other medical or personal data, while the second calls for the protection of genetic information to be separately regulated due to its specific nature (the so-called genetic exceptionalism advocated by Annas, Annas et al. 1995). Secondly, the legal protection of genetic information can take one of two forms: a) protection against genetic discrimination (limiting the use of genetic information); b) protection of genetic privacy (limiting access to genetic information). An example of the first approach is the Genetic Information Nondiscrimination Act (GINA), which was signed by the American President, George Bush, on 21 May 2008. Examples of the second approach can be found in regulations concerning the protection of genetic information stored in databases (Annas 1993).

The significant difficulties bound up with any attempt to isolate genetic data from data of a medical and personal nature mean that most legal systems, rather than solving the problem of protecting genetic information in separate special regulations, do this within the framework of other existing branches of law – the protection of personal data and the protection of medical information. However, regardless of these difficulties, the introduction of legal regulations prohibiting discrimination on the grounds of genotype fails to solve the problem of equality of opportunity with regard to access to basic social goods. A stance prohibiting discrimination is unable to solve this problem, because it fails to take into account that restrictions on equality of opportunity may result from the unequal starting positions of parties from, for example, poor families who cannot afford to provide adequate food and education or, in the case being discussed, genetic intervention facilitating success in life. For these reasons, many modern liberals follow Rawls' lead by calling for the redistribution of goods to 'level the playing field'.

8.5.2 'Levelling the playing field': social structure and the genetic lottery

Advocates of the egalitarian 'levelling the playing field' concept hold to the stance that equality of opportunity cannot be achieved simply by not restricting access to basic social goods. For this aim to be achieved, it is necessary, in their opinion, to correct the 'background of justice' containing the unjust inequalities influencing the outcome of the distribution of social goods. Two variants of the concept of guaranteeing equal opportunities by 'levelling the playing field' are distinguished: a) a variant envisaging the levelling of opportunity-limiting effects arising from an unjust social structure (termed the social structure view); b) a variant envisaging the levelling of opportunity-limiting effects arising from any factors beyond human control, that is, 'unchosen' factors (termed the brute luck view). In Rawls' *A Theory of Justice*, comments can be found relating to natural inequalities (relating to talent, health, etc.) that result from the genetic lottery. However, the author himself accepted the first variant of levelling opportunities, limiting himself to a redistribution of goods, eliminating inequalities arising from the functioning of social institutions and taking into the account the outcome of certain social groups beings discriminated against in the past (see Chapter 5). At the same time, he was aware that his concept was flawed due to it not taking into account all the inequalities relating to our decent and upbringing:

> The principle of fair opportunity can be only imperfectly carried out, at least as long as some form of family exists (Rawls 1999, 64).

The flawed nature of Rawls' equality of opportunity concept was also criticised by radical egalitarians demanding the inclusion of the family sphere within the justice system (Nussbaum 2006). The brute luck view adopted by such philosophers as Roemer or Cohen (Roemer 1996; Cohen 1993) is a response to these charges. In their view, true quality of opportunity can only be achieved when arbitrary natural inequalities between people that significant restrict their life prospects are levelled out.

According to Buchanan, both variants of 'levelling the playing field' may have similar implications for the issues associated with genetic enhancement technology being discussed here (Buchanan et al. 2007), as I shall briefly attempt to explain before I introduce some comments of criticism.

Since ancient times, it has been assumed within the traditional philosophical mainstream that social, rather than natural, factors are the object of justice (Plato 2004). This assumption involved making a distinction between the social, i.e. what is shaped by human decisions and choices, and the natural, i.e. what is given independently of human will. Natural inequalities with regard to talents or health were treated as the outcome of a game of chance bringing fortune or misfortune. The difference between injustice and misfortune is not, however, simply based on the distinction between what is dependent on or independent of human will, as Judith Shklar notes (Shklar 1990). In a situation where a natural disaster that could have been predicted (e.g. a flood) totally destroys the goods and chattels belonging to some inhabitants of a particular country, they may perceive this as an injustice if it was the state's duty to prevent this disaster or to employ appropriate cautionary measures to warn the inhabitants.

The distinction between misfortune and injustice matters, since the sense of injustice is something what protects us from oppression, gives us hope and trust in social order and encourages us to call for social changes. The sense of injustice is:

> [T]he special kind of anger we feel when we are denied promised benefits and when do not get what we believe to be our due. It is the betrayal that we experience when others disappoint expectations that they have created in us (Shklar 1990, 83).

According to Shklar, injustice, by contrast to misfortune, depends on what people may reasonably expect in a given society (Shklar 1990). It is hard to specify which expectations are valid (cf. von Hayek 1976), as they are defined within the social practices of a particular community and may differ from society to society, evolving across time. They need to be distinguished from a mere feeling of disappointment when we are surprised by an unpleasant outcome. These expectations are not solely concerned with the predictability and repeatability of certain events (like the expectation that the sun shall rise tomorrow morning, as it always does), but rather with the intended (desirable) functioning of social relations and structures (like the expectation that people keep promises etc.). The feeling of injustice challenges the frustration of being helpless and not being in control of one's own life. Thus, in order to overcome our own frustration, we respond to some misfortunes by seeking out others who could be blamed for them, transforming misfortune into injustice or tending to experience natural disasters 'as a personal offence, an evil act directed at us.' (Shklar 1990, 56). Shklar claims that we may consider our disability, pigmentation or sex as a misfortune since they are natural (sometimes limiting) conditions, but in a certain social context they may be used as social conditions for the committing of injustice. In other words, Shklar, much like Rawls, does not seek out injustice in natural differences or inequalities, but rather in how society exploits these differences.

According to Buchanan, the distinction between injustice and misfortune is changing in step with the development of human control over nature, which is broadening the scope of the requirements of justice:

> [N]ature mastered by human intelligence and directed to human purposes – is no longer the given, no longer that which must be accepted, and hence no longer the domain of fortune and misfortune. Paradoxically, nature brought within human control is no longer nature (Buchanan et al. 2007, 83).

The part of nature over which we gain control is also human nature, as Buchanan writes. In the author's view, the emerging possibility of controlling nature in the field of procreation is causing what was once the exclusive domain of chance (the genetic lottery) to become a domain of choice (reproductive decisions). This may lead to the notion of justice being transformed as a result of it being incorporated into the sphere of human procreation:

> [W]e think of justice as justice to persons. But we may soon have to contemplate the idea of justice in the designed creation of persons (Buchanan et al. 2007, 85).

Egalitarian conceptions of justice address the question of what equality should be applied to (equality of what?). One of the responses proposed in the literature is equality of natural resources. Two variants of this resource egalitarian view may arise: a) the Resource Compensation Principle; b) the Equal Resources Principle (Buchanan et al. 2007). The first of these principles is meant to indirectly guarantee the levelling out of natural resources through them being offset against social resources (e.g. the more talented should compensate the less talented for their inferior social position by redistributing wealth attained as an outcome of their privileged position). By contrast, the second of these principles is meant to directly guarantee the levelling out of opportunities via intervention in the distribution of natural resources, such as talent, something genetic intervention technology could make possible in the future.

When Jamaican athlete, Usain Bolt, wins successive races, we do not regard this to be unjust, even though we know that his successes are largely credited to his unquestionable talent. On the contrary, we admire him for this talent. A footballer in Poland's fourth league cannot regard it to be unjust that he was not born with Leo Messi's talent and does not play in the Barcelona team. The reasoning presented in the book *From Chance to Choice* presupposes, however, that if talents where at some point in the future to become an outcome of parental reproductive choices, then our understanding of justice would also have to change, because reproductive decisions would influence how we define our life prospects. If there were widespread access on the market to reproductive enhancement technologies, being born as an unenhanced person could, as the authors suggest, be a type of indirect discrimination if it restricted access to important social goods. Offspring enhancement could, to a certain extent, become a requirement of justice, by analogy with medical treatment, which is, in their view, a social justice issue.

Buchanan interprets, after Daniels (Daniels 1985), the right to access to healthcare as as justified by the principle of equality of opportunity (Buchanan et al. 2007), for he believes that the by purpose of treatment-related medical interventions or the correction of bodily dysfunction is to remove the restrictions it causes to equal opportunities in society:

> The significance of disease is that it limits opportunity in the most serious cases, at least, by preventing persons from developing the threshold of abilities necessary for being 'normal competitors' in social competition. (Buchanan et al. 2007, 74).

The author goes on to add that, since some natural inequalities, although they do not represent departures from normal species functioning, may place equally strong restrictions on opportunities within the context of social competition and therefore justify genetic interventions if it were necessary to limit these restrictions. In his view, in both cases, i.e. both the treatment of dysfunction and enhancement, we are dealing with intervention into the outcome of a natural lottery justifiable on the grounds of the equality of opportunity concept.

The author agrees that freedom of the individual should take precedence over the levelling out of opportunities in the case of medical interventions, which is meant to guarantee the requirement that patients give their informed consent to both treatment and enhancement. However, in the author's view, this problem disappears within the context of reproduction when the object of the genetic interventions is an embryo, and decisions are taken based on the informed consent of its parents.

However, the author himself notes the problems of implementing genetic equality of opportunity in the light of such issues as how to establish, as it were, what we acknowledge to be, or not be, a social asset. As the author correctly points out, assessments of this type are relative to social structure and subject to change (e.g. certain cognitive abilities may be an asset in societies based on highly advanced technology, but assets in societies based on manufacturing may be quite different). This also explains why authors attempt to point to a kind of 'genetic minimum' of qualities what would be of benefit under any social conditions, for example, certain IQ level (Buchanan et al. 2007; Kamm 2013).

There are a number of reasons why it would appear to be difficult to accept the authors' conclusions on the obligation to provide certain forms of genetic enhancement. First, the idea of justifying obligation to provide treatment by invoking the idea of levelling out opportunities would appear to be wide of the mark, as John Harris also pointed out, though he himself argued for the obligation to provide enhancement, albeit from a utilitarian reasoning standpoint (Harris 2013). The very idea of equal access to basic medical services can be justified by invoking the idea of guaranteeing equal opportunities (for treatment) in society. This does not, however, mean that the purpose of treatment is to guarantee for everyone that the basic requirements for social competition will be met.

Treatment goals are defined independently of social competition and, of these, the provision of relief from suffering, curing patients and returning them to the condition of health are singled out (Pellegrino & Thomasma 1993; Pellegrino 2004). The idea of caring for disabled people and making it possible for them to integrate into society need not be based on an unattainable ideal of equality of opportunity, but may be based on the ideal of solidarity and recognising disabled people as fully functioning members of society, even though they are incapable of fully participating in social competition for goods (see Chapter 5).

Second, the idea of levelling out opportunities through increasingly invasive intervention into what is given, continues to not only be an unattainable ideal, but also an *undesirable* utopia. Egalitarianism directed at the levelling out of natural inequalities offers justice that responds to differences in natural capacities, but is not sensitive to any ambitions people may have, so often provokes justified controversy. One potential problem could be society bearing the cost of the life choices of others and financing costly desires, when the boundary is blurred between what is given, and what is chosen. Furthermore, the idea of compensating for natural inequalities or intervening in the distribution of natural qualities is incapable of fully guaranteeing equality until the institution of family is completely abolished (cf. Plato 2004). The family is the first and basic source of the most valuable goods – it equips us with the required minimum of love, care and friendship, thus providing us with a sense of confidence and self-esteem. At the same time, it guarantees such basic human skills needed for life, as health, displaying emotions and feelings, developing the mind, imagination and senses, the creation of a personal conception of good and the formation of relationships. Some children are loved not enough or in a wrong way, poorly cared for or deprived of suitable role models, which undoubtedly affects their development and self-realisation in life. As Michael Walzer expresses it:

> [O]ur children (...) make their own way, bearing the unequal burdens of parental expectations and the unequal grace of parental love. These last inequalities cannot be eliminated; indeed, the family exists, and will continue to exist, precisely in order to make a place for them (Walzer 1985, 242).

The Platonic experiment abolishing the institution of family would by no means level out those priceless natural goods being discussed here, and would only make everybody equally devoid of them and therefore equally unfortunate. The family is and will continue to be the basic unit for distributing love and kinship (Walzer 1985), because any attempt to distribute these goods from above would be tantamount to depriving these goods of the valuable meaning we ascribe to them (cf. Sandel 2009, 2012). Nobody can be forced to love, because coerced love is no longer love, and lack of love cannot be offset against social goods. Therefore, instead of focusing on equipping our offspring with certain qualities guaranteeing them social success, we should instead be devoting more attention to promoting family relationships providing children with suitable conditions for their development.

8.6 Conclusions: the problem of domination as the result of reproductive decisions reconsidered

The advocates of genetic offspring enhancement cited in this chapter leave the final decision to parents. The obligation to provide enhancement is reduced in this argumentation to the State's obligation to make it possible for anyone, to a certain minimum extent and without resorting to coercion, to use these enhancements when they procreate. The will of future children is not taken into account in this case, on the assumption that the interests of parents and offspring will in principle be compatible, especially within the context of enhancements, which would not be called enhancements, as Harris writes, if they were clearly not something good (Harris 2013). However, as I stressed earlier, what is good for some may not be good at all for others, and children are undoubtedly separate people from their parents. The decision of parents to intentionally bring a handicapped child into the world (as mentioned in Chapters 1 and 5) for it to share its parent's disability, is most frequently regarded as morally wrong, the argument being that parents, in making such dysgenic decision, are making their child's situation worse. When focusing on the outcome of this decision, we are not able to differentiate this case from a situation where parents have failed to prevent the birth of a sick child (as was discussed in Chapters 1 and 3). Intuitively, most of us would differentiate these two cases, because outcomes are not the most important aspect of our moral judgements, which also take into account intentions. From an intention perspective, the decision of parents for their future child to realise their preferences with regard to a certain disability they perceive to be part of their identity rather than a deficiency resembles the decision of parents for their child to realise their preferences with regard to certain qualities (e.g. sex, cognitive abilities, height or strength). The pluralism of values and the parental preferences that follow from them make it unlikely that the decisions of the parents would lead to the disappearance of diversity and a complete standardisation of people on the population level which could have catastrophic consequences for that population's development. Nevertheless, the decisions of parents will lead to some standardisation within families or the social circles these families belong to. From a societal perspective, the decision of parents to equip their children with perfect pitch, enabling them to becoming involved in music, is a decision respecting pluralism of values, because it is envisaged that not all parents will want to have musically gifted children. However, from the perspective of the children resulting from these decisions, there is no question of pluralism of values coming into play when possessing specific traits like absolute pitch is the only criterion for them being brought into the world. So, if the ideal of individual freedom and self-realisation based on pluralism of values forms the basis of liberal democratic societies, we should also be supporting the kind of socio-legal solutions that would contribute to the autonomy of a child who, rather than being little more than the object of reproductive decisions, will in fact be one of the subjects in a parent-child relationship (see Chapter 9).

The obligation to provide genetic offspring enhancement not only fails to solve the problem of social injustice, but may become one of its most serious causes. Advocates of the egalitarian 'levelling the playing field' concept are making two significant errors in their conception of justice which might cause the total opposite of what they are meant to achieve. First, they are focusing on the inequalities themselves, believing them to be wrong and needful of correction. Second, radical egalitarians are unjustifiably expanding the 'playing field' to incorporate every sphere of social life, even the sphere of biological life subject to control. The inequalities in themselves, being a natural consequence of life and human freedom, are neither just nor unjust. As John Kane and Ian Shapiro emphasize: 'there is nothing in the meaning of justice that implies an egalitarian assumption' (Shapiro 2012, 296). Inequalities can only be unjust when: a) they are caused by an arbitrary decision;[4] b) they are unjustly exploited socially. In both cases, inequalities can facilitate domination, making inequalities unjust. Domination entails the use of power to control someone or something, and is akin to the management of private property.[5] The domination of people primarily restricts their autonomy, i.e. their opportunities for self-realisation and

---

4   Many intriguing psychological experiments confirm this intuition, demonstrating that people exhibit a strong tendency to level out, to a certain extent, the outcomes of some arbitrary decision, but this fails to apply to outcomes of random events (Blount 1995; Bellemare et al. 2011; Fischbacher et al. 2010). There are also studies showing that there is a deeply rooted intuition about justice that triggers a desire to level out the outcomes of cooperation, but this fails to apply to the outcomes of random events (Hammann et al. 2011; Warneken et al. 2011).
5   In the Roman Law one distinguished between the two kinds of power – the private one concerned with ownership (*dominium*) and the public one concerned with sovereignty and giving commands (*imperium*) (Weber 2002).

exercising control over their own lives. Such domination is exemplified by the relationships between master and slave or citizen and state in totalitarian and post-totalitarian systems (Havel 1978).[6] Within the context of access to basic social goods, domination may also rely on the assumption that there is one 'good X' that guarantees access to all the others (Walzer 1985). Societies based on such a 'gold standard' favour the formation of monopolies over the most valuable social goods concentrated in the hands of those possessing that most valuable good (in feudal societies, this was often noble birth, and in capitalist societies, it is money). Egalitarian concepts of justice, which Walzer terms the 'regime of simple equality', are incapable of guaranteeing equality, for, by focusing on the redistribution of the valuable good X, they are in effect eliminating a monopoly, rather than the phenomenon of domination itself (Walzer 1985, 14). The dominant good remains. All that happens is that access to it is widened or the dominant group changes. The phenomenon of domination as a form of injustice can only be countered by questioning the use of good X to guarantee access to every other social good. According to Walzer, this would involve replacing the gold standard with multiple standards relevant to the different spheres of life that are treated autonomously (Walzer 1985). This means that, rather than one important social good (like wealth) being converted into all the other important social goods (like healthcare, education, positions etc.), it should be kept within the sphere to which it belongs (e.g. wealth should guarantee a life of luxury, but healthcare should be allocated according to need).

In the view of advocates of genetic offspring enhancement, the possibility of increasing control over the outcomes of reproductive decisions is an argument for expanding the scope of justice into the sphere of reproduction. If we start from the assumption that justice serves to eliminate social domination, the conclusion might nevertheless be reached that the very idea of exercising control using offspring enhancement reproductive technologies is a form of injustice, because it enables domination in two ways. First, it enables the ones who enhance to dominate those who are enhanced by them, with the former controlling the natural

---

6   Havel emphasizes that of the most striking features of dominance in post-totalitarian systems, including consumer societies, is the tendency to total unification: 'Between the aims of the post-totalitarian system and the aims of life there is a yawning abyss: while life, in its essence, moves toward plurality, diversity, independent self-constitution, and self-organization, in short, toward the fulfillment of its own freedom, the post-totalitarian system demands conformity, uniformity, and discipline. While life ever strives to create new and improbable structures, the post-totalitarian system contrives to force life into its most probable states.' (Havel 1978).

resources of the latter and determining the scope of their autonomy according to their own preferences. This leads to the corruption of the parental relationship. Second, it enables the domination of some specific properties that are meant to guarantee access to the most valuable social goods (see Chapter 3). If we are to counter domination, we should instead be guaranteeing a social framework within which various human qualities will be able to guarantee access to various valuable social goods. The basic aim of the approach being proposed here is therefore not to level out natural goods, but rather to guarantee autonomy in their use. The idea of genetically enhancing offspring not only fails to guarantee this aim, but also stands in opposition to what I shall be developing further in the next chapter.

Acknowledgements

This text was originally prepared in Polish and some parts of it were published in chapter 4 in: Soniewicka M (2018) Selekcja genetyczna w prokreacji medycznie wspomaganej. Etyczne i prawne kryteria. Wolters Kluwer, Warszawa. Translated from Polish into English by Philip Palmer.

References

Agar N (1998) Liberal Eugenics. Public Affairs Quarterly 12:137–155.

Angrist M (2010) Here Is a Human Being. At the Dawn of Personal Genomics. Harper Perennial, New York.

Annas G (1993) Privacy Rules for DNA Databanks: Protecting Coded 'Future Diaries'. Journal of the American Association 270:2346–2350.

Annas G (2009) American Bioethics. Crossing Human Rights and Health Law Boundaries. Oxford University Press, Oxford & New York.

Annas G (2010) Worst Case Bioethics. Death Disaster, and Public Health. Oxford University Press, Oxford & New York.

Annas G, Glantz LH, Roche PA (1995) Drafting the genetic privacy act: science, policy and practical considerations. Journal of Law, Medicine and Ethics 23:360–366.

Annas GJ, Andrews LB, Isasi MR (2002) Protecting the endangered human: Toward an international treaty prohibiting cloning and inheritable alterations. American Journal of Law and Medicine 28(2–3):151–178.

Aristotle (2011) Nicomachean Ethics (trans: BartlettRC, CollinsSD). Chicago University Press, Chicago & London.

Bellemare CH, Kröger S, van Soest A (2011) Preferences, intentions, and expectation violations: A large-scale experiment with a representative subject pool. Journal of Economic Behavior and Organization 78:349–365.

Birnbacher D (2008) Posthumanity, Transhumanism and Human Nature. In: Gordijn B and Chadwick R (eds) Medical Enhancement and Posthumanity. Springer, Berlin, pp. 95–106.

Blount S (1995) When social outcomes aren't fair: the effect of causal attributions on preferences. Organizational Behavior and Human Decision Process 63(2):131–144.

Bostrom N (2008) Why I Want to be a Posthuman When I Grow Up. In: Gordijn B, Chadwick R (eds) Medical Enhancement and Posthumanity. Springer, Berlin, pp. 107–137.

Buchanan A (2011) Beyond Humanity? Oxford University Press, Oxford.

Buchanan A, Brock DW, Daniels N, Wikler D (2007) From Chance to Choice: Genetics and Justice. Cambridge University Press, Cambridge & New York.

Cohen GA (1993) Equality of What?: On Welfare Goods and Capabilities. In: Nussbaum M (ed) The Equality of Life. Clarendon Press, Oxford, pp. 9–29.

Daniels N (1985) Just Health Care. Cambridge University Press, Cambridge.

Daniels N (2013) Can Anyone Really Be Talking About Ethically Modifying Human Nature? In: Savulescu J, Bostrom N (eds) Human Enhancement. Oxford University Press, Oxford, pp. 25–42.

DeGrazia D (2012) Creation Ethics. Reproduction, Genetics, and Quality of Life. Oxford University Press, Oxford.

Fischbacher U, Eisenkopf G, Föllmi-Heusi F (2010) Unequal Opportunities and Distributive Justice, Research Paper Series. Thurgau Institute of Economics and Department of Economics at the University of Konstanz 57:1–28.

Fukuyama F (2002) Our Posthuman Future. Consequences of the Biotechnological Revolution. Farrar, Straus and Giroux, New York.

Glover J (2008) Eugenics: Some Lessons from the Nazi Experience. In: Beauchamp TL, Walters L, Khan JP, Mastroianni AC (eds) Contemporary Issues in Bioethics. Thomson Wadsworth, Belmont, pp. 215–220.

Gould SJ (2008) Carrie Buck's Daughter. In: Beauchamp TL, Walters L, Khan JP, Mastroianni AC (eds) Contemporary Issues in Bioethics. Thomson Wadsworth, Belmont, pp. 210–214.

Habermas J (2003) The Future of Human Nature. Polity Press, Cambridge.

Hamann K, Warneken F, Greenberg J, Tomasello M (2011) Collaboration encourages equal sharing in children but not chimpanzees. Nature 476:328–331.

Harris J (2013) Enhancements Are a Moral Obligation. In: Savulescu J, Bostrom N (eds) Human Enhancement. Oxford University Press, Oxford, pp. 131–154.

Hart HLA (1994) The Concept of Law. Clarendon Press, Oxford.

Havel V (1978) The Power of the Powerless (trans: WilsonP). http://vaclavhavel.cz/showtrans.php?cat=clanky&val=72_aj_clanky.html&typ=HTML (accessed: 1 July 2017)

Hume D (2010) An Enquiry Concerning the Principles of Morals. Project Gutenberg, ebook. https://www.gutenberg.org/files/4320/4320-h/4320-h.htm (accessed: 31 July 2018).

Kamm FM (2013) Bioethical Prescriptions To Create, End, Choose, and Improve Lives. Oxford University Press, Oxford & New York.

Kass LR (2002) Life, Liberty and the Defense of Dignity. The Challenge of Bioethics. Encounter Books, San Francisco.

Kevles D (2008) Eugenics and Human Rights. In: Beauchamp TL, Walters L, Khan JP, Mastroianni AC (eds) Contemporary Issues in Bioethics. Thomson Wadsworth, Belmont, pp. 205–207.

Lewis CS (2000) The Abolition of Man or Reflections on education with special reference to the teaching of English in the upper forms of schools. HarperOne, New York.

Mitchel CB, Pellegrino ED, Elshtain JB, Kilner JF, Rae S (1974) Biotechnology and the Human Good. Georgetown University Press, Washington, DC.

Müller-Hill B (2006) Lessons from a Dark and Distant Past. In: Khuse H, Singer P (eds) Bioethics. An Antology. Blackwell Publishing, Oxford, pp. 231–236.

Murray TH (1997) Genetic exceptionalism and 'future diaries': is genetic information different from other medical information? In: Rothstein MA (ed) Genetic Secrets: Protecting Privacy and Confidentiality in the Genetic Era. Yale University Press, New Haven & London, pp. 60–73.

Nozick R (1974) Anarchy, State and Utopia. Basic Books, New York.

Nussbaum M (2006) Frontiers of Justice: Disability, Nationality, Species Membership. The Belknap Press of Harvard University Press, Cambridge, MA & London.

Pellegrino ED (2004) Biotechnology, Human Enhancement, and the Ends of Medicine. The Center for Bioethics and Human Dignity, November 30. https://

cbhd.org/content/biotechnology-human-enhancement-and-ends-medicine. (accessed: 31 July 2018).

Pellegrino ED, Thomasma DC (1993) The Virtues in Medical Practice. Oxford University Press, New York & Oxford.

Persson I, Savulescu J (2012) Unfit for the Future: The Need for Moral Enhancement. Oxford University Press, Oxford.

Plato (2004) Republic (trans: Reeve CDC). Hackett Publishing Company Inc, Cambridge.

Ramsey P (1970) Fabricated Man. The Ethics of Genetic Control. Yale University Press, New Haven, London.

Rawls J (1999) A Theory of Justice. Revised Edition. Harvard University Press, Cambridge, MA.

Roemer J (1996) Theories of Distributive Justice. Harvard University Press, Cambridge.

Sandel M (2007) The Case against Perfection. Ethics in the Age of Genetic Engineering. The Belknap Press of Harvard University Press, Cambridge, MA & London.

Sandel M (2009) Justice, What's the Right Thing to Do? Farrar, Straus and Giroux, New York.

Sandel M (2012) What Money Can't Buy. The Moral Limits of Markets. Farrar, Straus and Giroux, New York.

Shapiro I (2012) On Non-Domination. University of Toronto Law Journal 62:293–336.

Shklar JN (1990) The Faces of Injustice. Yale University Press, New Haven & London.

Silver L (1985) Remaking Eden: Cloning and Beyond in a Brave New World. Avon Books, New York.

Singer P (2013) Parental Choice and Human Improvement. In: Savulescu J, Bostrom N (eds) Human Enhancement. Oxford University Press, Oxford, pp. 277–289.

Soniewicka M (2011) The Legal Challenges to Equality and Freedom in the Age of Genomic Medicine. In: Cserne P, Könczöl M (ed) Legal and Political Theory in the Post-National Age, CEE-Forum for Legal, Political, and Social Theory Yearbook. Peter Lang Verlag, Frankfurt am Main, pp. 77–88.

Taupitz J, Weschka M (eds) (2009) Chimbrids – Chimeras and Hybrids in Comparative European and International Research. Scientific, Ethical, Philosophical and Legal Aspects. Springer, Heidelberg.

von Hayek F (1976) Law, Legislation and Liberty, vol 2. The Mirage of Social Justice, Chicago.

Walzer M (1985) Spheres of Justice. A Defense of Pluralism and Equality. Basic Books, Oxford.

Warneken F, Lohse K, Melis A, Tomasello M (2011) Young children share the spoils after collaboration. Psychological Science 22:267-73.

Weber M (2002) Gospodarka i społeczeństwo. Zarys socjologii rozumiejącej. Wydawnictwo Naukowe PWN, Warszawa.

Wikler D (2013) Paternalism in the Age of Cognitive Enhancement: Do Civil Liberties Presuppose Roughly Equal Mental Ability? In: Savulescu J, Bostrom N (eds) Human Enhancement. Oxford University Press, Oxford, pp. 341-355.

Marta Soniewicka

9 Human self-understanding in the debate over moral human enhancement: autonomy and authenticity

9.1 Introduction

The term 'transhumanism' was coined by the English biologist, Julian Huxley, the brother of Aldous Huxley, the famous writer who wrote *Brave New World*[1]. He used the term as a title for an essay he published in 1957 in which he announced the appearance of a new 'cosmic self-awareness' which would decide the future of humanity (Huxley 1968, 73). He named humanity the 'managing director of the biggest business of all, the business of evolution' and, although we never actually asked to hold such a post, we cannot resign from it (Huxley 1968, 73). Humanity's 'cosmic duty' is to fully develop humans' possibilities as individuals, a community or ultimately, a species, acting to benefit the welfare of future generations and human progress (Huxley 1968, 76). The first task to be completed when realising this goal – essential for investigating the range of human possibilities – is an *exploration of human nature*, in which 'A vast New World of uncharted possibilities awaits its Columbus' (Huxley 1968, 74). Huxley's appeal to create an inner map of human possibilities did not have to wait long for a response. Scientists managed to sequence the complete human genome fifty years later, and world leaders hailed this discovery as the most important map for humanity and 'our own instruction book' (Collins 2006, 2–3). This discovery should pave the way to the implementation of the transhumanist assumptions Julian Huxley subscribed to, turning his dreams into reality:

> The human species can, if it wishes, transcend itself —not just sporadically, an individual here in one way, an individual there in another way, but in its entirety, as humanity. We need a name for this new belief. Perhaps transhumanism will serve: man remaining man, but transcending himself, by realizing new possibilities of and for his human nature (Huxley 1968, 76).

Undoubtedly, this belief, which Huxley also termed 'evolutionary humanism' (Bashford 2013, 160), has found its adherents among contemporary bioethicists

---

1 Both brothers were grandsons of the famous biologist and Darwinist, Thomas Henry Huxley, which explains their interest in the theory of evolution.

(Bostrom 2008; Agar 1998; Savulescu & Persson 2012; Harris 2007). One of these, John Harris, expressed his enthusiasm for the enhancement of evolution as follows:

> It is significant that we have reached a point in human history at which further attempts to make the world a better place will have to include not only changes to the world, but also changes to humanity, perhaps with the consequence that we, or our descendants, will cease to be human in the sense in which we now understand that idea. (...) This new process of evolutionary change will replace *natural selection* with *deliberate selection*, *Darwinian evolution* with *'enhancement evolution'*. (Harris 2007, 3–4)

Proponents of transhumanism, such as Persson and Savulescu, argue that the enhancement of human nature is a moral duty, and therefore essential, if we wish to prevent the destruction of the human race (Persson & Savulescu 2008). In their view, the psychophysical evolution of the human species is not keeping pace with human technological advancement and the possibilities this brings, which could be used to either enhance human beings or bring about the self-destruction of the world's inhabitants. Science and technology should therefore be used, in the authors' view, to take evolution into our own hands and enhance human nature to such an extent that people would be able to meet contemporary global challenges.

Transhumanism's opponents, who are referred to as 'bioconservatives' and include Leon Kass, Jürgen Habermas and Francis Fukuyama (Habermas 2003; Fukuyama 2002; Kass 2002), see more danger than promise in biotechnological interventions targeted at human nature enhancement. In this chapter, I shall attempt to demonstrate that the primary cause of the conflict between transhumanists and bioconservatives are differing assumptions relating to the understanding of what it means to be human. I shall highlight the problem by primarily focusing my reflections on the transhumanists' most controversial postulate – the notion of the moral human enhancement.

9.2 Moral enhancement

Persson and Savulescu understand moral enhancement to be intervention aimed at creating suitable dispositions to make accurate judgements and take action that accords with them:

> To be morally enhanced is to have those dispositions which make it more likely that you will arrive at the correct judgement of what it is right to do and more likely to act on that judgement (Savulescu & Persson 2012, 5).

Tom Douglas refers to the propensities these authors write about as motives conceived as psychological stimuli causing a person to act in a desirable fashion:

> There are various ways in which we could understand the suggestion that we morally enhance ourselves. To name a few, we could take it as a suggestion that we make ourselves more virtuous, more praiseworthy, more capable of moral responsibility, or that we make ourselves act or behave more morally. (...) Rather, I will take it as a suggestion that we cause ourselves to have morally better motives (henceforth often omitting the 'morally'). I understand motives to be the psychological — mental or neural — states or processes that will, given the absence of opposing motives, cause a person to act (Douglas 2008, 229).

The author understands 'better motives' to be stronger stimuli more likely to guarantee desirable behaviours. Douglas presupposes that a moral act arises from identifiable mental or neural states. For example, he emphasises that aversion to members of certain racial groups and brutal aggression are genetically conditioned psychological states that can be investigated and better understood by referring to their biological (neuro-mental) aspects. This leads the author to conclude that:

> [T]here are some emotions such that a reduction in the degree to which an agent experiences those emotions would, under some circumstances, constitute a moral enhancement (Douglas 2008, 231).

The same applies to emotions whose strengthening would be correlated with the appearance of propensities toward socially desirable acts. For example, he mentions at this juncture propensities toward caring for and showing concern for others, which are correlated with an appropriate level of oxytocin (a hormone which research indicates is most abundantly secreted by women in an early stage of pregnancy and people who are in love) (see Churchland 2012). Similarly, propensities toward altruism, truthfulness or rudimentary justice enabling cooperation are perceived as psychological states grounded in neurobiology and genetics (see Churchland 2012; de Waal 2016, Haidt 2013, Greene 2013).

Transhumanists understand moral enhancement not only to be emotional conditioning aimed at the creation of a temperament prone to cooperative behaviour, but also as an expansion of human cognitive capabilities bound up with dispositions toward moral behaviours (Savulescu, Sandberg & Kahane 2011; Douglas 2008; Walker 2009)[2]. Cognitive enhancement incorporates the

---

2   There is ongoing debate among naturalists over whether distinctive abilities specifically associated with morality exist or whether we are also dealing with general cognitive abilities formed by a combination of evolution and social training; this second position seems to predominate (Piłat 2013).

expansion of memory and raising intelligence levels or improving self-control skills (DeGrazia 2012). All these qualities are correlated, as the authors claim, with the ability to make the correct moral decisions, although they are of course no guarantee of this. Transhumanists claim, on the assumption that the core psychological stimuli enabling cooperation (altruistic predispositions) are innate rather than acquired (see Tomasello 2009), that genetic interventions will be the most effective enhancement method in the future.

The notion of enhancement of human nature, thus conceived, can raise many justified doubts of an empirical nature. First, the exact relationship between the influence on humans of environmental and genetic factors continues to attract controversy (Arnhart 2010). Many contemporary studies indicate that the expression of innate tendencies is largely dependent on the experience that shapes it (see Kidd, Palmeri & Aslin 2012). Second, it would be absurd to maintain that the genes correlated with certain moral virtues forming part of the human character can be identified. And as far as such complex phenomena as intelligence or character are concerned, grave reservations are expressed about the possibility of investigating their genetic background, not to mention modifying or controlling it. Third, genes are not external to the components of being human, and every genetic modification can affect the human genotype in its entirety. For this reason, a genetic intervention designed to enhance something can in effect give rise to unpredictable changes jeopardising a person's normal development.[3]

Reservations at least as grave are expressed about this notion from a moral/political standpoint (see Chapter 8). There are no clear-cut standards relating to virtues and we have no way of knowing who would decide which virtues should be promoted and how should they be interpreted. In this case, the risk also arises of political misappropriation, already familiar from history, when social engineering was carried out on a mass scale with catastrophic results for the victims. It also doubtful whether any kind of standardisation would be appropriate or whether the same tendencies would be of equal benefit to everyone.

All these reservations would appear to constitute enough evidence to discredit the transhumanists' eugenic ideas. However, this chapter has a different

---

3 The role played by interconnected genes as information carriers is very complex – genes we consider to be correlated with certain character traits can simultaneously be linked to a greater susceptibility to certain diseases, something that is currently a focus of scientific research. Studies in mice have showed, for example, that increasing learning and memory skills using genetic modifications simultaneously increased sensitivity to pain (DeGrazia 2012).

purpose. I wish to focus on the reductionist naturalistic assumptions regarding human nature and the moral agency on which the notion of enhancement is based. By undermining these assumptions, important arguments can be formulated that not only contradict the notion of human moral enhancement through biomedical intervention, but also the notion of genetic engineering envisaging the design of children. I shall critique these assumptions by employing the Aristotelian understanding of virtue and Kantian understanding of agency – both these approaches combine the notion of human moral integrity rooted in reflexivity and intentionality, which is insufficiently developed from a reductionist naturalistic standpoint and the consequential ethical doctrines adopted by the transhumanists.

9.3 The problem of our species' self-understanding – the elusiveness of human nature

Animal nature is completely determined by natural factors, enabling us to define what specific animals are by referring to their biological traits and the conditions within which they function. Having defined their nature, we are able to respond to the question of what animals of a specific type need to flourish in the variant of life they lead. With people, however, it is somewhat different since, as Hannah Arendt points out, the natural conditions of our existence 'can never 'explain' what we are or answer the question of who we are for the simple reason that they never condition us absolutely.' (Arendt 1998, 11).

The two interrelated questions of 'Who am I?' and 'What am I?' have been borrowed by Arendt from St Augustine (Arendt 1998, 10; Augustine 2008). We can only answer the first question, which relates to personal identity, i.e. what makes each of us unique, by living our lives, something I shall be considering later in this chapter. The second question, 'What am I?', relates to human nature and asks what is common to all humans and what distinguishes people from other species. The answers to both of these questions are inextricably bound up with a question relating to moral obligation: 'What should I do?'. For, as Charles Taylor rightly points out, our identity orients each of us in moral space – in order to know who we are, we also need to know what is meaningful in our lives and to what we should attach value. Our moral topography is inextricably bound up with our understanding of what it means to be a human being (Taylor 2001).

When the question arises of what is human, we present an unsolvable problem to ourselves, because answering this question requires us to adopt an outside perspective on ourselves (Arendt 1998). The problematic question of human nature reached its apogee, as Max Scheler emphasises, with the rejection of metaphysics, whether it be the Christian version (where relating to God guarantees an outside perspective) or the secularised version (where an outside perspective, a 'view from nowhere', can be achieved through the transcendental self) (Scheler 1991).

Reductionist naturalism attempts to overcome this problem by proposing that human nature be explained from the outside perspective of science. The naturalist perspective is based on the theory of evolution and physicochemical reductionism, in which self-replicating life is understood to be the outcome of a series of physical chance events combined with the natural selection mechanism. According to Thomas Nagel, reductionist naturalism has achieved the status of an unassailable, almost sacrosanct dogma, because it would appear to be the sole alternative to theism (Nagel 2012; cf. Mitchel et al. 2007). In his view, critiquing this stance is politically incorrect in western societies, even though it is incapable of offering an explanation for phenomena irreducible to physical phenomena, such as consciousness, meaning, value, intentionality, agency, thought, mind, etc. From a reductive naturalistic standpoint, these are a random side effect of nature. Evolutionary naturalism adopts the stance that the appearance of conscious beings capable of mental life is a biological side effect of the physical order providing us with self-understanding that undermines the credibility of our cognitive abilities while at the same time undermining our confidence in the scientific picture of the world which gave rise to these abilities (Nagel 2012; Plantinga 2011; Habermas 2008; Spaemann 2017; Jonas 1987). The same applies to the sphere of morality explained solely by means of the theory of evolution, which not only weakens the authority of reason, but also, significantly, our moral abilities, as I shall demonstrate in this chapter.

9.3.1 The question of the meaning of humanity

The notion of enhancing human nature is inextricably bound up with a question formulated by the father of transhumanism, Julian Huxley: 'What are people for?' (Huxley in Bashford 2013, 161). This is the question about the meaning we attribute to humanity. This question is of a teleological nature, as Arendt observes.

The classical moral reasoning model, as Alasdair MacIntyre emphasises, is comprised of three elements:

a) Empirical assumptions concerning the nature of man ('man-as-he-happens-to-be');
b) Normative assumptions concerning the nature of man ('man-as-he-could-be-if-he-realized-his-essential-nature');

c) Moral norms (representing the best way of moving from point a to point b; in other words, the best way to achieve certain ideals) (MacIntyre 2007, 52–53).

In modern times, the ideal rooted in metaphysics has been rejected, yet the norms that functioned in this model are still preserved. In MacIntyre's view, the main reason that the Enlightenment failed was that it created an incomplete moral theory, which focuses on what principles should be observed, but is unable to justify them.

Taylor also draws attention to this problem, writing about the internal contradiction residing in a reductionist naturalism that renounces the strong moral valuations on which it is based (Taylor 2001). In the post-Enlightenment reductive-naturalistic model from which the transhumanists draw, attempts are made to deduce norms from empirical assumptions relating to humans and then use the latter to justify the former. This is problematic, because the meaning of humanity cannot be extracted from purely descriptive aspects of human functioning in the world. The problem of what is meaningful for humans (and what this constitutes) is not being determined by nature, but rather by humans capable of taking a stance on nature. Even if we use empirical research to prove that people have an innate ability to empathise, a propensity for altruism, experience mutual sympathy, or take pleasure from the successes of others, this does not automatically mean that that these predispositions should be promoted in people. If we wish to put forward the thesis that predispositions correlated with the possibility of interpersonal cooperation should be promoted, we first need to refer to the moral horizon that reductionist naturalism rejects, as Taylor correctly points out (Taylor 2001). The moral horizon comprises what are termed strong valuations or ideals constituting a criterion for moral discernment, i.e. the assessment of what is valuable, right or wrong. Our strong valuations do not arise from our predispositions, desires or choices. In fact, they constitute a *criterion for their evaluation*. Reductionist naturalism renounces its own moral sources, for its theory is not equipped to either articulate or justify them if it wishes to continue to comply with the assumption of objectivity and empirical verifiability behind its claims (Soniewicka 2017).

The naturalistic reasoning employed by the transhumanists can be reproduced in somewhat simplified form as follows:

a) Humans are beings possessing natural (innate) altruistic tendencies and natural (innate) cooperation skills (these are evolutionary adaptations, whose primary function is the adaption and survival of the species);
b) by following their natural tendencies, people are striving for the common good (on the assumption that a harmony of interests exists);

c) given that the conditions for our species' functioning have undergone radical change, driven by technological development with which evolution is failing to keep pace, we need to enhance human beings' natural moral tendencies and skills if our species is to survive.

The change in conditions of cooperation mentioned in *point c* involves changes in both the scope and form of this cooperation, since modes of human co-existence have been transformed. Societies which once functioned in relatively small family/tribal groups now function within political communities numbering many millions, which requires more sophisticated forms of labour division. Furthermore, the effects of technology-assisted action can be much more far-reaching, both in time and space, which is causing these groups to intermingle. They are becoming interdependent and need to cooperate with each other on a global scale. This requires the correction of the tendencies and abilities expressed in *point a* and better coordination of the objective mentioned in *point b* through the application of procedural reason (the ability to establish hierarchies of preference, select suitable means for the realisation of goals and calculation of costs and benefits) in such a manner as to incorporate the universal community of people, both present and future generations. This also gives rise to proposals to adopt utilitarianism as the ethical doctrine best equipped to express and realise this goal (Greene 2013). However, when applying a utilitarian criterion, it should be acknowledged that any means that will turn out to most effectively maximise happiness in the world should be taken advantage of, including genetic interventions which could increase the statistical probability that people will be more inclined to cooperate in the face of global challenges (Persson & Savulescu 2012).

Serious philosophical charges may be levelled at this manner of reasoning. *Points a and b*, which are of an empirical nature, include implicit normative premises. If it is accepted that altruistic tendencies are an evolutionary adaptation aiding the survival of the species, it does not follow in the least that this should guide the actions of representatives of this species (specific people), especially if this would be at the cost of individual sacrifices or self-preservation in extreme circumstances. However, proponents of transhumanism would appear to claim otherwise, since the altruistic tendencies they describe are not only physiological responses or neuronal states. They are also the *correct* (or desirable) responses supporting their pursuit of the ideal of universal harmony of interests. The adaption and preservation of the species should in fact be understood not only as functions of our abilities, but also, at the same time, as *constitutive* components of a goal which is regarded, by this reasoning, as appropriate. Since the goal of enhancement is to enable wider cooperation and altruism, the main assumption here is not that people are simply altruistic by nature and willing to cooperate, but rather that they really *should be* such, i.e. that they should be striving to harmonise their interests on a global scale and working toward the universal good of mankind, even at the cost of making individual sacrifices.

Attention should be drawn at this juncture to the distinction between functionality and teleology (Spaemann 2017). Certain mechanisms are observable in nature that have specific function. For example, the function of pain is to signalise dysfunction in an organism. However, it may be excessive or last longer than necessary to perform the function of a signal. But this signal is not always able to reveal to us what dysfunction it is drawing our attention to. If altruistic tendencies are treated as evolutionary adaptations whose function is to enable, as far as possible, the species to adapt and survive, it should also be acknowledged that these tendencies, for better or worse, fulfil this function, yet are not in themselves either necessary or important.

9.3.2 Nature's normativity

If we claim, on the basis of empirical research, that altruistic tendencies are innate and egoistic tendencies are acquired through social interaction (see Tomasello 2009), drawing the normative conclusion from this that we should be more altruistic than egoistic could be almost tantamount to acknowledging that nature is binding, which would resolve the problem of justifying the aforementioned ideal. The assumption that nature is normative was present in various metaphysical conceptions, from the ancient conception of the cosmic order (adopted in the philosophy of Plato, Aristotle and the Stoics) to Christian deistic conceptions (Taylor 2001). According to these conceptions, we could find indications in nature as to what we should be, because humans were perceived to be both part and a reflection of the rational order of the universe (the ontic *logos*) or as a work of creation (creationist ideas).

The possibility exists of adopting a secularised version of these conceptions, and the recognition that nature, along with all its beauty and danger, transcends us impels us toward religious reverence and respect (see Dworkin 2013). Similar assumptions form the basis of the normative idea of human nature from which the notion of inalienable human dignity as the foundation of and justification for human rights is derived. It may then be claimed that genetic enhancements violate human nature, thus undermining the idea of human rights (Fukuyama 2002), leading Georg Annas to conclude that heritable genetic interventions should be termed a 'crime against humanity' (Annas 2009). For a crime against humanity (*genocide*), as Arendt notes, entails the undermining of our normative status as humans (Arendt 2006).

According to DeGrazia, the fallaciousness of this line of reasoning resides in the fact that since human rights are supposed to protect all human beings by virtue of their species affiliation – irrespective of any presented traits, such as consciousness, the ability to take autonomous action and rationality – genetic enhancements would have to lead to the creation of a completely new species to make this a real threat (DeGrazia 2012; Birnbacher 2008). In other words, change introduced by means of genetic engineering would have to be drastic, transcend typically human properties and accumulate in a large proportion of the population. Even if this type of change were to occur, DeGrazia does not see anything wrong in such a change. He only perceives the possibility of such a change having negative consequences if this would lead to the domination of individuals who had been enhanced over those who had not (see Chapter 8). However, it is possible to prevent this without rejecting out of hand the idea of genetic enhancement.

Transhumanism's proponents accuse bioconservatives of attributing a moral value to something natural (the Independent Worth of Nature Claim), pointing out that not everything that is natural is regarded as good and worthy of preservation, the best example being illnesses or genetic defects (Kamm 2013). Transhumanism's opponents do not, however, accept that everything that is natural is good which would be absurd. This misunderstanding arises from the fact that the advocates of both positions are invoking different conceptions of human nature. In the case of transhumanism's opponents, this a normative conception of human nature viewing the individual as a moral agent (Spaemann 2017; Habermas 2003). For transhumanists, this is a descriptive conception of human nature as a collection of characteristics typical of people (Buchanan 2011). When transhumanists reject metaphysical conceptions along with ideas such as the sanctity of human life, human dignity and normativity of nature, they are unable to adopt the assumption that any aspect of nature (e.g. altruistic tendencies) is binding.

Rejecting the idea of the normativity of nature is not tantamount, however, to acknowledging that both every intervention and no intervention into nature are equally justified, because significant doubt then arises as to the direction and safety of these changes, as I shall discuss in the next section.

9.3.3 The 'playing God' and unknown consequences arguments

George Annas draws attention to the problematic nature of establishing what enhancement would entail and what could be understood by the term 'enhanced' within this context (Annas 2009). If the earth was flooded by natural disasters, it would perhaps be necessary to create human beings equipped with gills; if air pollution made life on earth impossible, the only hope for human survival would possibly be to modify human lungs, so that people would be able to breathe carbon dioxide (Annas 2009). The whole problem with this is that nobody can be certain of what will be better for the next generations, or what adaptive traits will prove to be important. Given this lack of certainty, irreversible decisions should not be made in the name of humanity.

Alan Buchanan opposes this line of argument by claiming that it is just as difficult to estimate the genetic benefits of enhancements necessary for adapting to the harmful effects of environmental change as it is to estimate their risk (Buchanan 2011). This does not mean, in his view, that it is rational to adopt a solution based on risk aversion and a tendency to preserve the *status quo* (see Chapter 11). Furthermore, Buchanan, Brock, Daniels and Wikler believe that it is possible to determine which human qualities no one sound of mind would reject and only enhance these. They call these general-purpose means:

> [U]seful and valuable in carrying out nearly any plan of life or set of aims that humans typically have (Buchanan et al 2007, 167).

However, the existence of such incontestably beneficial genetic properties is as controversial as the issue of what they entail or whether they will complement any plan of life. I shall be reflecting on this further in this chapter.

If we are willing to listen to the transhumanists' advice and take control over procreation and the further evolution of the human species, the fundamental question arises of who would decide, and on what basis, what is better for our species, or will be better over the next 100 or 1000 years. We would need to be omniscient to know what will be good for future people, which brings to mind the famous argument against genetic engineering formulated as 'playing God'.[4] The famous geneticist, James Watson, who participated in

---

4   This also explains the existence, contradicting Kamm's line of reasoning, of a difference between parents who pray to God for their child to become a good person, and parents who employ genetic engineering to the same end, because in the first situation, the parents are entrusting their children's fate to the will of God, on the assumption that God knows better than them what will be good for their child (cf. Kamm 2013, 345). See also Chapter 6 of this book.

the sequencing of the human genome and astonished people with his radical views on genetic engineering, ironically shrugged of this accusation by claiming: 'I'm not hesitant to say we're playing God. Someone should.' (Watson in Angrist 2010, 49). However, doubts may be harboured as to whether the Creator's perspective is accessible to parents, or in fact any group of scientists or philosophers (Habermas 2003). It is for these reasons that such philosophers as Michael Sandel reject the idea of human enhancement by means of genetic interventions with unknown and uncertain consequences on the basis of its arrogance (*hubris*) (Sandel 2007). This could lead to the violation of our species' ethical self-knowledge (Habermas 2003), and therefore to the genetic genocide Annas mentions (Annas 2009).

The proponents of the idea of genetic enhancement claim that it should be directed by the principle such as the one introduced by John Harris which states: 'more of eveything' (Harris 2007). Yet this principle is not only empty but also nonsensical since it means 'more of who knows what'. Gilbert K. Chesterton aptly described this kind of approach in an ironic manner:

> We are fond of talking about 'liberty;' that, as we talk of it, is a dodge to avoid discussing what is good. We are fond of talking about 'progress;' that is a dodge to avoid discussing what is good. (...) The modern man says, 'Let us leave all these arbitrary standards and embrace liberty.' This is, logically rendered, 'Let us not decide what is good, but let it be considered good not to decide it.' He says, 'Away with your old moral formulae; I am for progress.' This logically stated, means, 'Let us not settle what is good; but let us settle whether we are getting more of it.' (Chesterton 1908, 33).

Paraphrasing Chesterton, one may add that transhumanist say, 'Neither in religion nor morality, my friend, lie the hopes of the race, but in biomedical enhancement.' This clearly expressed, means, 'We cannot decide what is good, but let us give it to our children.' (Chesterton 1908, 33).

The further paradox of the transhumanists' argumentation lies in the fact that it presents us with an alternative to surrendering to the control of nature or that of other people, yet both options would appear to be difficult to accept. The first option presupposes that species self-knowledge is at least partially accessible to us on the basis of observation, because it can be inferred from the biological categories conditioning our nature. Against the background of these assumptions, any intervention into the species' biological structure would appear to be self-defeating. For if what is good can be inferred from innate tendencies, and we manipulate the innate tendencies of future generations to comply with what we regard as good, rather than controlling nature, we are actually becoming its tools, as C. S. Lewis wrote (Lewis 2001). Transhumanists' idea to take evolution into our own hands and broaden the scope of human control over nature then leads to a paradox, because:

> Man's conquest of Nature turns out, in the moment of its consummation, to be Nature's conquest of Man (Lewis 2001, 68).

The second option, which rejects the idea of species self-knowledge, would appear to much more closely resemble the idea of transhumanism. It envisages the possibility of the completely unobstructed shaping of human nature, conceived as a collection of desirable qualities dependent on social needs. Upon reconciling themselves to the idea of biomedical moral enhancement, they are then forced to accept that those who would decide on the enhancement of future generations would know better than future generations which traits they should possess for their future benefit. This means that:

> [W]hat we call Man's power over Nature turns out to be a power exercised by some men over other men with Nature as its instrument (Lewis 2001, 55).

In later sections of this chapter, I will take a closer look at the normative conception of human nature viewing the individual as a moral agent so as to deepen my critique of the reductionist assumptions of the notion of genetic human enhancement.

9.4 Naturalistic reductionism with respect to morality: the issue of the agent's reflexive engagement

In the Genetic Virtue Program proposed by Mark Walker (Walker 2009), the author invokes the philosophy of Aristotle, according to which an act of virtue must arise from our permanent, unchanging character (Aristotle 2011). The proposed programme is meant to be an interdisciplinary project combing the efforts of philosophers, psychologists and geneticists which aims to investigate and enhance the genetic correlates of virtuous behaviour using biotechnology. Walker's idea is based on the following assumptions:

a) Virtues are part of the human character, comprising, in particular, character traits conceived as permanent predispositions towards certain behaviours;
b) character traits are heritable (genetically conditioned);
c) evil is a function of human nature;
d) our fundamental moral obligation is to eliminate evil (Walker 2009).

The author concludes from these premises that our moral obligation is to use biotechnology to morally enhance human nature. Having equipped ourselves with the appropriate psychological and genetic knowledge, we should, in Walker's view, introduce the Genetic Virtue Program using such means as the genetic selection of embryos of a desired genotype or applying suitable genetic modification. Just as embryos are being tested today for the genetic defects responsible for diseases and disabilities, we should, in the author's view, use preimplantation diagnostic techniques to select for genetic moral tendencies in the future. Since we are willing to apply biotechnology to the enhancement of our physical or mental faculties, the author writes, we should be even keener to promote the idea of moral enhancement on which humanity's future fate may depend. The author acknowledges, at the same time, that not all virtues have to be correlated with genetic predispositions and certain role in the shaping of character should be attributed to socialisation processes. Walker holds the view that his programme is a desirable condition, but not enough in itself to make people better. The hope of this programme 'is not to make persons virtuous but to make them better equipped to *learn* how to be virtuous' (Walker 2009, 39). He also alludes to Aristotle's claim that virtues are not innate:

> So virtues arise in us neither by nature nor contrary to nature, but nature gives us the capacity to acquire them, and completion comes through habituation (Aristotle 2011, 1103a, 23).

Some people are more capable of acquiring virtues and others, less so, and it is this 'susceptibility to virtues' that can, and should in Walker's view, be corrected. A transhumanism programme thus conceived, envisages that biomedical technologies are a new, assistive means of achieving this very goal, which has only been achieved to date through nurturing and socialisation.

In the following paragraphs, I shall attempt to demonstrate that the transhumanist idea to genetically enhance virtues does not tally at all with the assumptions of Aristotle's moral philosophy.

9.4.1 The reductionist understanding of moral virtues

It should be noted that Aristotle's moral philosophy can only be fully comprehended when we take into account the conceptual framework within which it was embedded – the aforementioned metaphysics of the cosmic order within which nature has a normative meaning. The Aristotelian form is the internal structure of matter rather than a material superstructure (Spaemann 2017). Human beings are given an internal structure that reflects nature. Aristotle introduces a distinction between life and a good life in which an individual's *telos* is realised. These assumptions form the basis of Aristotle's concept of virtue, which he understood to be established tendencies to act and feel in a certain way, making it possible for individuals to attain their *telos* (Aristotle 2011).

The concept of virtue the transhumanists evoke does not so much pass over this conceptual framework as intentionally reject it, as was mentioned before. This stance is also bound up with the adoption of a different understanding of moral virtue, which can lead to misunderstandings. The Darwinian approach adopted by transhumanists assumes that moral virtues are evolutionary adaptations by means of which 'certain instinctive impulses accounting for our needs as a species are expressed' (Kołakowski 2014, 118). Moral virtues are therefore equivalent to species utility and are of a purely instrumental nature. In fact, they are external means to a completely separate end – the success of the species. Much the same applies in the case of utilitarianism which reduces virtues to stimuli triggering socially desirable human behaviour. Benjamin Franklin expressed this idea as follows: 'a virtue is a quality which has utility in achieving earthly and heavenly success' (Franklin in MacIntyre 2007, 185). In other words, moral virtues like, for example, altruistic tendencies, are only as important as the goal that is to be achieved – a harmony of interests and the well-being of the community. It follows from consequential reasoning that the so-called behaviouristic component (behaviour conforming to a virtue, e.g. altruistic behaviour) is a condition sufficient to describe behaviour as virtuous (desirable for realising a goal). Furthermore, if that species or social success could be achieved using other, more effective means, these virtues would become redundant.

The approach to virtues is completely different in Aristotle's philosophy, because the practising of virtue is an *internal* means to achieving the end of leading a good life. This means that 'the end cannot be adequately characterized independently of a characterization of the means', as Thomas Aquinas interprets Aristotle's thought (MacIntyre 2007, 184). If we are to understand what the virtuous life entails, we need to evoke the virtues without which it cannot be achieved. Practising virtues is part and parcel of the virtuous life, so such practising of virtues is not good in a functional (utilitarian) sense purely because of the need to achieve some external goal (success). Virtuous behaviour is good in itself, so virtuous people are happy of the very fact of performing virtuous deeds.

Furthermore, according to Aristotelian philosophy, the fact that an act conforms to a virtue is not enough in itself. For that act to be regarded as virtuous, the agent needs to comply with three further conditions, which are listed as follows:

a) Acts with knowledge;
b) acts from rational choice (rational choice of the actions for their own sake);
c) actions from a firm and unshakeable character (Aristotle 2011, 1105a, 28).

The behaviouristic component does not in this case suffice, and habituation does not in itself equate to moral competence. Aristotle writes about the conscious and reflexive temperament resulting from practice. Moral excellence (*arête*) is not reduced to conduct that accords with a virtue, but instead entails right conduct out of the virtue.

Walker perceives the difference between the reductionist naturalism takes on virtue, and the much more demanding concept adopted by Aristotle, yet claims that they are not mutually contradictory, because the Aristotelian conception takes the biological conception further, creating the possibility of genetic intervention, as illustrated by the following thought experiment:

> One hundred people have been genetically conditioned to be inclined to tell the truth, with sixty of these actually doing this. The behaviourist condition is met in the case of the latter, but this does not suffice when the Aristotelian approach is applied. It is only possible to assess if their behaviour is truly virtuous by investigating whether the other three conditions are met in their case. It turns out that 55 of the 60 people take pleasure in speaking the truth, 50 of them meet the knowledge condition and 45 of them meet the rational choice condition (5 were compulsive truth-tellers). This Aristotelian sorting method thus reveals that out of the 60 people who are virtuous on utilitarian grounds, 45 are truly virtuous, and these two positions are not, according to Walker, in conflict with each other (Walker 2009, 37–38).

There is absolutely no need for the assumptions behind his programme to accept that the behaviouristic condition is the sole condition for virtue, but it is assumed that it is a condition that may be genetically interfered with.

Walker's argumentation is applied to the statistical distribution of specific traits across a group. Yet a group is incapable of referring to its own virtue reflexively in order to practise it, so the reflexive condition will never be met in this case. If individuals are taken into consideration, Walker's argumentation is not able to demonstrate that genetic manipulation of qualities correlated with virtues could have any effect whatsoever on the 'enhanced' individuals' ability to refer to them reflexively and decision to follow the path of virtue. It is unable to do this because Walker is using a naturalistic conception of moral virtue as a superstructure rooted in biology which is inconsistent with the Aristotelian understanding of moral virtue as the realisation of internal normative human structure. For virtue, rather than being an example of biological conditioning or a habit arising from biological conditioning, is the outcome of reflexive self-referentiality grounded in action.

This aspect of our reflections may be ably summarised using the following observation by Robert Piłat:

In short, advocates of ethical naturalism make valid points, but they are not relevant to the issue at hand. Moral norms are of an absolute nature; they are not reliant on the statistical probability of choosing a cooperation strategy. Habituation is not a norm, even if its influence is strong enough to be continuously operative. Moral normativity requires a strong relation that binds being a suitable agent to the observance of suitable norms (Piłat 2013, 177).

9.4.2 First and second nature

The difference between the ethics of virtue rooted in Aristotle's philosophy and the transhumanists' approach can be better understood by invoking the distinction between bald naturalism and second nature naturalism proposed by John McDowell (McDowell 2002). Such a division into first (biological) nature and a second nature associated with customs, habits and nurture has been familiar since antiquity. In ancient philosophy, a life lived according to second nature was understood to be a life that was free rather than being subordinated to biological and physiological needs, which were thought to express enslavement. However, the emancipation process from first nature to second nature had to take place within a framework staked out by first nature. If we compare second nature to *software*, first nature should be compared to *hardware*; the secondary system can only function efficiently and endure when it is compatible with the flexible primary system (Spaemann 2017). Human biological functions forming part of first nature, e.g. eating or sexual relations, become personal acts of second nature, acquiring a specific meaning within its bounds (Spaemann 2017). Likewise, personal relations can be based on biological relations without being reduced to them, e.g. a kinship relation that incorporates relations not arising from biological ties (shared affinities or child adoption). Even if the biological function dies out, a personal relationship can last a whole lifetime and take on an intrinsic meaning.

As McDowell points out, although the notion of moral virtue cannot be understood without invoking our innate tendencies and predispositions, that is, our biological nature, its meaning cannot possibly be derived from it (McDowell 2002). For moral virtue is acquired through habituation, which determines our second nature. Second nature is rational and cannot be reduced to first nature, so it cannot be explained or modified by the empirical sciences, as is the case with first nature (which includes human organs, mental states, etc.). The virtue of truthfulness is not something that happens to people who have an innate tendency toward speaking the truth; the virtue is not like having an innate preference for certain tastes or smells. Even the claim that moral virtues supervene on our biological dispositions is not enough to acknowledge the existence of some purely descriptive, empirically cognisable component of moral virtue (cf. Audi 2013, 2014, 2015; Kramer 2009), for example, truthfulness.

Let us take a look at the virtue of courage, which both Plato and Aristotle distinguished from impudence. From Aristotle's perspective, courage comprising a virtue is bound up with action contributing to the realisation of an ethical ideal (a person's *telos*), which can no longer be equated with impudence. The issue of concern in this case is therefore not actually the ability to master fear and risk one's life, but the ability to master fear and risk one's life for a *worthy cause*. One example of moral heroism is sacrificing one's life to save that of a stranger. The attitude of someone prepared to sacrifice their life can neither be understood through reference to the purely descriptive level nor inferred from any of that person's physical or biological properties. For sacrificing one's life does not possess vital significance, but it may possess moral significance when values adopted by the protagonist engaged in that act are being realised (Spaemann 2017). What is needed to understand the moral significance of this deed is a conceptual framework alluding to second nature (McDowell 2002).

In other words, the genetic modification of human nature cannot be understood as moral enhancement, because moral excellence forms part of our separately formed second nature, which cannot be derived or explained in terms of our biological system. Comparing second nature to first nature is like comparing a musical composition to a scientific description of sounds. A scientific description tells us what makes possible that sounds can simply come into being, but tells us nothing about the content of the composition or its meaning for us.

For these reasons, the thesis should be rejected that biomedical enhancement is nothing more than the continuation of traditional rearing methods that have always been practised. I shall be returning to this in a later section of the chapter. As McDowell aptly expresses this:

> Moral education does not merely rechannel one's natural motivational impulses, with the acquisition of reason making no difference except that one becomes self-consciously aware of the operation of those impulses. In imparting *logos*, moral education enables one to step back from any motivational impulse one finds oneself subject to, and question its rational credentials. Thus it effects a kind of distancing of the agent from the practical tendencies that are part of what we might call his first nature (McDowell 2002, 188).[5]

---

5   McDowell's approach is not antinaturalistic, for he does not evoke metaphysical ideas to define moral virtue, instead pointing to a broader conception of naturalism that transcends the reductionist derivation of moral virtues from biological human nature.

9.5 Transcending human nature – the issue of autonomy

The moral agent is distinctive for its ability to distance itself from its first nature while retaining awareness of its own capabilities and limitations arising from first nature, as well as its ability to transcend them, while also being both the agent and object of its own action, something I shall be developing in this section. Unlike other species, humans are not identical to their biological nature. It may be stated, after Robert Spaemann, that humans are not so much their biological nature as the *possessors* and shapers of their nature (Spaemann 2017).[6] Humans are the agents of intentional acts that can transcend their innate abilities and condition – for example, they can dream about flying (Spaemann 2017) – something the advancement of culture has certainly made possible (cf. Tomasello 2009). Therefore, it is not so much self-preservation or survival that express people's exceptionality, but rather the human aptitude for self-transcendence, by which they transcend themselves and the conditions of their existence (Spaemann 2017).

Thought about self-transcendence is deeply embedded in the philosophical tradition. A famous passage from Giovanni Pico della Mirandola's *Oration on the Dignity of Man* contains the following dialogue between the Creator and his creation – the human being:

> Once defined, the nature of all other beings is constrained within the laws We have prescribed for them. But you, constrained by no limits, may determine your nature for yourself, according to your own free will, in whose hands We placed you. (…) [Y]ou may, as the free and extraordinary shaper of yourself, fashion yourself in whatever form you prefer. It will be in your power to degenerate into the lower forms of life, which are brutish. Alternatively, you shall have the power, in accordance with the judgment of your soul, to be reborn into the higher orders, those that are divine (Pico della Mirandola 2012, 117).

Pico della Mirandola compares humans to Proteus due to their ability to transform themselves, thus acknowledging that not fully determined human nature is their distinguishing trait, enabling them to recreate themselves anew. It could appear that this manifesto of Renaissance humanism accords with the transhumanists' conception.[7] After all, they underline that pursuit of excellence is one of the

---

6   This does not mean that they can shape themselves with complete freedom, only within a certain given context and scope.
7   The very name transhumanism, which contains the prefix *trans* (across, through, beyond) alludes to the idea of transcending the human (or what is typical of the species) (see Chapter 8).

human species' distinguishing traits, and that the theory of evolution is the best metanarrative for this goal (Bashford 2013), something I shall attempt to question in a later section of this article.

The idea of transhumanism should not be regarded as a mere secularised version of the notion of human dignity rooted in the Platonic-Christian tradition, for it actually continues to stand in open opposition to it. When Pico della Mirandola postulates that the human species should be transcended, he is not thinking in terms of biological advancement, but rather the *spiritual* advancement distinguishing human beings from other animal species. This pertains to ethical transformation, in-depth reflection and a pursuit of excellence based on the assumption of moral action for which freedom is a necessary condition. For we read in the above quotation that a person endowed with freedom is born with potential that can be both used (becoming similar to God) and squandered (remaining an animal). In this vision, humans are called upon by God to live and act in a manner that complements the act of creation and to participate in it, taking full advantage of the freedom they have been granted to this end. The order of existence here is a given. It is hierarchical, and the role and goal of humans (striving for the Good in Plato or sanctity and redemption in Christianity) are predetermined. In the disenchanted, post-Enlightenment world, humans retain their creative role, but its goal is not determined in advance. People have to find it themselves, usually doing this by searching for it inside themselves (Taylor 2001). The idea of transhumanism is not, however, a continuation of this strand of philosophical thought, because transhumanism, as opposed to the traditional philosophical approach, claims that humans are not agents enhancing themselves, but rather the *objects* of this process of enhancement. Transhumanists reached this position by adopting utilitarian ethical assumptions and a reductionist naturalistic conception of humanity and morality.

Traditional morality distinguishes between what we do and what happens to us; also of importance are the intentions and an understanding of the social practices and relations that determine the selection of suitable means of action. All these aspects of morality are irrelevant from the standpoint of consequential utilitarian ethics, on the basis of which action is evaluated from the perspective of outcomes, applying a cost-benefit analysis. If we achieve the same desirable outcome, e.g. self-control, using appropriate genetic intervention rather than education or persistent exercise of the will, there is no reason for a utilitarian to reject the first of these methods. Instead, the utilitarian should select the most effective method, leading to the conclusion being drawn that moral human enhancement using biomedical interventions is superior to traditional methods of rearing, socialisation or self-improvement, which are more costly, time-consuming and less effective (Walker 2009). This is encapsulated in the words of one of the characters in Aldous Huxley's *Brave New World*, who praised the benefits of the pharmacological treatment 'soma' as follows:

> And there's always *soma* to calm your anger, to reconcile you to your enemies, to make you patient and long-suffering. In the past you could only accomplish these things by making a great effort and after years of hard moral training. Now, you swallow two or three half-gramme tablets, and there you are. Anybody can be virtuous now. You can carry at least half your morality about in a bottle. Christianity without tears–that's what *soma* is (Huxley 2000, 400).

The question arises as to why we should value mastery achieved through arduous effort and training over that which is the outcome of medical therapy not requiring any effort, or even participation, on our part. This difference is not justifiable in terms of the special value of the effort, as transhumanists think, but can be justified in terms of an in-depth understanding of moral character which cannot be described purely on the basis of the outcomes of actions, but this notion should be associated with the normative relation linking a specific agent with his/her action goal (Piłat 2013).

9.5.1 Two perspectives: theoretical and practical, collective and individual

There are two important philosophical traditions which, when quoted, enable a better understanding to be obtained of where the difference lies between the conceptions of man promoted by advocates and opponents of transhumanism. Although these traditions are rooted in ancient philosophy, I shall, for simplicity's sake, call one of them Kantian philosophy, and the other, Darwinian philosophy, to emphasise the core of the dispute. These traditions accentuate the passive and active sides of human nature in a completely different manner.

As Christine Korsgaard emphasises, humans as rational beings can, in Kant's view, perceive themselves from two different perspectives:

a) As objects of theoretical study (wholly determined by natural forces, the mere undergoers of their experiences);
b) As agents (free and responsible, the authors of their actions) (Korsgaard 1989, 120).

The first of these perspectives is the domain of empirical research in which humans are perceived as beings going through different experiences (that is, as passive beings) whose behaviour can be studied by explaining their motives and using these findings to predict how they will behave in the future. The second (practical) perspective, which, for Kant, is the domain of morality, places emphasis on the active side of human nature, understanding people as agents – creating their own thought and steering their own lives. In this domain, it is crucial to understand the reasoning agents use to justify their actions. The Darwinian approach, in which consequential ethics, including utilitarianism, is rooted, adopts the first perspective, accentuating the passive nature of humans as objects of study. While from the Kantian perspective it is what we do and why we do it that is of most importance in morality, the Darwinian perspective focuses on what happens to us (Habermas 2003). From a Darwinian standpoint, moral action is a certain kind of experience that humans go through.

The same applies to the conception of freedom as a sense of liberty we experience, making use of our own powers, as David Hume writes. This also explains why John Stuart Mill claims that freedom is necessary since it makes as happy (Mill 2003). Kant comprehends this notion completely differently. For him, freedom is the power to initiate something, that is, the power to be an originator. Internal freedom, or autonomy, is not directly reducible to independence or freedom of choice, for Kant understands it to be the rational ability to subordinate one's will to universal moral law (Kant 2002). Freedom, thus conceived, is the key to understanding human dignity, the assumption that people hold the status of moral agents, and therefore every human being is valuable for its own sake and human worth is immeasurable, incomparable, non-cumulative. Rather than being treated as a mere means to an end, it should always be treated as an end in itself (Kant 2002; see Audi 2016; Kołakowski 2014). Human dignity is therefore something to be respected rather than maximised. Autonomy is something good in itself. It is not tied to facts, but rather relates to our perception of ourselves as free and responsible beings when we choose to take a practical reasoning perspective and decide what should be done. As Korsgaard writes:

> In fact, it is only from the practical point of view that actions and choices can be distinguished from mere 'behavior' determined by biological and psychological laws (Korsgaard 1989, 120).

Both these perspectives are derived from different relations to agency, while differences in choosing one of these perspectives lead to fundamental differences in the understanding of morality, as Korsgaard indicates. From the Darwinian perspective chosen by the transhumanists, the species is 'the real subject and the object of behaviours that can be evaluated in terms of morality' (Kołakowski 2014, 118). However, the Kantian perspective presupposes that 'the human person is both an agent of will and ultimate object of every moral intention' (Kołakowski 2014, 118). From the first perspective, the individual can be perceived functionally as a carrier of the species' values. However, from the second perspective, the individual is normative, rather than functional, in nature (Habermas 2003), possessing intrinsic value. From a Darwinian perspective, inherent human dignity is a notion that is either worthless or even an expression of 'speciesism' manifested in the biased attribution of special value to the human species that other species do not possess (Singer 2011; see Chapter 13). However, from a Kantian perspective, human dignity is a regulative idea without which the normative meaning of humanity cannot be comprehended. In other words, the Darwinian approach offers a collective perspective on morality (applicable to the entire species or a specific population), while the Kantian approach emphasises an individual perspective on morality. Clearly, Julian Huxley's aforementioned question, 'What are people for?', will encounter a completely different response from each of these two positions, which is of crucial importance for any viewpoint adopted on the human enhancement issue.

From a Kantian perspective, as Korsgaard notes, comprehending one's own personal identity is inextricably linked to the notion of autonomy:

> If I can overcome my cowardice by surgery or medication rather than *habituation* I might prefer to take this less arduous route. So long as an authentic good will is behind my desire for greater courage, and authentic courage is the result, the mechanism does not matter. But for the Kantian it does matter who is initiating the use of the mechanism. Where I change myself, the sort of continuity needed for identity may be preserved, even if I become very different. Where I am changed by wholly external forces, it is not. This is because the sort of continuity needed for what matters to me in my own personal identity essentially involves my agency (Korsgaard 1989, 123).[8]

Freedom is here understood to be an action being acted and, at the same time, a necessary condition for having a life of one's own in which we identify with what

---

8   It should be added here that Kant's ethics assume that acting on an inclination, irrespective of whether this is the outcome of a natural predisposition or the use of pharmacology (e.g. under the influence of 'soma'), is not completely autonomous and does not constitute a moral agency, because for this to be the case, these actions would need to be bound by obligation and involve practical reason on every occasion.

we understand to be our moral obligation (Korsgaard 1989; Korsgaard 1992; Audi 2016), something I shall be returning to below.

9.5.2 Free to fall

According to the Kantian approach to morality, the transhumanists' moral paternalism is untenable. Attention was drawn to this by John Harris, who, although he is an advocate of human advancement, treats the idea of moral advancement with scepticism, choosing the prospect of freedom over the prospect of survival of the species (Harris 2011, see Chapter 10).

The author emphasises that morality is based on an assumption of freedom, both to do good and to fall, as illustrated in the famous passage from the third book of Milton's *Paradise Lost*, where God says about man:

> .... [W]hose fault?
> Whose but his own? Ingrate, he had of me
> All he could have; I made him just and right,
> Sufficient to have stood, though free to fall (Milton 2000, line 96).

Harris interprets the above quote as follows:

> One thing we can say with confidence is that ethical expertise is not 'being better at being good', rather it is being better at knowing the good and understanding what is likely to conduce to the good. The space between knowing the good and doing the good is a region entirely inhabited by freedom. Knowledge of the good is sufficiency to have stood, but freedom to fall is all. Without the freedom to fall, good cannot be a choice; and freedom disappears and along with it virtue. There is no virtue in doing what you must (Harris 2011, 104).[9]

He goes on to clarify that the same character tendencies that would appear to lead us towards weakness and immorality also enable the opposite tendency to coexist – morality grounded in freedom that arises from the tension among our internal contradictions (what we are and what we should be, as mentioned above). Tennessee Williams expressed this idea well in an interview: 'If I got rid of my demons, I'd lose my angels' (Williams in Devlin 1986, 245).

I shall use the example of Alex – the main protagonist in Anthony Burgess' novel *A Clockwork Orange* (Burgess 1995), splendidly adapted for the screen by Stanley Kubrick – to show the Kantian approach is largely intuitive and consistent with a common-sense approach. Alex displayed psychopathic tendencies

---

9   It would also be possible here to quote Huxley's *Brave New World*, whose main protagonist demanded the right to be imperfect and unhappy (Huxley 2000). Also see Chapter 10.

and ended up in prison for using brutal violence. To get his sentence shortened, he agreed to submit to an experimental resocialisation method that caused violence to trigger a nausea reflex and provoke anxiety in him. When conditioned against aggression, Alex was not able to physically harm anyone, and was not even able to defend himself against aggression directed at him by others. From a moral standpoint, it would be difficult to assess such a person physically unable to commit aggression as good.

Transhumanists responded to the charge that their ideas negatively impacted on freedom by arguing that biomedical moral enhancement does not involve the elimination or even limitation of freedom, because certain genetically conditioned tendencies do not, by reserving the sphere of free choice for enhanced individuals, comprehensively determine their choice of whether their superior genetic system should or should not be used to a moral end like preserving the species (Persson & Savulescu 2012). Some of the transhumanists even took their argumentation a step further, claiming that autonomy can be enhanced by biomedical interventions honing cognitive abilities, mainly the ability to reason (Schaefer, Kahane & Savulescu 2014). The crux of the problem, however, resides in the face that when talking about freedom in a Kantian spirit, we are not speaking of freedom of choice; one may be not autonomous when all the selection options are imposed in advance, even if it is possible to choose between them. If we are not conditioned in our actions by social or genetic factors, that does not mean that we are autonomous in a Kantian sense. If our choices are left to complete chance or we are guided by strong tendencies, we will not be totally autonomous, something I shall be returning to later. Kantian autonomy does not equate either to the freedom to choose among our preferences or freedom of action according to them. Other animal species are also free in the sense that they have the freedom to choose from among various preferences and the freedom to act in accordance with this choice. Under normal circumstances, Buridan's famous ass would not die of thirst or hunger if it was placed at an equal distance to the hay and water; even a donkey that is as hungry as it is thirsty will be able to choose whether it should first quench its thirst or satiate its hunger. The freedom being discussed here within the context of morality should in fact be understood as the special ability to manage one's own life according to one's own perception of good and, at the same time, as the ability to assume full responsibility for failure in this undertaking. A person enhanced in such a manner as to be equipped with certain preferences will not be totally autonomous because, from a Kantian standpoint, what choices are made from among preferences is not the only important factor. It is also important whether a choice is the outcome of the rational involvement of the will and where the preferences come from.

If we are to better understand the significance of autonomy for the comprehension of the moral agent, it is worth referring to the argumentation of Habermas (Habermas 2003), who uses it as a basis for the formulation of arguments that are critical toward any form of genetic human enhancement, as I shall be discussing in the next section.

9.5.3 Genetic lottery and genetic intervention – the unavailability of the human beginning as a condition for autonomy

In ancient philosophy, freedom was realised in our social nature by mastering our biological nature, as was mentioned earlier. In modern times, attention has been drawn to the fact that the social conditions for human life can be just as compelling as any pressure exerted by biological necessity. Yet the modern conception of freedom has turned toward inner spiritual sources (the concept of free will) which was rooted in Christianity (Taylor 2001). This process was most influentially articulated by Kant who was keen to emphasise individuation rather than socialisation in his philosophy. Human action is autonomous when, rather than being caused by either internal tendencies or external social pressure, it is instead triggered by instrumental reason enabling our ego to abstract itself from its social and biological conditioning. However, while the will of others limits our freedom, making our action heteronomous, the necessary laws of nature, including human nature, rather than limiting human freedom, merely define its context and create the conditions for its existence.

Habermas draws attention to the fact that a scientificistic worldview based on the theory of evolution changes conceptions of freedom, transforming the Kantian realm of necessity into the realm of chance (Habermas 2003). It then becomes tempting to use instrumental reason not only to shape the external conditions for human existence, but also the internal conditions, as Harris, quoted in the introduction to this chapter, postulated (Harris 2007). Human biological nature has begun to be perceived as an internal environment that can be objectified and shaped, much like the external environment in which people live. This is leading, in Habermas' view, to the technologizing of human nature and the altering of human self-awareness and the structure of moral experiences (Habermas 2003). Regulating our internal nature comes at the cost of destroying the notion of the self (Habermas 2008). He claims that genetic engineering, which instrumentalises and optimises the biological bases for human existence, poses a threat to human autonomy by transforming it into heteronomy. In other words, the unconstrained regulation of human life for the purposes of trait selection, is leading to the violation of human dignity – the moral basis of human equality.

Habermas' argumentation is disputed by such philosophers as Thomas Nagel, who point out that no one chooses their genes, so their random selection offers no more freedom than parental selection (Habermas 2003; cf. Kamm 2013). Habermas responds to the question of why the chance selection of a set of tendencies resulting from a genetic lottery should favour personal autonomy (more than a gene set we would receive from a planner intervening in our reproduction) by pointing out the difference between creation and birth. He also refers to Arendt's notion of 'natality' as a human beginning which is not at our own disposal (Arendt 1998). In nature, as Arendt notes, human conception of birth and death do not exist, since the world of nature is replicable. The birth and death of human beings are more to us than ordinary natural events, because they concern unique, irreplicable individuals. Humans not only possess life in the biological sense (*zoe*), but also life in a socio-historical sense (*bios*), thanks to which we can say that they have their own biographies. Something radically individual emerges with its own beginning and end from nature's replicable process of dying and being brought back to life – human life. For Arendt, birth as a means of finding oneself in the world is the most important aspect of the human condition and forms the basis of the theory of agency, according to which humans perceive themselves as agents equipped with the ability to give a beginning to things and events (Kant 2000, B478, 488; Arendt 1998).

Habermas draws on Arendt's thought to advance the thesis that the experiencing of one's own freedom requires us to relate to something which is not at our disposal – the fact of birth as a means of finding oneself in the world and the boundary between what is given (natural fate) and what is subject to our actions (social fate). Action in the world is possible precisely because we are both embodied and socially embedded (Pugh 2015). However, we relate to each of these dimensions differently when we assume that the first dimension is granted to us, whereas we consciously participate in the second. My organic nature is granted to me and defines the scope of my possibilities, acting as a starting point rather than limiting my freedom, because 'Being determined is a constitutive support of self-determination' (Seel in Habermas 2008, 160). Our biological nature should not therefore be treated in a purely instrumental manner, objectivising it, because my own body, with which I identify, is a condition for being the agent through which my body acts. Rather than being abstract beings equipped with a body and reason, we are embodied, rational beings, for whom our embodiment and reason are not so much properties as a form of being (Spaemann 2017). The social dimension of our existence that influences the shaping of our identities is of a different nature. For socialisation takes place in interaction with an agent, through acts of communication in a shared symbolic world (Habermas 2003). The agent in this process takes part actively and may relate to it by consciously identifying with its own socialised nature – an act of assimilation is, in this case, an expression of consent to define oneself. It may also reject this identification, constructing its own identity based on differences to what has been rejected – an act of opposition is, in this case, an expression of rebellion.

Freedom is conditioned by a need to comprehend the boundary between what we are and what we are becoming or may become under the influence of the will of others. What we are is a distinguishing feature of our uniqueness, because it is expressed in our actions and choices, and not in what happens to us without any participation of our will. This entails the acceptance of responsibility not only for our own actions, but our own qualitative constitution if it is co-created by our action (Spaemann 2017). Experiencing one's freedom therefore largely entails relating it to something that is not subject to disposal according to the will of other people – a random act of fertilisation that generates the unpredictable genetic combination of the organism that comes into being in this manner (Habermas 2003). The fact of birth, thus conceived, grants us a sense of autonomous existence that precedes any influence of socialisation, enabling us to relate to it and thus conceive of ourselves as the creators of our own lives. If, instead of being born, humans were created (i.e. other people took complete responsibility for the conditioning of our own structure), our sense of autonomy would be threatened. For genetic interventions blur the boundary between the autonomous and heteronomous, as well as between people and things. As a result, the personal relationships of free and equal beings are disrupted, creating new social relations and leading to the self-instrumentalisation of the species (Habermas 2003). This is caused by transforming procreation from the dimension of agency (*praxis*) to the dimension of manufacture (*poiesis*) (Ramsey 1970).

Even if we do not accept all the assumptions of Kantian philosophy, it is worth noting that, by adopting the above reasoning, we are expressing an important intuition relating to the difference between our attitude toward what arises from chance and what arises from someone's decision. The outcome of a genetic lottery is neither just nor unjust, unlike someone's purposeful distribution of genetic endowments (see Chapters 5 and 8). In the case of genetic enhancement, genetic intervention realises the preferences of parents, e.g. the desire to possess a musical child. This burdens the child with excessive expectations on the part of parents who may limit the child's future freedom, as Dena Davis claims (Davis 1997). According to this line of argument, if the parents decide to equip their children with excellent hearing, they will have a greater claim to what their children will achieve in life than when their talent is the outcome of a genetic lottery. They thus become the unwelcome co-authors of their children's lifestory, as Habermas writes (Habermas 2008).

In Davis' view, such parents will exert much more pressure on their children to develop the talents in which they invested when making their choice.

Advocates of transhumanism respond to this charge by claiming that the mastery of the skills in question will also depend on the will of the child. When a child as musical as its parents is born to a family of musicians, the realisation of its potential still depends on its own efforts, and it is to the child rather than its parents that we attribute the claim to success. Will the situation with genetic interference not have precisely the same outcome? The whole point is that the differences between these situations does not depend on the outcome or even the probability of achieving a particular outcome, but they regard our understanding of the parent-child relationship, for which the parents' intentions are of crucial importance. In the first case, the parents are reconciled to the fact that their child may or may not be musical, and their reciprocal relationship envisages the initiating of an interaction between independent and autonomous agents, although the child's autonomy is entrusted to the parents' care until it has fully developed. However, in the second case, the parents are bringing about the birth of a child with specific traits, which leads to a redefinition of the parental relationship – the parents' relation to the child resembles that between creator and created. The point here is not that the parents are depriving the child of any chance to make a choice, but rather that they are predefining the context of this choice. The decision to distribute natural properties according to parental preference is arbitrarily determining the space for the child's personal development.

From a Kantian perspective, the fact that I cannot jump through a fourth-floor window without doing myself any harm does not mean that I feel less free as a result. Whereas if someone locks me in a room on the fourth floor of a building, my freedom will then be curbed drastically even if I can do many other things in that room and take many important life decisions there. In other words, there is a significant difference between the context of freedom determined by nature and that determined by the arbitrary decisions of other people, even if they want what is best for the child. Only in the second case can we speak of someone's autonomy being limited.

9.6 Enhancement and nurturing

We have to agree that both genetic and environmental factors have an influence on our personality. There is absolutely no need to question the influence of genetic factors in the process of human development to demonstrate the significant qualitative difference between nurturing and biomedical enhancement. The essence of the charge against biomedical moral enhancement lies in a difference between personality and moral character. The transhumanists' approach does not distinguish between personality and character and presupposes that they are the outcome of what is given to us (biological determinants) and what we experience (social determinants). Criticism of this approach based on the philosophical considerations presented above presupposes that a person's moral character is shaped within the sphere of action (*praxis*), in which the key role is played by that person's *will*. Human personality, on the other hand, could be explained by references to biological and social factors only.

Advocates of biomedical enhancement claim that the difference between nurturing and genetic advancement is only a matter of degree, because the nurturing process takes very little account of the will of the child and its effects are largely irreversible. Sending a child to a particular school or sending it to ballet classes will lead, in their view, to the same irreversible psychophysical changes as genetic intervention before the child is born. We have to agree that purely mechanical 'training' of a child, with the parents employing physical or psychological violence to control its development fails, much like prenatal interference with its genotype, to respect the child's will. If the person rearing the child treats their ward like an artist does an artwork, it will not essentially make much difference what means are used to achieve this (prenatal or postnatal, psychotropic methods or the belt). In both cases, the (existing or future) child is merely the object of specific operations with a concrete aim (usually the maximisation of parental preferences concealed under the guise of what is supposedly for the child's good). Within a population context, it is meaningful to talk of the great similarity between the idea of genetic engineering (so-called designer babies) and that of social engineering (e.g. communist enterprise of re-making mankind).

Nurturing can, however, be understood differently if, rather than concentrating on the observable outcomes of this process, we attempt to comprehend the process itself and the crucially important relationship between the person rearing the child and their ward, in which case Habermas' aforementioned reflections on socialisation would appear to be relevant. This relationship is conceived in subjective terms in which emphasis is placed on the child's active participation in the rearing process. The child's participation in its own upbringing is not only a fact, but a necessary condition for the aforementioned freedom to be oneself. We can only perceive ourselves as free people responsible for ourselves and our own choices if we understand our own characters to be the outcome of an individuation process rather than one of socialisation alone. Character formation must take into account the rationales that we wish to be guided by in our lives. A rearing process based on intersubjective communicability presupposes the possibility of presenting the rationales to a child that lie behind specific rearing decisions. The child can relate to these rationales, assimilate them and agree to define themselves, as was mentioned earlier. It is therefore one thing to apply rearing methods and another to utilise pharmacological treatment (e.g. giving a child Ritalin when it is hyperactive), although this may turn out to be essential in exceptional cases (President's Council on Bioethics 2003). These methods rely on the parents or carers attempting to explain to the child how it should behave by offering suitable rationales or examples, or attempting to comprehend the context behind the child's behaviour if it diverges from the models that have been provided. The precedence given to these rearing methods over medical interventions arises from a specific conception of the moral character of an individual whose development requires *the reflexive engagement of the person in question*. Engaging children in the rearing process does not involve them fulfilling their desires only. Instead, this develops in them the ability to self-reflect, enabling them to take a stance on their desires, what they are doing and who they are (Piłat 2013). Genetic interventions take place without the child's participation, anticipating its agreement and not presenting it with any rationales. When a child is the object of genetic interventions, the child is not only not in a position to relate to them during their application, but is also not able to distance itself from them as much as it would be able to from the effects of rearing. The best example of this is the decision of sex selction of progeny (see Chapter 3). If I am born a woman, I can take advantage of my sexuality and understand it in various ways, but I cannot either fully distance myself from my sex or reject it. However, if I was reared in the manner that boys are reared, I could distance myself from this and reject it if it turned out to be inconsistent with my biological sex and self-understanding.

For the above reasons, Habermas claims that the genetic enhancement of offspring instrumentalises the parent-child relationship, which has a destabilising effect on their awareness of being free and unique people. In his view, the relationship between parents and child should be based on recognition of the otherness of a child who, rather than existing just to realise parental preferences, is a separate being from its parents, revealing its unique personality in interaction with its environment (Habermas 2008). Similar conclusions are reached by Sandel, who is keen to emphasise the importance of the child's relationship with its parents for its normal development (Sandel 2007). This relationship should be one of mutual trust based on the affirmation of the person who has been born, irrespective of their genetic makeup. This affirmation is expressed through parents' readiness to accept the gift of life unconditionally while being 'open to the unbidden', as the author writes (Sandel 2007).

This special relationship between parents and child is also subject to legal protection. Parental rights are, by definition, paternalistic. If it is accepted that parents care about their child's good, they are entrusted with relatively large freedom to decide what they consider to be for the good of their child. Children's rights are the responsibility of their parents until they possess first, partial, and later, full, legal capacity, thus Feinberg describes them as 'rights-in-trust' (Feinberg 1982). They are in fact the rights of future adults that have been entrusted to parents on the assumption that they will guard them while taking into account that they will in the future be fully autonomous individuals. In Feinberg's view, this requires of the parents that they be guided in their decisions by 'the child's right to an open future' (Feinberg 1982). By this, he understands that any parental decision should guarantee the child as many open opportunities that it could benefit from in the future as possible. When bringing up a child, parents should take decisions in such a manner as to leave the child as much freedom as possible to independently determine its life ideals when it is adult, including the opportunity to reject the parents' vision, at least to an extent. If this parental vision cannot be rejected and its formation cannot be actively participated in, as would be the case with biomedical interventions, this may provoke legitimate doubts.

9.7 Authentic identity – the issue of intentionality and individual expression

In this chapter, I have attempted to demonstrate that the reductionist naturalism the transhumanists invoke is incapable of offering us a full understanding of either ourselves or our moral experiences. The transhumanists, still firmly under the spell of instrumental reason, assume that humans can be reduced to the focus of objective scientific research and their nature can be manipulated. A deep understanding of our subjectivity is epistemologically inaccessible to scientific research, because our reason is deeply embedded in our nature (Habermas 2008; Spaemann 2017; Nagel 2012). An agent cannot be described completely objectively, that is, in isolation from the manner in which the agent interprets its own experiences and understands itself (Taylor 2001). In-depth articulation of our experiences takes into consideration that they are deeply embedded in intentionality, that is, our attitude towards ourselves and the world. For, rather than living in a world of facts, we live in a world of choices to which we assign specific meanings and values. Our understanding of ourselves not only influences what we are experiencing, but also how we experience this and what we understand from these experiences.

Naturalists would like to reduce reflection to a neutral description of our behaviours or desires, an approach which is at odds with the concept of reflection as an active attitude of will capable of influencing our actions and changing our feelings or desires. In other words, a scientificistic worldview overlooks an extremely important aspect of the contemporary conception of our identity – authenticity based on self-expression and autocreation, which are associated today with a fulfilled life. It is therefore finally worth taking a closer look at the notion of authentic identity and its importance for the comprehension of morality.

9.7.1 Numerical identity and qualitative identity

Philosophers today refer to two distinct concepts of identity – qualitative identity and numerical identity. The concept of identity accepted by radical naturalists is termed *qualitative*, because it is atomic empirical data (relating to quality and impressions) that are ontologically original. Identity is secondary to empirical data, because it is a synthesis of them that constitutes a constructive addition, giving us a sense of our 'self'. A person's identity therefore becomes, according to radical naturalism, a kind of a fiction generated by the brain to integrate our impressions and experiences. This conception is derived from John Locke's conception of punctual subjectivity. Locke conceived subjectivity as a radically disengaged ego based on a continuity of memories guaranteeing psychological continuity across time. This conception attracted extensive criticism from such philosophers as Hume (see Spaemann 2017; Taylor 2001). Aware of this criticism, Derek Parfit modified Locke's conception by envisaging a psychological conception of identity based on pure mental connectedness instead of mental continuity (Parfit 1987, 206).

Qualitative conceptions of identity are contrasted with *numerical* conceptions, which presuppose the continuity of existence of a subject of impressions which is ontologically prior in relation to impressions (Spaemann 2017). Change in a person's qualitative constitution does not change their identity according to this stance, which guarantees the existence of on *a priori* unity of identity. Numerical identity is bound up with the continuity of existence of a living being and can be understood in two ways: naturalistic (organic continuity) or antinaturalistic (organic-spiritual). In both cases, one's identity is determined at the moment it comes into being, which, in the case of humans, is the moment of conception, when an individualised living organism comes into being (DeGrazia 2012).

The difference between the two kinds of numerical identity resides in the fact that, in the naturalistic version, a distinction is made between the biological existence of a human organism and its socio-personal existence, which is bound up with its *narrative identity*, which is, in a sense, a superstructure arching over instrumentally conceived organic functioning. The biological conception of numerical identity is, in this case, a necessary condition, but is insufficient for a narrational identity to emerge. Narrational identity is conceived as an individual conception of ourselves – an autobiography we write based on what we regard to be valuable which incorporates our social roles, meaningful relationships, choices and actions. In the antinaturalistic version, it is presupposed that it is impossible to separate personal from biological existence (Spaemann 2017), while narrative identity, which comes into being in dialogue with others and is associated with mental life, is on every occasion deeply embedded in corporeal life. From this perspective, our self is not something that is possessed in the way that we possess our organs or qualities. Rather than being the sum of our qualities, it is the mode of our life in which our qualitative constitution is expressed. It is related to a specific location and time of living and determines the uniqueness of our person. Numerical identity is not dependent on self-knowledge, because part of our identity is also comprised of those events which we do not remember (like our birth) or are not aware of (e.g. our suppressed traumas).

The assumption that certain biological predispositions will increase the likelihood of moral judgements and actions that are consistent with them (Douglas 2008) is based on a qualitative conception of identity. If we assume that the self is a fiction integrating mental states, what these states are and where they come from is of no significance to our sense of being ourselves. The charge of inauthenticity directed at biomedical enhancements presupposes the existence of a genuine 'self' preceding such enhancements, so it makes sense if we adopt a numerical conception of identity. Authenticity is most frequently understood as 'being true to oneself and presenting oneself to others as one truly is' (DeGrazia 2012, 75). We express ourselves through our actions, decisions and choices. Inauthenticity involving self-deception or the deception of others may be expressed, for example, through our pretending to be someone we are not to achieve social acceptance. However, as DeGrazia rightly points out, inauthenticity need not be the result of dishonesty. It may also arise from the failure of our autonomy, when, for example, we succumb to addictions or environmental influences by acting in a conformist manner (DeGrazia 2012). In the author's view, biomedical enhancements, whether they be postnatal or prenatal, have no influence on numerical identity, which is independent of the changing qualitative constitution (DeGrazia 2005, 2012). They can only influence our narrational identity, but this is not ethically problematic, in his view, if we reject the assumption that there is some set of qualities that constitute the core of our personalities (the essentialist approach) – who we are and how we understand ourselves.

The problem lies in the fact that DeGrazia sees no difference between biomedical self-enhancement and being enhanced by genetic interventions of the others, because his conception of narrative identity as a superstructure arching over biological identity varies little from the approach adopting the conception of qualitative identity. In his view, it is of no concern to our identity whether what we relate to in it is the outcome of a genetic lottery, our actions or those of others. However, as I have been attempting to demonstrate by invoking Habermas' argumentation, if our qualities are the outcome of someone's else's intervention and therefore the expression of someone else's preferences and value system with regard to the qualities we should possess, this is in fact important to our identity (cf. Bolt 2007).

The earlier discussed Kantian concept of the moral agent is bound up with the antinatural version of the numerical conception of identity. When we perceive ourselves as identical with ourselves across time, this happens because we not only understand ourselves as beings to which something happens, but, first and foremost, as beings who initiate events and cause something to happen as well as the creators of their own ideas and lives. This approach appears to accord with our common understanding of ourselves and, according to Korsgaard, by no means requires the adoption of powerful metaphysical assumptions (like the concept of the transcendental self adopted by Kant). The only requirement is acknowledgement of the practical integrity of the personality in action (Korsgaard 1989). It is worth adding at this juncture, after Spaemann, that perceiving ourselves as the beginning of events is a pragmatic fiction enabling us to act (Spaemann 2017). For we never begin from scratch. Our action is always situated in some context, as was mentioned before. However, our 'self' is not in this case a fiction, because it refers to a real, concrete being living in a specific space and time, the subject of intentional acts. Intentionality not only presupposes that we are able to identify our own desires, but that we are able to take a stance on them, and thus influence them and transform them into rationales motivating action. It is also of concern to us where these desires come from.

9.7.2 Intentionality: two levels of volition and the alienation of the will

The problem of intentionality, crucial for the issue of authentic identity, can be better understood by evoking the analytical distinction between two volitional levels presented by Harry Frankfurt (Frankfurt 1971). By evoking the example of a drug addict, Frankfurt not only shows that our desires can come into conflict with each other, but also that we will fail to understand that conflict if we fail to indicate that those desires lie on different levels. Frankfurt terms the powerful physiological need felt by a drug addict to take another dose of a drug a first-order volition. This same person may also desire to free himself from this addiction, a phenomenon Frankfurt calls a second-order volition. A second-order volition refers to the first-order volition – for the drug addict desires not to desire the drug. The lack of coherence between these two levels of desire leads to alienation of the will, making the person, in Frankfurt's view, not fully autonomous. Another example of such an alienation of the will is the earlier mentioned protagonist from *A Clockwork Orange*, who, as the result of an enhancement experiment feels aversion on a physiological level (first-order volition) towards aggression, yet on a reflexive level (second-order volition) still desires to do evil.

The above example from Korsgaard would appear to suggest that if I were to conclude, with all my perceptual faculties intact, that the most effective method of mastering my fear would be to take suitable medication enabling me to take an important decision demanded by a particular situation, then that pharmacological stimulation would not undermine the autonomous nature of my action,[10] for my personal moral integrity would be preserved. However, if I had been genetically conditioned to not feel fear, that would not mean in the least that I possesses the virtue of courage, because my inability to feel fear would not be the outcome of my desire to be brave for a specific, legitimate purpose. What is more, being fearless would even prevent me of developing a courageous character for which anxiety plays an important role. I could even suffer like Wagner's Siegfried due to feeling no fear.

By assuming that certain biological predispositions increase the likelihood of moral judgements and actions that are consistent with them, it is presupposed that the sole role of reflection is to integrate our desires, granting us a sense of our mental states being relatively coherent. This approach presupposes that second-order volitions accommodate themselves to first-order volitions. Reason here performs the function of a 'press secretary', justifying our desires and the actions they cause (Haidt 2001). This concept does not accord with the concept presented by Frankfurt, who assumes that 'a person is free to have the will he wants' (Frankfurt 1971, 20). Therefore, it is not only a lack of compatibility between first- and second-order volitions that leads to us feeling alienation

---

10 However, self-enhancement using neurocognitive interventions could also lead to alienation of the will when this results in one being cut off from one's own emotions, or when they are administered to conform to others' needs or social norms that we mistakenly perceive to be our own (Elliott 1999, 2003; Bolt 2007; President's Council on Bioethics 2003).

of will, but also our awareness that their coincidence is not our own doing, as Frankfurt notices (Frankfurt 1971). Frankfurt's reasoning can be illustrated using the example of action under the influence of hypnosis, where both volitional orders would coincide but not through any conscious design. It would be difficult to regard such a hypnotised person as an autonomous agent if that person did not remember, following hypnosis, that he is acting under its influence (a situation of this type could also be grounds for excluding him from bearing legal responsibility for the act).

A somewhat different problem is presented by situations of self-deception that lead to a reconciliation of the two levels of volition, and, although this coincidence is of their own making, it can be acknowledged that, since they were under the influence of illusions, they were not completely free. This last example shows that the channelling of our desires does not equate to an act of will, as Spaemann writes (Spaemann 2017). Second-order volitions do not alter the content of first-order volitions, nor are they in competition with each other. Spaemann compares second-instance volition to a review panel that may send back a verdict given by a court of lower instance for reconsideration by that court, pointing out various oversights without changing the content of the verdict (Spaemann 2017). Therefore, the directing of will, rather than being a second-order act of will, is actually the *attitude* that Kant termed good will (a specific conception of respect toward moral law), and St Augustine called the order of love (*ordo amoris*).

9.7.3 Ordo amoris: the inner shaping of the will

The emotions transhumanists would like to correct, indicating their correlation with undesirable behaviours, can also be well correlated with desirable behaviours, as Peter Strawson notes (Strawson 1962). This can be exemplified by the aforementioned aversion that can be correlated with both displaying dislike for people different from us and displaying an aversion toward brutal violence. The transhumanists' error lies in a mechanistic comprehension of human action, where certain emotions are perceived as the causes of certain behaviours, leading transhumanists to fall into the illusion that it is possible to control human behaviour by manipulating people's emotions or predispositions. This, however, is an unwarranted simplification that enables scientists to erroneously assume that they are capable of explaining anything using the laws of physics (Nagel 2012). Human action can be interpreted differently, as I have been showing in this chapter, by not identifying emotions in any way with their causes. We are then in a position to state that my anger, rather than causing my unpleasant reaction toward another person, became apparent in my behaviour – in other words, that I expressed my anger through my action.

Emotions and feelings are neither good nor bad in themselves. It is rather such issues as what stance we take towards them, what we do with them and which emotions or feelings guide our actions that are subjected to moral assessment. It is a truism today to claim that we need our emotions to fully understand and express ourselves, and this also applies to moral action. Many perfectionistic ethics, especially in the Judeo-Christian tradition, stress that self-improvement or education, rather than leading to the suppression of feelings or emotions, should result in an inner transformation in which these emotions and feelings will be ordered and channelled in an appropriate manner. Rational philosophy from Plato to Descartes assigned this task of ordering the emotions to reason.

Another path is taken by the Christian tradition developed by St Augustine, in whose view access to the most vital moral sources should be sought with one's heart. He described the virtue enabling us to live well as the order of love (*ordo amoris*) (Augustine 2000, 1575). Continuing this line of reason, which was also developed by Pascal, Max Scheler advanced the thesis that there is an objectively correct order of *movements of love and hate*, which constitutes the spiritual aspect of human life (Scheler 1999). What is of concern here is man's axiological structure (Stróżewski 2013), which may be termed ethos, that is, the rules of the value preferences describing our outlook on the world and our manner of participating in it. According to Scheler's concept, this structure is objective, radically individualistic, hierarchical, dynamic, complex and teleological, and 'may be characterised by both the harmony and disharmony of its elements' (Stróżewski 2013, 258). Taylor terms this structure an orientation toward good which is the basis of our identity (Taylor 2001). *Ordo amoris* is neither a representation of the hierarchy of our natural desires according to the criterion of their intensity nor an ordering of natural desires according to purely rational reasoning, but rather a personal orientation toward good integrating rational, emotional and corporeal factors. Ethos, rather than be given to man, is *assigned* to him. It is at once potential and actual – both normative and descriptive in nature. Living in harmony with oneself involves living in harmony with the order of one's heart. It requires the ability to bring this order to fruition by living one's life, something often termed self-realisation. As Władysław Stróżewski notes, 'Man-the creator is above all a creator of his own self' (Stróżewski 2013, 266), his axiological structure is dialogic and dynamic. It is created throughout one's life and in interaction with others. Creating oneself and living in harmony with oneself therefore not only require autonomy, but also the recognition of others (Taylor 2001; Spaemann 2017).

9.8 Concluding remarks

In this chapter, I have attempted to demonstrate that the idea of genetically enhancing human nature is based on a reductionist conception of the moral agent, action and identity that fails to offer us a satisfactorily deep concept of self-understanding. This is why Habermas believes that a naturalistic vision of the world reduced to physical facts, rather than being science, is poor metaphysics (Habermas 2008). The transhumanists' naturalistic assumptions are derived from a Darwinian standpoint that perceives the one in a passive manner (as an object) where freedom is understood to be a kind of experience, and moral virtues are reduced to species utility. This is incompatible with both the Kantian and neo-Aristotelian approach to morality, where the one is understood in terms of agency (as an agent) whose freedom is a necessary condition, while virtues are perceived as values in themselves (internal to a virtuous life, which cannot be understood without them) requiring active and reflexive engagement that cannot be derived from biological properties or described in these terms.

Neither Aristotle's nor Kant's concepts exert such an effect on us when presented in their original form rooted in metaphysics. Nevertheless, the insights into what and who we are contained in these great ethical doctrines would appear to better correspond with how we understand ourselves. For the philosophical thought derived from these traditions offers a deeper interpretation of our actions, desires and convictions as well as the meanings we confer on these. A fuller understanding of ourselves as autonomous agents engaged in self-development and sincere self-expression provides as with major arguments against the idea of enhancement using prenatal genetic interventions which should not be ignored if such values as freedom or authenticity are meaningful to us.

Aldous Huxley expressed a special attachment to these values in his famous dystopic novel *Brave New World*, in which he presented the bleak vision of interference in evolution postulated by his brother mentioned at the beginning of this chapter – Julian Huxley. The writer presented a world driven by the idea of standardising humankind established by means of an artificial reproduction programme and conditioning directed at the creation of socialised human beings (i.e. those who would take pleasure from their social destiny). The civilisation he describes, which 'has chosen machinery and medicine and happiness' (Huxley 2000, 395) has no need for moral virtues, traditionally conceived, because only unstable societies need heroism, nobility or enlightenment. The utility of human existence is thrown into doubt in the novel by a desire for freedom, but not just the freedom to be happy, rather the freedom to be happy in one's own way.

Similar fears about the idea of making people happy using the forces of reason are presented by Stanisław Lem in his short story *Altruizine OR A True Account of How Bonhomius the Hermetic Hermit Tried to Bring About Universal Happiness, and What Came of It*. The story's main protagonist wishes to make people altruistic by administering a wonder drug to them called Altruizine which increases empathy in people within a range of fifty yards:

> According to its discoverer, ALTRUIZINE will insure the untrammeled reign of Brotherhood, Cooperation and Compassion in any society, since the neighbors of a happy man must share his happiness, and the happier he, the happier perforce they, so it is entirely in their own interest that they wish him nothing but the best. Should he suffer any hurt, they will rush to help at once, so as to spare themselves the pain induced by his (Lem 1974, 136).

However, the outcome of rendering 'others happy by revolutionary means' (Lem 1974, 139) turns out to be the opposite of what was expected, because strong empathy stripped of any deeper moral motivation on a reflexive level leads to persecution and slaughter aimed at minimising empathetically experienced suffering and maximising empathetically experienced pleasure. The protagonist came to understand from this experience that happiness, like moral virtues, can only be arrived at by following a path of one's own that requires reflexive engagement.

Acknowledgements

This text is a combined and broadly extended version of two papers previously published in Polish: Soniewicka M (2015) Biologiczne podstawy moralności w kontekście genetycznego ulepszania człowieka. In: Stelmach J, Brożek B, Kurek Ł, Eliasz K (ed) Naturalizacja prawa: interpretacje. Wolters Kluwer, Warszawa 2015, pp. 279-298; Soniewicka M (2015) Transhumanizm: kilka uwag na temat filozoficznych źródeł sporu o ideę biomedycznego ulepszania moralnego. Ethics in Progress, 6(1) 2015: 202-213. Translated from Polish into English by Philip Palmer.

References

Agar N (1998) Liberal Eugenics. Public Affairs Quarterly 12:137–155.

Angrist M (2010) Here Is a Human Being. At the Dawn of Personal Genomics. Harper Perennial, New York.

Annas G (2009) American Bioethics. Crossing Human Rights and Health Law Boundaries. Oxford University Press, Oxford & New York.

Arendt H (1998) The Human Condition. The University of Chicago Press, Chicago & London.

Arendt H (2006) Eichmann in Jerusalem: A Report on the Banality of Evil. Penguin Classics, New York.

Aristotle (2011) Nicomachean Ethics (trans: BartlettRC, CollinsSD). Chicago University Press, Chicago & London.

Arnhart L (2010) Can virtue be genetically engineered? Politics and the Life Sciences 29(1):79–81.

Audi R (2013) Moral Perception. Princeton University Press, Princeton.

Audi R (2014) Naturalism, Normativity & Explanation. Copernicus Center Press, Krakow.

Audi R (2015) Reasons, Rights, and Values. Cambridge University Press, Cambridge.

Audi R (2016) Means, Ends, and Persons. The Meaning and Psychological Dimensions of Kant's Humanity Formula. Oxford University Press, Oxford.

Augustine St (2000) The City of God (trans: DodsM). The Modern Library, New York.

Augustine St (2008) The Confessions. (trans: ChadwickH). Oxford University Press, Oxford.

Bashford A (2013) Julian Huxley's transhumanism. In: Turda M (ed) Crafting Humans. From Genesis to Eugenics and Beyond. Vandenhoeck & Ruprecht, Göttingen, pp. 153–167.

Birnbacher D (2008) Posthumanity, Transhumanism and Human Nature. In: Gordijn B, Chadwick R (eds) Medical Enhancement and Posthumanity. Springer, Berlin, pp. 95–106.

Bolt LLE (2007) True to Oneself? Broad and Narrow Ideas on Authenticity in the Enhancement Debate. Theoretical Medicine and Bioethics 28:285–300.

Bostrom N (2008) Why I Want to be a Posthuman When I Grow Up. In: Gordijn B, Chadwick R (eds) Medical Enhancement and Posthumanity. Springer, Berlin, pp. 107–137.

Buchanan A (2011) Beyond Humanity? Oxford University Press, Oxford.

Buchanan A, Brock DW, Daniels N, Wikler D (2007) From Chance to Choice: Genetics and Justice. Cambridge University Press, Cambridge & New York.

Burgess A (1995) A Clockwork Orange. W. W. Norton & Company, New York.

Chesterton GK (1908) Heretics. John Lane: The Bodley Head, London.

Churchland P (2012) Braintrust: What Neuroscience Tells Us about Morality. Princeton University Press, Princeton.

Collins FC (2006) The Language of God. A Scientist Presents Evidence for Belief. Free Press, New York.

Davis DS (1997) Genetic Dilemmas and the Child's Right to an Open Future. Hastings Center Report 27(2):7–15.

DeGrazia D (2005) Enhancement Technologies and Human Identity. Journal of Medicine and Philosophy 30:261–283.

DeGrazia D (2012) Creation Ethics. Reproduction, Genetics, and Quality of Life. Oxford University Press, Oxford.

Devlin AJ (ed) (1986) Conversations with Tennessee Williams, University Press of Mississippi.

de Waal F (2016) Primates and Philosophers: How Morality Evolved. Princeton University Press, Princeton.

Douglas T (2008) Moral Enhancement. Journal of Applied Philosophy 25(3):228–245.

Dworkin R (2013) Religion Without God. Harvard University Press, Cambridge.

Elliott C (1999) A philosophical disease: Bioethics, culture and identity. Routledge, New York.

Elliott C (2003) Better than well: American medicine meets the American dream. Norton, New York.

Feinberg J (1982) The Child's Right to an Open Future. In: Aiken W, LaFollette H (eds) Whose Child? Children's Rights, Parental Authority, and State Power. Rowman and Littlefield, Totowa, NJ, pp. 124–153.

Frankfurt HG (1971) Freedom of the will and the concept of a person. Journal of Philosophy 68:5–20.

Fukuyama F (2002) Our Posthuman Future. Consequences of the Biotechnological Revolution. Farrar, Straus and Giroux, New York.

Greene J (2013) Moral tribes. Emotion, Reason, and the Gap Between Us and Them. The Penguin Press, New York.

Habermas J (2003) The Future of Human Nature. Polity Press, Cambridge.

Habermas J (2008) Between Naturalism and Religion. Polity Press, Cambridge.

Haidt J (2001) The Emotional Dog and its Rational Tail: A Social Intuitionist Approach to Moral Judgment. Psychological Review 108(4):814–834.

Haidt J (2013) The Righteous Mind: Why Good People Are Divided by Politics and Religion. Vintage, New York.

Harris J (2007) Enhancing Evolution. The Ethical Case for Making Better People. Princeton University Press, Princeton, NJ.

Harris J (2011) Moral Enhancement and Freedom. Bioethics 25(2):102–111.

Huxley A (2000) Brave New World. RosettaBooks, New York.

Huxley J (1968) Transhumanism. Journal of Humanistic Psychology 8(1):73–76.

Jonas H (1987) Macht oder Ohnmacht der Subjektivität. Insel Verlag, Frankfurt am Main.

Kamm FM (2013) What is and What is Not Wrong with Enhancement. Evaluating Sandel's View. Bioethical Prescriptions To Create, End, Choose, and Improve Lives. Oxford University Press, Oxford & New York.

Kant I (2000) Critique of Pure Reason, GuyerP, Wood AW (trans and ed). Cambridge University Press, Cambridge.

Kant I (2002) Groundwork for the Metaphysics of Morals (trans: WoodAW). Yale University Press, New Haven & London.

Kass LR (2002) Life, Liberty and the Defense of Dignity. The Challenge of Bioethics. Encounter Books, San Francisco.

Kidd C, Palmeri H, Aslin RN (2012) Rational snacking: Young children's decision-making on the marshmallow task is moderated by beliefs about environmental reliability. Cognition 126(2013):109–114.

Kołakowski L (2014) Niepewność epoki demokracji. Znak, Krakow.

Korsgaard CM (1989) Personal Identity and the Unity of Agency: A Kantian Response to Parfit. Philosophy & Public Affairs 18(2):101–132.

Korsgaard CM (1992) The Sources of Normativity, The Tanner Lectures on Human Values, delivered at Clare Hall, Cambridge University, November 16 and 17, 1992.

Kramer MH (2009) Moral Realism as a Moral Doctrine. John Wiley & Sons, Oxford.

Lem S (1974) Altruizine OR A True Account of How Bonhomius the Hermetic Hermit Tried to Bring About Universal Happiness, and a What Came of It. In: Lem S (auth) The Cyberiad. Fables for the Cybernetic Age (trans: KandelM). The Seabury Press, New York.

Lewis CS (2001) The Abolition of Man or Reflections on education with special reference to the teaching of English in the upper forms of schools. HarperOne, New York.

MacIntyre A (2007) After Virtue, 2nd ed. Notre Dame University Press, Notre Dame, IN.

McDowell J (2002) Two Sorts of Naturalism. In:McDowell J (auth) Mind, Value, and Reality. Harvard University Press, Cambridge, MA & London, pp. 167–197.

Mill JS (2003) Utilitarianism and On Liberty. Including Mill's 'Essay on Bentham' and selections from the writings of Jeremy Bentham and John Austin, 2nd ed. Warnock M (ed). Blackwell Publishing, Oxford.

Milton J (2000) Paradise Lost. Paradise Lost, Leonard J (ed). Penguin Books, London.

Mitchel CB, Pellegrino ED,Elshtain JB, Kilner JF,Rae S (1974) Biotechnology and the Human Good. Georgtown University Press, Washington, DC.

Nagel T (2012) Mind and Cosmos. Why the Materialist Neo-Darwinian Conception of Nature Is Almost Certainly False. Oxford University Press, Oxford.

Parfit D (1987) Reasons and Persons. Clarendon Press, Oxford.

Persson I, Savulescu J (2008) The Perils of Cognitive Enhancement and the Urgent Imperative to Enhance the Moral Character of Humanity. Journal of Applied Philosophy 25(3):166–167.

Persson I, Savulescu J (2012) Moral Enhancement, Freedom and God Machine. The Monist 95(3):399–421.

Pico della Mirandola G (2012) Oration on the Dignity of Man: A New Translation and Commentary, Borghesi F, Papio M, Riva M (eds). Cambridge University Press, Cambridge.

Piłat R (2013) Refleksja i kompetencja moralna. In:Piłat R (auth) Powinność i samowidza. Wydawnictwo UKSW, Warszawa, pp. 169–188.

Plantinga A (2011) Where the Conflict Really Lies: Science, Religion, and Naturalism. Oxford University Press, New York.

President's Council on Bioethics (2003) Beyond Therapy: Biotechnology and the Pursuit of Happiness. President's Council on Bioethics, Washington, DC.

Pugh J (2015) Autonomy, Natality and Freedom: A Liberal Re-Examination of Habermas in the Enhancement Debate. Bioethics 29(3): 145–152.

Ramsey P (1970) Fabricated Man. The Ethics of Genetic Control. Yale University Press, New Haven, London.

Sandel M (2007) The Case against Perfection. Ethics in the Age of Genetic Engineering. The Belknap Press of Harvard University Press, Cambridge, MA & London.

Savulescu J,Persson I (2012) Unfit for the Future: The Need for Moral Enhancement. Oxford University Press, Oxford.

Savulescu J, Sandberg A, Kahane G (2011) Well-Being and Enhancement, In: Savulescu J, ter Meulen R, Kahane G (eds) Enhancing Human Capacities. Wiley–Blackwell, Oxford, pp. 48–88.

Schaefer GO, Kahane G, Savulescu J (2014) Autonomy and Enhancement. Neuroethics 7:123–136.

Scheler M (1991) Die Stellung des Menschen im Kosmos. Bouvier Verlag, Bonn.

Scheler M (1999) Ordo amoris w znaczeniu opisowym i normatywnym (trans:Czapliński W). Kwartalnik filozoficzny 26(4): 123–158.

Singer P (2011) Practical Ethics. Cambridge University Press, Cambridge–New York.

Soniewicka M (2017) 'Promissory' naturalism – comments on moral sources. Polish Law Review 3(1): 259–275.

Spaemann R (2017) Persons: The Difference between 'Someone' and 'Something'. Oxford Studies in Theological Ethics. Oxford University Press, Oxford.

Strawson P (1962) Freedom and Resentment, In: Watson G (ed) Proceedings of the British Academy 48: 1–25.

Stróżewski W (2013) Axiological Structure if Human Being. In: Kołodziejczyk ST (ed) Existence, Sense and Values. Essays in Metaphysics and Phenomenology. Peter Lang, Frankfurt am Main.

Taylor C (2001) Sources of The Self. The Making of the Modern Identity. Harvard University Press, Cambridge, MA.

Tomasello M (2009) Why We Cooperate. The MIT Press, Boston University Press, Princeton.

Walker M (2009) Enhancing genetic virtue: A project for twenty-first century humanity? Politics and the Life Sciences 28(2): 27–47.

Wojciech Lewandowski

10 Genetic enhancement and moral perfection

To have a better life, to be a better person – these are one of the most often analysed human aspirations in ethics. Thanks to advances in the biomedical sciences which allow us to not only combat diseases, but also provide people with additional, unprecedented opportunities, both of these pursuits have gained a completely new perspective. This is the context surrounding the modern discussions on human enhancement. Most often, this category is referred to the augmentation of human capabilities above and beyond the usual level. This could mean any change on a person's biological or psychological level that would increase species-specific capabilities above a certain statistically determined level (Savulescu, Sanders & Kahane 2011, 7). The scope of human enhancement includes cognitive enhancement, aiming at expanding memory or increasing intelligence, enhancing mood, allowing the adjustment of the intensity and type of experienced emotions, physical augmentation, including increased height, strength or stamina, as well as extending human life. a new category of human enhancement, which this article is devoted to, is moral enhancement. The greatest hopes among the currently analysed methods of human enhancement, aside from pharmaceutical and surgical interventions, are raised by genetic enhancement, also including eugenic selection.

There are two competing positions in the discussion on improving the human species. The first, called transhumanism, says that the enhancement of human species should be promoted. Based on this position, the obligation – or at least the admissibility – is justified of using available knowledge and resources for better men, or beings better than men, to live in the future. The second stance, referred to as bioconservatism, considers enhancing the human species as unacceptable. Striving for a better life and being a better person should take place in the traditional way, for example, through upbringing and one's own efforts.

One of the arguments used against human enhancement by bioconservatists is a conviction based on traditional perfectionism, that the fundamental aspect of human excellence is moral perfection. To be a good person, one does not need to have a great memory, super strength, or live for 200 years. The idea is to live one's life as well as possible. Focusing on enhancement will not only not help, but it may destroy our ability to live autonomously. Transhumanists respond that moral refinement using pharmaceuticals, surgical intervention, or genetic selection and modification, constitutes only a correction of what remains imperfect in the human condition, while retaining the valuable achievements of evolution. The possibility of future existence of physically, mentally and morally enhanced individuals may, according to them, represent the last stage of humanity's moral development. The issue of moral enhancement using biomedical measures seems to be the critical point of the entire discussion. On the one hand, it allows transhumanists to fend off some of the allegations made by the supporters of bioconservatism, and on the other – it is an attempt to take some of the moral intuitions referred to by the latter into consideration.

In this chapter, I wish to answer the question of whether it is possible to develop a compromise stance, reconciling a certain version of the transhumanist project enhancing the human condition with a traditional vision of human development, as an individual and autonomous pursuit of moral perfection. Due to the complexity of the ongoing discussion on this subject, this question will be confined to the genetic enhancement of future persons in the context of reproductive decision-making. I will begin by presenting the way in which the category of moral enhancement appeared in the discussion on improving the human condition. The second part of the text presents the transhumanist arguments for biomedical human enhancement in the moral dimension, together with an account of the dispute over the nature of such enhancement. The third part relates four issues connected with the matter of moral perfection to the problem of genetic enhancement: the issue of the right to imperfection, the justification of sacrifices, the moral judgement of an agent's characteristics, and the reasons for moral enhancement.

10.1 Procreative beneficence

Julian Savulescu is one of the most fervent supporters of the genetic enhancement of future people. In a 2001 article, *Procreative Beneficence*, he provides a justification for the moral obligation to conduct genetic selection in order to bring the birth of children with better-than-average genetic endowment. Savulescu begins his argument with the following example. Four embryos have been created as a result of *in vitro* fertilization. Let us assume that a test exists which allows to conclude that if the embryo possesses type A and B alleles, the likelihood of the child's intelligence quotient being above 140 as a result of ordinary education is above 50%. However, if the embryo has type C and D alleles, the probability of achieving such IQ us much lower. According to Savulescu, in such a hypothetical situation, it would be a rational and legitimate decision to employ such a test and utilise its results to select the embryo with a better genetic endowment for implantation (Savulescu 2001, 414).

Reasonableness in relation to the above example is mainly found in using all available information to choose the option with the largest likelihood of achieving the best result. It would both be unreasonable not to perform the test, as well as carry it out, but fail to utilise its results. According to Savulescu, the situation of a parent is hence like that of a participant to a game of chance[1]. The premise of this argument is that having a baby, aside from other important moral and social reasons, constitutes a benefit for the potential parents, which justifies taking action aiming at the child's conception. Striving to achieve this benefit appears to be subject to every condition of rationality. Deciding between having a more talented and less talented child, a parent would act to their detriment by selecting the latter or not trying to find out about the available opportunities. Adopting such an assumption does not necessarily imply that the motivation is in itself selfish, that a less able child would be loved less, whereas a more capable one would be under constant pressure to succeed. If it turned out that, despite the increased likelihood of achieving above 140 IQ, a child would have an average intelligence quotient, it would still be loved. R.M. Green justifies this by saying that 'parental love almost always prevails' (Green 2007, 114). Parents who dream of a daughter do not have to love their son less, and parents who dream of an outstanding athlete do not have to think less of a child lacking any sporting talent. Genetic enhancement can provide some added value, allowing to maximise the expected benefit of the parents, but without determining their attitudes toward the child. In addition, the requirements of rationality do not restrict the parents' reproductive autonomy. According to Savulescu, if parents had any reasons to choose an embryo with a predisposition to asthma for implantation, and other considerations did not preclude it, they could do it. According to proponents of genetic enhancement, it would be difficult to justify only dependence on blind chance and failure to take advantage of the opportunities provided by progress in genetics.

Genetic enhancement is justified not only by the requirements of rationality in the pursuit of one's self-interest, but also by moral requirements. What differentiates a parent from a participant to a game of chance, is that parents do not play to win only for themselves, but also for their child. In this context,

---

[1] M. Hayry (Häyry 2010, 236–240) thinks that this is just one of the equivalent ways to encompass reality. Not taking advantage of the test does not have to be regarded as irrational if one considers other arguments than increasing the probability of winning. See Chapter 2.

Savulescu indicates the moral dimension of genetic enhancement by formulating the Principle of Procreative Beneficence.

> Procreative Beneficence: couples (or single reproducers) should select the child, of the possible children they could have, who is expected to have the best life, or at least as good a life as the others, based on the relevant, available information (Savulescu2001, 415).[2]

The rationale for this principle is based, on the one hand, on one of the solutions to Parfit's 'non-identity problem', and on the other – on the argument about the absence of a morally significant difference between treatment and enhancement. The 'non-identity problem' formulated by Parfit is expressed in the question, whether an action can be rated as better or worse for persons whose identity depends on our decisions (Parfit 1986, 361–364). In accordance with the traditional stance, the effects of alternative actions can be compared only if there is someone for whom our action would be better or worse. Most moral assessments pertain to actions performed in respect of already existing people, therefore comparing the possible effects of these actions does not pose a problem. Possible difficulties may relate only to estimating the value of individual effects. It is different in the case of actions that result in the creation of new people. The possible effects of the decision to have a child in the near or far future cannot be compared in the same way, because either choice would result in bringing a different child to this world. According to Parfit, none of these alternatives is better or worse for anyone. To conceive a child with a lesser expected quality of life is not worse for it, because the alternative would be for the child never to exist. To conceive a child with a better expected quality of life is not better for it, as it is not possible to indicate any other possibility of existence with a worse quality of life. Therefore, Parfit asserts to use impersonal principles that disregard personal identity when making comparisons concerning future persons, whose identity depends on our decisions. In accordance with these principles, a better action is one which results in more happiness or that which makes life worth living, regardless of who is the person enjoying this life. The Principle of Procreative Beneficence is such a rule – based on the category of a 'better life'. Living with a higher intelligence quotient is better than living with a lower intelligence quotient, even if it is not better for the same being[3].

---

2   Savulescu and Kahane present aslightly modified version of this principle (Savulescu & Kahane 2009, 274).

3   Savulescu does not directly favour the impersonal justification of the Principle of Procreative Beneficence, allowing to have it based on the so-called Wide Person-Affecting Principle, which imposes the selection of such an option, that would be better for a certain person, than the alternative for another person. (Savulescu & Kahane 2009,

The second element that constitutes the rationale for the obligation to ensure better life for future children is to reject the moral difference between genetic enhancement and uncontroversial therapeutic activities. According to the proponents of this stance, one cannot indicate a clear moral difference between gene therapy and improving human genome, as there is no moral difference between wearing glasses and using binoculars (Harris 2007, 20). It makes no significant difference what kind of measures do we use to raise human capabilities: mechanical, chemical, or genetic ones[4]. Most people do not oppose vaccines, though they should probably be regarded as an enhancement of the human immune system, and not therapy. Similarly, most people would not mind if it were discovered how to genetically modify human organisms so as to be resistant to AIDS or various types of cancers, instead of inventing a vaccine for these diseases (Harris 2007, 21–22).

The Principle of Procreative Beneficence has met with considerable criticism. The emerging allegations concerned, among others, that it was too demanding for potential parents (Herissone-Kelly 2006, 166–169), that the category of 'the best life', on which it is based, seems vague (Parker 2007, 279–280), that it cannot be reconciled with unconditional parental love, which requires to accept every child as a gift (Sandel 2009, 47–50), or that it leads to a reduction of the child's autonomy. One way to rebut these allegations is to demonstrate that they do not apply to moral enhancement (Douglas 2008, 228–229).

10.2 Procreative altruism

Imagine that your child abuses a dog. Your attempts at explaining why it is bad, encouraging empathy, or even the threat of punishment, do not bring any results. Assume that there is a product whose application makes a child sensitive to the suffering of others. You administer the product and the child shortly comes to a sincere belief that hurting animals is bad, and can even provide compelling reasons in support of that judgement. Imagine that further biomedical progress

---

277) Savulescu's arguments for the necessity of moral enhancement, presented later in this chapter, imply, however, identical outcomes in the case of both the impersonal position, as well as the wide person-affecting position. The lack of aclear solution to the non-identity problem inclines certainauthors to completely reject the Principle of Procreative Beneficence (Bennett 2013). See also Chapters 4, 5 and 12.

4 According to Steven Rose, the ban of steroid use in sports or the use of memory-enhancing drugs is only the expression of a certain prejudice towards overcoming limitations, just as it was at the beginning of the scientific revolution (Rose 2006, 74).

allows to carry out procedures, which allow to permanently affect the moral condition of future children, for example through genetic selection of embryos or interference in the embryo's genetic material. Would the use of such procedures be acceptable?

The controversy surrounding genetic enhancement and the category of a 'better life' seem to pale in comparison to the need to improve the moral aspect of future people, as indicated by transhumanists. According to Persson and Savulescu, most of humanity's existence was spent living in relatively small and closed communities, with primitive technology that allowed us to influence only the immediate environment and future. The human psyche, common moral intuitions and typical behaviours were adapted to these conditions and remained so even when the development of science and technology completely changed human life. Global population has exceeded 7 billion individuals; people now use mass-produced high-tech devices. In this new reality, it is relatively easier to cause huge harm than bring about a comparable benefit. The existence of weapons of mass destruction makes it possible to harm millions of people by a relatively small group. In addition, catastrophic consequences, such as overpopulation or exhaustion of essential natural resources may be caused by an accumulation of the effects of individual actions. These problems cannot be solved on a purely technological level. According to Persson and Savulescu, humanity possesses the means to eliminate hunger or make clean energy available globally even today. The fact that these issues remain unsolved, in their opinion, is caused by pushing them to the outer rim of our moral consciousness (Persson & Savulescu 2012, 103). We care too little for people outside our immediate surroundings, especially if their number is very high, we treat negligence too leniently and pay to little attention to those effects of our actions that extend beyond the immediate future (*Ibid.* 104). Therefore, the human condition requires improvement not only in the cognitive dimension, but also in the moral one. Traditional methods of moral enhancement, based on moral upbringing or striving towards one's own virtues, are not sufficient. Progress made in terms of reflection on morality over the last two and a half thousand years seems to pale in comparison to technological and scientific progress (*Ibid.* 106). Modern people are still not sufficiently willing to make sacrifices for the benefit of the public good or future generations.

The argument of the inadequacy of natural moral dispositions towards modern conditions of life can also be referred to the problem of applying the Principle of Procreative Beneficence so defended by transhumanists. Human motivation in procreative decisions is adjusted to natural procreation. People care about the well-being of their own children. Therefore, if they had methods of genetically improving them, they would probably take advantage of them in order to ensure the best possible start for their offspring, as well as an advantage, regardless of the success, or even other people's detriment. The existence of people enhanced in terms of intelligence could, for example, lead to an unwarranted impairment of the situation of 'ordinary' people on the labour market or to their discrimination in other areas (Douglas 2008, 229). According to Katrien Devolder and Thomas Douglas, the Principle of Procreative Beneficence should, therefore, be widened.

> Procreative altruism: If couples (or single reproducers) have decided to have a child, and selection is possible, they have significant moral reason to select a child whose existence can be expected to contribute more to (or detract less from) the well-being of others than any alternative child they could have (Douglas & Devolder 2013, 403).

Among the features that affect the success of others, Douglas highlights dispositions associated with motivation towards morally valuable activities in particular. Therefore, the category of a 'better life', up until now based on the value of success, takes on a moral significance, which brings the concept of genetic enhancement closer to a traditional vision of moral excellence.

> A person morally enhances herself if she alters herself in a way that may reasonably be expected to result in her having morally better future motives, taken in sum, than she would otherwise have had (Douglas 2008, 229).

The above definition assumes the ability to compare a set of motivations that affect the actions of the person concerned, if they have been subjected to moral enhancement, and a set of motivations that person would possess without undergoing moral enhancement. This comparison does not apply as to whether that person would actually have better motivation towards morally valuable actions, but the probability of having such motivation. According to Douglas, it is possible to determine this probability on the basis of research on the biological underpinnings of aggression or racial bias. A reduction of the occurrence of such emotions in a given person could meet the definition of moral enhancement (*Ibid.* 231).

The concept of moral enhancement based on modifying human motivation was met with criticism even among authors generally favourable towards biomedical enhancement of man. John Harris presents three objections to this concept. Firstly, the primary cause of prejudice against certain social groups based on race, gender, and sexual orientation is not found on the emotional level, as aversion to spiders is, but involves feeding false beliefs about these groups. Preconceptions underlying morally bad actions should, therefore, be eliminated by employing methods of classical education and changes on a cognitive level (Harris 2010, 105). Secondly, even if the grounds for morally wrong actions are often nested in negative emotions, then the project of eliminating them or weakening their intensity seems to be very risky. Negative emotions occupy an important place in the moral life of man, and their elimination would probably adversely affect interpersonal relationships. Morality would not be possible without strong negative feelings towards those who hurt us or our loved ones (Ibid. 106). Thirdly, Harris sees moral biomedical enhancement as a threat to human freedom. Citing John Milton's 'Paradise Lost', he reminds that man is a moral entity, because they have been made '*Sufficient to have stood, though free to fall*' (Milton 2000, line 96ff). Without that possibility of collapse, a morally enhance person would only be an automaton devoid of autonomy, acting due to innate motivations, and not because of moral reasons.

Savulescu and Person include Harris's postulate not to disregard cognitive enhancement when defining moral enhancement, however, they also do not forgo the emotional aspect. Their definition is as follows:

> To be morally enhanced is to have those dispositions which make it more likely that you will arrive at the correct judgement of what it is right to do and more likely to act on that judgement (Persson & Savulescu 2010, 405).

In accordance with this definition, genetic enhancement in terms of morals would include both the development of cognitive and emotional capabilities, as well as dispositions for altruistic activities. Assuming the premises of preference utilitarianism, Savulescu and Persson state that an agent enhanced in these respects will be able to better estimate the consequences of their actions and their impact on other people's preferences. In addition, they will have the dispositions to act according to their own moral judgement, which allows to eliminate the problem of poor will. Finally, an enhanced agent will manifest the desire to sacrifice their own preferences in order to fulfil those of other people (*Ibid.* 406).

Savulescu and Persson reject Harris's argument that moral enhancement of human dispositions may pose a threat to freedom. Therefore, the discussion concerning the place of traditional moral excellence is already beyond the bioconservatism-transhumanism conflict, and constitutes the subject matter of a dispute within transhumanism itself. Another topic raised in this discussion is the problem of the identity of the enhanced agent, the social consequences of improving the human condition, and the issue of value pluralism, which could be against the unification of future people in terms of only a single moral profile. All these problems already assume the settlement of what can and should be enhanced in order for future moral entities to be best prepared to undertake appropriate actions. What remains interesting is how such a morally-enhanced agent will look at their life and the relationships they are in, and whether the postulates of modifying human abilities on a cognitive and emotional level, formulated from an impartial point of view, can be transposed into the language of individual pursuit of one's own excellence.

10.3 Imperfect procreation and moral perfection

The current state of the discussion on moral enhancement of people shows that the traditional vision of moral development, providing, among others, for the freedom of the moral agent, still retains a significant argumentative value. Based on the above analysis, one could indicate four areas of difficulties related to the reconciliation of the category of genetic enhancement and moral excellence. The first is the matter of the right to be morally imperfect. With regard to traditionally understood perfection, this problem has already appeared in the context of justifying the obligation to strive for moral excellence. In the case of moral enhancement, it appears in the discussion concerning freedom. According to Harris, providing an individual with the 'possibility of falling', that is, acting on bad intents, is the condition for moral enhancement. According to Savulescu and Persson, there is no reason for accepting bad intentions. If it a machine were invented in the future that would affect human motivations in such away as to modify evil intentions without interfering in any morally acceptable ones, they think it would allow to reconcile the good consequences arising from the elimination of evil actions with almost complete freedom. Every subject would be free in choosing all morally acceptable options. Freedom would be limited only to evil intentions in order to prevent serious harm, injustice, or other deeply immoral behaviour (Persson & Savulescu 2010, 406). What is more, if the subject voluntarily agreed to use this machine or benefit from other ways of biomedical moral enhancement, then their freedom would be complete (*Ibid.* 412). In other cases, in which adults would not agree to use an intention-modifying machine, according to Savulescu and Persson, one should give priority to preventing catastrophic consequences or significant harm over the autonomy of the individual, understood as the freedom 'to fall'.

This argument has some limitations. From the agent's point of view, the decision whether to participate in the clinical enhancement project or agree to use the intention-controlling machine is based not solely on balancing the value of one's own freedom and probability of avoiding harm made to others, but on determining whether the agent has the obligation to grant such consent. Regardless of whether they assume the assumptions of consequentialism or other ethical theories, their vision of moral development can be based on one of the following four principles:

1) I do not have the right to be imperfect and I do not have an obligation to strive for excellence.
2) I have the right to be imperfect, thus I do not have an obligation to strive for excellence.
3) I do not have the right to be imperfect, so I have an obligation to strive for excellence.
4) I have the right to be imperfect, but I also have an obligation to strive for excellence.

Of the above sentences, only sentence no. 1 is internally inconsistent. The recognition that nothing justifies my imperfections contradicts the statement about the lack of moral obligation to eliminate this faulty state. However, the subject of Savulescu and Persson's criticism, seems to be sentence no. 2, suggesting that the right to be imperfect is absolute and lifts the moral requirements concerning the agent itself. The transhumanist concept based on principle no. 3, completely rejecting the possibility of tolerance for imperfections, however, would lead to the conclusion that one should use scientific and technological progress in order to break free from imperfections. It would impose a moral obligation on parents to use the available achievements of biomedicine, including genetics, in order to ensure the greatest likelihood of having a polite child that is willing to cooperate and make sacrifices. In theory, the ability to formulate a compromise position between transhumanists and bioconservatists is provided by rule no. 4, which sets up a conditional right to be imperfect, allowing people to tolerate each other's defects, provided that they try to overcome them. The critical point, however, lies in a different approach of both these stances to the efficiency of conquering one's flaws. In a bioconservatist approach, although tolerance for defects, similarly to forgiveness or effort put in the pursuit of being better for others, do not provide immediate results, they constitute important factors in creating bonds between people. Transhumanism says, however, that moral enhancement should take place by means giving hope for effectively achieving the purpose as soon as possible. Although transhumanists assume that moral enhancement will not eliminate those relation-building elements, but only make their creation easier and more effective, however, on the other hand, it is difficult to apply this idea to the perspective of utilising such moral enhancement presented by them. If a moral agent found itself in a situation where it had to choose an activity that required effort in overcoming their disadvantages, and an activity supported, for example, by pharmaceuticals that affected the change of motivation, then from transhumanism's point of view, it would be too risky and unreasonable to select the first option. However, if this choice were to be justified by a positive and long-term impact on the relationship between the agent and the person whom a given activity concerns, then moral enhancement is not needed. This represents a significant difficulty in reaching a compromise that considers the traditional dimension of moral excellence as part of the moral enhancement project.

The second area of similar problems faced both by the concept of moral enhancement, and moral excellence, is the matter of sacrifice. Traditionally understood moral excellence is often associated with the ability to make sacrifices for the benefit of others. In most moral tradition, sacrificing one's own interest for other people constitutes the ideal of moral perfection. Moral development perceived from this perspective is a process that ranges from struggling with one's flaws, through the exercise of dispositions to fulfil moral obligations and coping with increasingly difficult moral challenges, up to forming an attitude allowing for moral heroism. The most pronounced example of heroic sacrifice is the sacrifice of life. It is understood traditionally as valuable not only because of the positive effects it has for others, but also as a conclusion of moral development. A decision which leads to an individual's death is also a decision, in which all of their past life finds fulfilment. For each type of sacrifice, the traditional concept of moral excellence takes into consideration the overall meaning of human life, along with its intrinsic aim, which is to achieve self-fulfilment as a person. This is the justification for the asymmetry of moral judgements that allow to decide about sacrificing one's goods for other people, and forbid from sacrificing another person's goods without their consent, even if it would contribute to an increase of the total sum of values.

According to Persson and Savulescu, the ability to make sacrifices is also one of the most important factors of moral self-enhancement, both in the consequential perspective, and in less demanding moral theories (Persson & Savulescu2010, 406). The idea of moral enhancement, however, assumes a different perspective. In accordance with the Principle of Procreative Altruism, the primary reason for moral enhancement is to increase the future prosperity of the child and others. This changes the vision of moral development in a significant manner. Sacrifice is no longer something that fits in the meaning of a person's life, but it is simply a rational way out of a conflict of interest. Such a perspective also does not allow to justify the asymmetry in sacrificing oneself and sacrificing others, and excludes the moral judgement of the freedom of the sacrificing subject, which leads to another issue.

The third problem area is the issue of moral evaluation of qualities resulting from genetic enhancement. In the traditional sense, moral evaluation applies to traits that form the moral character of a subject, and thus are directly or indirectly associated with the moral choices made by them. In this context, attempts made by Douglas, Harris, Persson, and Savulescu to define moral enhancement seem to go in the direction of including this fact. At the same time, however, adopting the maximisation of overall well-being as the single criterion of moral evaluation causes that it no longer matters whether the ability to formulate true moral judgements and dispositions to act in accordance with these judgements are the result of decisions taken by the subject, or are they only the result of genetic intervention. Breaking the link between moral evaluation and decision implies interesting, if not always convincing arguments. As an example, consider the case of creating and selecting embryos to give birth to a 'saviour sibling', i.e. a child who would be able to be a tissue donor for the older brother or sister. The justification for bringing them forth would be that already at the starting point, their very existence allows to save someone's life. Adopting the assumptions described above would allow one to conclude that the life of a 'life-saving sibling' is not only good at the outset, but also 'morally good'. Even if this is not the result of the child's autonomous decision, its existence and qualities (tissue compatibility) deserve a positive moral assessment ('born to be a hero'). The project of genetic enhancement and the traditional vision of human excellence stand here in conflict. In order to reconcile them, one should either recognise that moral enhancement is to have any features that positively affect the well-being of others – then tissue compliance should be judged, in moral terms, equally to the disposition towards altruistic behaviours – or consider the relationship between moral value and the subject's decision, forfeit the moral evaluation of the changes made to one's genetic endowment, and accept that moral enhancement may only be achieved through individual effort.

The fourth problematic area includes issues related to justifying the aim of moral enhancement from the parents' point of view. One may notice a certain analogy in substantiating one's own individual development and genetic enhancement of moral dispositions. Table 10.1 compares these two perspectives:

One could assume that genetic enhancement will to some extent be subject to the same criteria as self-enhancement.

The following assumptions support the rejection of reasons A1–A3 and B1–B3:

i. The reasons justifying the pursuit of excellence/genetic enhancement include, respectively, the personal reasons of the agent or their parents[5].

---

5 This view assumes that, from the view of the agent, personal arguments will always outweigh impartial arguments.

Tab. 10.1: Kinds of reasons justifying enhancement

No.	A. Reasons for agent's individual excellence from their own perspective	B. Reasons for a child's genetic enhancement from the point of view of their parents
1.	Maximising overall well-being	Maximising overall well-being
2.	Outclassing others	Having a better child than others
3.	Achieving success	Having a child who achieves success
4.	Creative development of the most valuable qualities one finds within oneself	Providing the child with the best possible qualities, which it may develop according to their own outlook on life

ii. Striving for excellence/genetic enhancement should encompass the value of a person subject to enhancement, and not making them dependent on the result of enhancement.

iii. One of the basic conditions for personal excellence/genetic enhancement is the inclusion of persons with whom the agent has special relations.[6]

Both from the perspective of the subject of moral enhancement, as well as from the parents' perspective, impartially understood maximisation of values seems to be too weak reason, especially since in the case of parents, choosing genetic enhancement could lead to a situation where – due to its enhanced motivations – a child would be internally determined to choose to the interests of others over their own. David DeGrazia attempts to combine personal and impartial perspective. In his opinion, the key factors influencing moral behaviour include freedom, moral motivation, and moral beliefs. Freedom, as the foundation of moral subjectivity, has a special value, however also important is the final product – morally right behaviour of a person. Any possible restriction of liberty resulting from an enhancement at the motivational or cognitive level may, according to DeGrazia, be justified by the desire to live in a better world (DeGrazia 2014, 367). However, DeGrazia does not indicate a criterion that allows to calculate what expected positive effects resulting from moral enhancement would compensate the possible restriction of the individual's freedom. Moreover, the fact that personal

---

6   Although there is a dispute in contemporary ethics on how to understand special relationships and whether they actually constitute a source of arguments for moral obligations, the general statement that an agent has responsibilities towards their children does not raise any objections. See Chapter 6.

development cannot be subject to the same balancing as well-being constitutes an argument against reducing the problem to impartial reasons. While it is possible to give up one's own well-being in order to ensure more for others, the same exchange is not possible in relation to own moral development. It would be difficult to give an example of an action resulting in a moral retrogression of one person, compensated by moral progress in the lives of others. An impartial exchange could involve increasing or decreasing chances for moral development, however, causing uneven chances of being a morally good person is even more controversial than causing unequal opportunities to achieve prosperity.

Rejecting the priority of impartial reasons is not sufficient to conclude that from the parents' point of view it is impossible to find other reasons for the genetic enhancement of moral dispositions. However, such a reason cannot be found in the value of having a child that is better than others, because it assumes conditioning the child's value on comparing it with others. These arguments relate to the same degree to individual enhancement. It is somewhat more difficult to reject reasons A3 and B3. Striving for success is an important part of personal development. It would certainly be inappropriate to subject the recognition of one's own value to achieving success and granting it priority over other elements of development, such as developing relationships with other people, for example. The argument seems to be even stronger if applied to the parents' perspective – if the ultimate reason for genetic enhancement was the value of projected successes of the child for its parents or the child itself, then it would constitute subjecting the recognition of its value to future successes and carry the risk of the parents fulfilling their own ambitions through the child and, in extreme cases – enter into a relationship with the child or break it away depending on the future success.

Reasons A4 and B4 could be a good justification for our own development and genetic enhancement. First of all, it should be noted that B4 excludes the Principle of Procreative Beneficence – ensuring the best opportunities for a child can be the reason for genetic enhancement, rather than the will to have the best child. Here, the result in the form of a good life is subordinated to the creative development of one's capabilities in relation to other people. The value associated with the creative and autonomous development of one's own qualities sets out the perspective of searching for a compromise concept of genetic enhancement. However, using this reason to justify the genetic enhancement project faces serious limitations. A4 presupposes that the agent discovers valuable traits in themselves while B4 assumes designing them. This fact is crucial in assessing the impact of moral enhancement on the parent – child relationship. If moral enhancement is accomplished through the selection of embryos, it already assumes our preference for certain qualities. Parents would not take the decision to enter into a relationship with a child, if it did not have these qualities or had them to a lesser extent. Genetic enhancement consisting in a manipulation of the embryo's genetic material implies the pursuit towards revealing desired characteristics in the future. Recalling the analogy to a game of chance formulated by Savulescu – if the parents' choice of genetic enhancement is maximising the chances of winning, then the desired qualities' failure to manifest equals a certain failure. The reaction to this failure will depend, of course, on the intensity of expectations and the probability of winning, and in most cases Green's argument that 'parental love almost always prevails' would certainly apply. In addition, the adoption of B4 would exclude the possibility of blaming this failure on the child – it would equally apply to the child and its parents. Nevertheless, due to the fact that the genetic enhancement project aims to tap into the deepest level of moral subjectivity, having to come to terms with the fact that the child does not have the qualities it could have possessed seems to speak against such interference. Traditional morality involves a network of interpersonal relationships, which determine the manner of dealing with moral evil. On the agent's side, it is the recognition of a morally unjust action accompanied by a sense of guilt, taking the responsibility for the committed evil and an attempt at redress. On the wronged person's side – the possibility of forgiveness, and from the perspective of third parties – the pursuit of justice. The project of genetic enhancement that involves impact on factors constituting biological foundations of morality does not take into consideration the need to develop new ways of dealing with moral faults, or even new models of social relations. From an impartial point of view, one could treat this necessity as the cost of genetic enhancement, however, it is difficult to estimate, and the fact that it is rarely considered in transhumanist proposals only testifies to the deficiencies of this project.

10.4 Conclusions

The project of genetic modification pertaining to moral dispositions is based on a vision that encompasses the elimination of many social problems, beginning with the eradication of anti-social behaviours and reducing the occurrence of crime, to eliminating the effects of racial hatred and increasing the motivation to solve the problem of world hunger. The difficulties of transposing the global vision of solving these problems to the individual situation of parents presented in this chapter are caused not only by the theoretical problem of aligning impartial and personal reasons, but also the specificity of methods used to enhance the human condition. Therefore, it seems that a compromise position concerning the genetic selection of embryos is not possible, just as the possibility of formulating such a stance in relation to other methods of genetic enhancement seems doubtful. On the other hand, the matter of facilitating moral dispositions using other biomedical measures remains an open question, as long as they take into consideration the reasons indicated in the ongoing discussion relevant from the point of view of a moral agent.

Acknowledgements

The article originally appeared in Polish in: *Etyka* 47 (2013): 67–83. Translated from Polish into English by Aeddan Shaw.

References

Bennett R (2014) When intuition is not enough. Why the Principle of Procreative Beneficence must work much harder to justify its eugenic vision. Bioethics 28(9):447–445.

DeGrazia D (2014) Moral enhancement, freedom, and what we (should) value in moral behaviour. Journal of Medical Ethics 40(6):361–368.

Douglas T (2008) Moral enhancement. Journal of Applied Philosophy 25(3):228–245.

Douglas T, Devolder K (2013) Procreative altruism: beyond individualism in reproductive selection. Journal of Medicine and Philosophy 38:400–419.

Green RM (2007) Babies by design. The ethics of genetic choice. Yale University Press, New Haven; London.

Harris J (2007) Enhancing evolution. The ethical case for making better people, Princeton University Press, Princeton, NJ.

Harris J (2010) Moral enhancement and freedom. Bioethics 25(3):102–111.

Häyry M (2010) Rationality and genetic challenge. Making people better. Cambridge University Press, Cambridge.

Herissone-Kelly P (2006) Procreative beneficence and the prospective parent. Journal of Medical Ethics 32(3):166–169.

Milton J (2000) Paradise lost, Leonard J (ed). Penguin Books, London.

Parfit D (1986) Reasons and persons. Clarendon Press, Oxford.

Parker M (2007) The best possible child. Journal of Medical Ethics 33(5): 279–283.

Persson I, Savulescu J (2010) Moral enhancement, freedom and the god machine. The Monist 95(3):399–421.

Persson I, Savulescu J (2012) Unfit for the future: The need for moral enhancement. Oxford University Press, Oxford.

Rose S (2006) Brain Gain. In: Miller P, Wilsdon J (eds) Better humans? The politics of human enhancement and life extension. Demos, London, pp. 69–72.

Sandel M (2009) The case against perfection. Ethics in the age of genetic engineering. Harvard University Press, Cambridge, MA; London.

Savulescu J (2001) Procreative beneficence: why should we select the best children? Bioethics 15(5–6):413–426.

Savulescu J, Kahane G (2009) The moral obligation to create children with the best chance of the best life. Bioethics 23(5):274–290.

Savulescu J, Sandberg A, Kahane G (2011) Well-being and enhancement. In: Savulescu J, ter Meulen R, Kahane G (eds) Enhancing human capacities. Wiley-Blackwell, Chichester; Malden, MA.

Wojciech Lewandowski

11 Bioconservatism and the preference for *status quo*

Against the background of all bioethical debates, the divide between the supporters and opponents of enhancing the human condition does not come as a surprise and may be interpreted as a new ground for the disputes between the proponents and opponents of the widest possible use of the achievements of biomedical sciences that have gone on for many years. To the former, the project concerning the enhancement of human capabilities in physical, cognitive or moral terms is the next step of applying constantly evolving knowledge and technology in order to improve the quality of human life. To the latter, any intervention should be preceded by careful reflection that allows to identify the possible risks and moral limitations of such of practices. Unlike most other bioethical discussions, the debate concerning the enhancement of human condition refers to interventions that, in most cases, are yet unavailable. Both sides use arguments based on the expected further development of biomedical sciences and technology, and the expected consequences of this development. An argument concerning the future impact of new activities, for which there is no empirical evidence of effectiveness, is always fraught with risk of utopian thinking or an *a priori* rejection of any changes. Between these extreme positions, there are those that offer arguments based on comparing the enhancement of the human condition with therapy and traditional ways of improving human capabilities. However, this middle path does not eliminate polarisation completely. Proponents of improving human nature often assume that there is no morally significant difference between therapy and enhancement. On the other hand, its opponents claim that interventions cross the safety threshold, beyond which the existing sources of objective values, such as human nature, autonomy, or dignity, will be exposed to a significant risk (Kass 2002, Fukuyama 2002, Habermas 2003, McKibben 2004, President's Council on Bioethics 2003, Sandel 2007).

Most commonly, bioconservative stances are accused of using rhetoric instead of arguments, ignoring biological facts when referring to the concept of nature, and formulating theses on the current or future human psyche without backing them up with empirical evidence (Buchanan 2011b, 2–10). One of the most interesting arguments against bioconservatism is based on an attempt to demonstrate that opposition against the human enhancement project is based on an error related to an unjustified preference of the current state of affairs. In this article, I will present possible ways of defending a bioconservative position against this argument. In the first part, I will cover the argument formulated by Nick Bostrom and Toby Ord referring to the status quo bias, and afterwards I will elaborate on how this argument affects the risk of inconclusiveness of bioconservatism's justification. At the end, I will present an attempt to defend bioconservatism based on Bernard Williams' category of 'human prejudice'.

11.1 The *status quo* bias

The essence of the accusation of making a *status quo* error lies in indicating the fact that the preference of the current state of things may wrongly affect the estimation of the possible benefits and losses. According to Bostrom and Ord, in the context of human capability enhancement, this error can be made when answering the question, whether we have any reasons to believe that the balance of long-term consequences of improving human capabilities will be beneficial. The authors limit this question to the matter of enhancing cognitive abilities, such as fluidity of speech, memory, abstract reasoning, social intelligence, directional awareness, the ability to count or musical talent. According to the authors, the fundamental difficulty in the question about the moral assessment of enhancing interventions is the radical uncertainty about both their effects, and the value of those effects. The authors claim that we face this kind of radical uncertainty in many situations – when deciding to get married or supporting significant social reforms. The unpredictability of individual human life and social systems cause that these types of decisions are not based on hard scientific evidence, but on subjective, intuitive judgement. The quality of this judgement depends on whether it is based on the knowledge of facts needed to decide or on prejudices.

The most famous description of the status quo bias was formulated by Tversky and Kahneman. Based on a series of psychological experiments, they have proved that the preference for maintaining status quo is a consequence of the aversion towards loss. In most cases, choices made between wins differing in size and probability of occurrence were not based on actual calculation of these values, but on the estimated size of emotional sense of loss in the case of a lost game (Kahneman & Tversky 1979). Tversky and Kahneman's theses are supported by biological (increased effort in order to avoid losses than to achieve benefits is common to people and other animals), sociological (opposition towards reforms), and economical observations (Kahneman 2011, 304–306).

According to Bostrom and Ord, the *status quo* bias in bioethical discussions can be identified by the following test.

Reversal Test: When a proposal to change a certain parameter is thought to have bad overall consequences, consider a change to the same parameter in the opposite direction. If this is also thought to have bad overall consequences, then the onus is on those who reach these conclusions to explain why our position cannot be improved through changes to this parameter. If they are unable to do so, then we have reason to suspect that they suffer from status quo bias (Bostrom & Ord 2006, 664–665).

In accordance to the test above, authors who oppose increasing the average intelligence quotient in the human population should demonstrate whether decreasing this value in the population would also be unfavourable. It seems that most bioconservative arguments would pass this test quite easily. If, according to Jürgen Habermas, forming the genetic endowment of children does not make them treated as a party to the communication process, or as autonomous authors of their own way of life, then it does not matter whether genetic intervention increase or reduce cognitive capabilities. On this basis, it may seem that – at least in some variants of bioconservatism – the criticism of enhancing interventions is not based on an erroneous calculation of the results caused by aversion towards losses, but on deontological restrictions constituting arguments rivalling consequentialist ones.

There are at least three responses to this type of defence. First, it can be concluded that the deontological nature of arguments against enhancing intelligence is illusory, and in fact based on identifying the adverse consequences of this type of changes. The premise of the normativeness of human nature can be considered synonymous with the statement that the present condition remains in a state of balance, which allows to pursue all values highlighted by bioconservatists. If, according to them, destabilising this balance one way or the other were groundless, then the lack of sufficient substantiation that it would be impossible to pursue these values after the change would allow to assume that this position was based on the *status quo* bias (Żuradzki 2014, 219). Additionally, it is possible to reduce deontological restrictions by pointing out that if biomedical interventions were the only way of eliminating possible natural hazards associated with the deterioration of the human condition, then the same arguments would allow to justify these interventions for purposes other than medical treatment (Bostrom & Ord 2006, 673). Furthermore, it is possible to accept the consideration of deontological constraints, but only to an extent that the value of a certain state could be reduced, if that state was caused by a violation of these constraints (Bostrom, Ord 2006, 656–657). Standing by the absolute validity of deontological constraints could also be a consequence of the *status quo* bias.

It should be noted that the reversal test is not based on a precise criterion. The ability to substantiate both conclusions can be understood very broadly as providing any reasons to justify changes, or very narrowly – as providing compelling reasons. The former causes that most bioconservative standpoints could be accused of the *status quo* bias. The second is associated with the fact that, in the context of the dispute about the modification of any parameter, the lack of a reason satisfactory to one party to the dispute, would allow them to formulate a suspicion of committing the *status quo* bias, bringing an argument based on this test down to an *ad personam* argument, and the entire debate concerning the enhancement of the human condition – to the psychology of scientific discourse. Critics of bioconservatism avoid this trap, recognising that there are certain arguments opposing the enhancement of the human condition, but at the same time stating that these arguments are not sufficient to justify the cessation of research on human enhancement.

11.2 The problem of conclusive reasons

The proponents of enhancing human capabilities admit the existence of various kinds of arguments. While explaining his famous Procreative Beneficence principle, Julian Savulescu states that the obligation to carry out these interventions is a *prima facie* obligation. This type of obligation means having good reasons to select improving changes, however these reasons would be decisive only if there were no other reasons opposing these changes. Following the same logic, one may consider that the bioconservatists' objections referring to the right to an 'open future' or 'openness to the unbidden' are not based on the assumption that a world, in which the intelligence quotient is 180 would be a worse world than the current one, but on the assumption, that there are reasons not to choose interventions designed to create such a world.

According to Allen Buchanan, authors such as Fukuyama, Kass, or Sandel, opposing the widespread access to future technologies enhancing the human condition, rest their reasoning not on considering the arguments for and against enhancing the human condition, but on formulating arguments against such interventions. On this basis, Buchanan concludes that all of them adopt the so-called conclusive reasons view (Buchanan 2008).

Conclusive reasons view: Any conclusive reason outweighs all countervailing reasons.

According to Buchanan, bioconservative reasons against the enhancement of the human condition can hardly be considered conclusive. If enhancing the human condition threatened human nature, lead to alienation and the loss of our true 'I' or expressed ingratitude and a lack of openness to the 'unknown', then precisely the same reasons would have to be conclusive also in the case of all interventions, including those that do not involve bio-medical enhancement of the human condition (Buchanan 2011a, 150–151). According to Buchanan, the only way to avoid this absurd conclusion is to recognise that these reasons are not conclusive and cannot be considered in any other way than by balancing them with reasons for enhancing interventions.

Rejecting the model of weighing reasons for and against enhancing interventions may raise further suspicion that bioconservatists make the *status quo* error. However, in ethics it seems that the position of conclusive reasons is adopted often enough in the context of other moral problems, that such a suspicion may be rejected this time also. It is most often considered that conclusive reasons include those that refer to the projection of possible harm led to by given actions. Tom Douglas made an interesting attempt to apply this category to the issue of human condition enhancement. According to Douglas, one may indicate at least five possible harms resulting from enhancing interventions. First, harmful utilisation of enhancing technologies, for example in military operations. Second, harm associated with enhanced people achieving competitive advantage over unenhanced ones. Third, the prospect of forced enhancement tied to the fact that an increase in the number of enhanced people may exert pressure on the unenhanced or lead to the enactment of a law establishing enhancement as an obligation. Fourth, increasing the susceptibility to harming others, consisting in the fact that people possessing enhanced capabilities may have less sensitivity and empathy when compared to unenhanced ones if cognitive enhancement is not accompanied by an emotional enhancement[1]. Fifth – increasing the acceptability of permissible harm, that is, a potential risk of indicating circumstances that would justify harming people, who have not been subjected to enhancing interventions or excluding unenhanced people from public discourse and levelling their civil rights to those of children. According to Douglas, the above reasons could be considered conclusive if all enhancing interventions resulted in unjustifiable harm of others or if most of those interventions had such consequences with no concurrent form of state regulation allowing to eliminate harmful interventions and permit safe ones (Douglas 2015, 25–27).

Another strategy of demonstrating the conclusiveness of reasons that oppose the enhancement of the human condition is found in referencing the precautionary principle found in ethics. According to Neil Manson, each version of this

---

[1] According to John Harris, cognitive enhancement alone will allow to avoid those consequences without having to interfere at the motivational level (Harris 2010).

principle has a three-part structure: the damage condition, which refers to the effect in virtue of which precautionary measures should be utilised, the knowledge condition, which pertains to the possibility of establishing a causal relationship between a given act and the considered damage, and the remedies that should be taken in response to the activity to prevent damage (Manson 2002, 263–265). In the context of the discussion on enhancing the human condition, it would be the bioconservatists' task to prove that the first two conditions are met, whereas the appropriate remedy is to refrain from this type of intervention. The precautionary principle would also support the view that the burden of justifying the enhancement of the human condition, along with protective measures allowing to avoid potential harm, rests on those who believe that efforts should be made to carry out a risky policy or project. Rebutting the allegation of a *status quo* error would consist in adopting a weak or strong variation of the precautionary principle. Both, however, have their own problems.

> *The Strong Precautionary Principle*: When a project is associated with a serious risk, even in the lack of scientific evidence of such risk, it should not be pursued, regardless of its expected benefits.[2]

The main argument against this version of the principle is based on the comparison between undertaking a risky action and the potential benefits. If a given activity is risky, but preserving the *status quo* is even riskier, then the strong precautionary principle implies a wrong choice. If, on the other hand, the strong precautionary principle is to be applied to all choices, and if each one of them carries a significant risk, then it should be considered that none be selected (Sunstein 2005, 42–48).

> *The Weak Precautionary Principle*: When choosing between alternative strategies, we should pay more attention to the risk associated with a given strategy than the possible benefits.[3]

Generalising this principle unto all choices would imply equally cautious treatment of risk associated with catastrophic and irreversible consequences, and the risk related to acceptable and reversible damage. One way to defend the bioconservative position would be to recognise that the present human condition is a value whose loss would be disastrous. The most famous attempt to apply this strategy is Hans Jonas's heuristics of fear, based primarily on the qualitatively higher value of the existing heritage of evolution in the form of the opportunity to learn the truth, valuation, and freedom (Jonas 1984, 32–33). A potential

---

2 Different varieties of this principle are presented by Sunstein (2005), 19–20.
3 Variations of this principle: Sunstein (2005), 18–19.

loss of these possibilities constitutes, according to Jonas, a sufficient reason not to include them in any calculation allowing the risk of losing them. Hence, the basic principle of the precautionary principle seems to be the particularly valuable state of the present human condition. It is characteristic for this kind of argument to assign infinite size to protected values, which allows to reason that enhancing human capabilities using biomedical intervention does not increase the objective value of neither the species, nor individual units. This justification allows to state that risk is the only factor that must be taken into consideration. However, this argument can be reversed: if biomedical interventions can neither reduce, nor increase the intrinsic value of the human species, then balancing other benefits and losses is a sufficient criterion for these interventions. In addition, the allegation of a *status quo* bias can be related to assigning lexical superiority over all other values to the current human condition.[4]

It seems that it is not necessary to justify the objective value of the human species in order to avoid the rebuke of inconclusiveness based on the *status quo* bias. Referencing various types of practical arguments allows to state that even if a comparison of the benefits and losses speaks for enhancing interventions, the objections against such interventions do not prove irrational prejudice.

11.3 'Human prejudice' towards enhancing interventions

Is such a situation possible in which an agent or a group of agents, committing the *status quo* error or not, possessed conclusive reasons not to select a certain change, even if afterwards they would consider it justified and desirable? To determine whether conservatism associated with the enhancement of human condition is a result of bias, one may compare the two ways of formulating the question about the rationale of individual interventions:

1. 'Should interventions enhancing human capabilities be carried out?'
2. 'Does an agent have good reasons to decide about carrying out an intervention that improves their capabilities?'.

The first question can be interpreted in at least two ways:

1a. 'From an impartial point of view, should interventions enhancing human capabilities be used?'.
1b. 'From our point of view, as the representative of the *homo sapiens* species, should interventions enhancing our capabilities be used?'.

---

4   Other aspects of this argument are presented by Hainz (2012).

The first interpretation, adopted by the proponents of enhancing interventions, implies the possibility of evaluating changes from an impartial point of view or, in other words, 'from the point of view of the universe', which does not consider individual characteristics and preferences of the agent carrying out the evaluation[5]. The second interpretation includes asking this question from the point of view of the representatives of a species, in which these changes are introduced. The basis of the rebuke based on the reversal test seems to be the recognition that the point of view of the representatives of the *homo sapiens* species may be biased and based on prejudices. With regard to the issue of radical enhancement, namely – introducing features that no representative of the human species has ever had, this allegation would have exactly the same structure as the accusation of speciesism[6]. In line with this accusation, favouring the interests of the representatives of one's own species over the interests of other species results from a bias (Singer 1995, 6–9).

The argument formulated by Bernard Williams in his article 'The Human Prejudice' (Williams 2006) allows one to reject both the accusation of speciesism, as well as the accusation of prejudice against interventions enhancing the human condition. According to Williams, agents which ask questions about giving preference to individuals from their own species, do it in the context of values already expressed by them. From this point of view, preferring the representatives of one's own species would not be a recognition of absolute superiority of humans over animals, but only a consequence of the fact that the co-representatives of the same species are more important *to us* than individuals from other species.

According to critics of this position, in order to maintain it, one should indicate arguments for preferring humans to animals. Without any arguments, such preference would still be an unjustified bias, such as sexism or racism, in respect of which the only criterion for behaviour in relation to others is whether they are 'like us' (Singer 2009, 572–573). According to Williams, however, there is a difference between attempts to justify racism and sexism, and the attempts to substantiate preference based on species membership. In the first case, we are dealing with an effort to warrant discriminatory practices *ad hoc* by referencing incorrect arguments, for example, based on false assumptions about the worse intellectual capabilities of the discriminated group. In the second case,

---

5   Some concepts of moral enhancement assume modifications that improve human dispositions toward solving moral problems precisely from this point of view. Savulescu, Persson (2012).

6   This argument is analysed in the context of other biomedical interventions by DeGrazia (2007).

the statement 'this is a human being' does not require any additional reasoning associated with characteristics that differentiate people from animals. The ability to use complex languages ridden with abstract concepts, creating and communicating culture, as well as technological development seem to have no connection with our preference towards other people. According to Williams, we have a reason to expand our sympathies to other groups of people or animals, but only when we perceive them as aspects of human life (Williams 2006, 147).

Williams transposes the explanation of species preference into enhancing changes by formulating the following fictitious example. Let us assume that representatives of an advanced extra-terrestrial civilisation come to Earth. The visitors are friendly, reasonable, and have extensive experience in creating peaceful societies. Because their experience shows that species-specific preference and autonomy in creating culture has a destabilising and destructive effect on the community, they offer to painlessly remove these factors. Williams notes that people in favour of such a change would have to either use arguments formulated from the 'human point of view', which could be understood by the opponents of such changes, or arguments common to both humans and aliens. The first option would put supporters of changes in a paradoxical situation of finding in the human point of view elements for its rejection[7]. In the second case, even if there were moral rules common to all rational beings, one could doubt whether they would support making changes[8]. According to Williams, the reason for this is found in the fact that these rules do not say how to arrange one's life after changes (Williams 2006, 151)[9].

In this aspect, the dispute between bioconservatists and transhumanists can be interpreted as a dispute about the category of human beings' 'real interests'. The former, sometimes relating this idea to the concept of nature, believe it to be a constant foundation of common human traits and behaviours. On this basis, they justify the acceptability of medical interventions aimed at the restoration of features caused by illness or other pathological state, which allow to function in the context of that nature. The latter, however, relate the concept of 'real interests' to the maximisation principle, arguing that if a given feature present on a certain level were valuable (e.g. it allowed to obtain a certain number of goods), then all interventions that raise those features to a higher level would be objectively desirable. In both above models, it is possible to identify examples that

---

7   According to Nicholas Agar, the inability to resolve this paradox argues for the adoption of species relativism (Agar 2010, 12–15).
8   An opposing position is presented by Savulescu (2009).
9   Detailed examples of such difficulties are presented by Agar (2014).

may be interpreted in the category of the *status quo* bias. A patient who refuses to take advantage of medical capacities that would restore their health can be suspected of making this error. Even in this case, however, the reversal test will not necessarily lead to true conclusions. The desire to remain in the current state can be justified by excessively high cost of adapting to new opportunities or the lack of a connection between these possibilities and an individual's meaning of life. Therefore, it is necessary to formulate formal terms allowing to distinguish between situations, in which an agent has a reason not to opt for changes, and those when their decision is motivated, for example, by fear of an objectively desirable change.

According to Williams, the issue of improper discernment of real interests lies not only in the agent not having sufficient knowledge that could help in making a decision. If the agent was not aware that a change could be in their interest, and if they concluded that it was in their interest in result of this change, then it would constitute proof only if the change of perspective could be explained by a reference to *general incapacity*, which they were subject to in their original condition, and which was eliminated or mitigated by that change (Williams 1993, 42–43).

The definition of 'general incapacity' must, according to Williams, meet two conditions. First, the incapacity cannot be defined exclusively on the basis of conditions justifying the change. If some religious sect were to justify the need to undergo brainwashing by the fact that after its end, each and every one of them would be able to honestly recognise their prior failure to accept the proposed religious claims, then that type of reasoning would not satisfy the first condition. Secondly, the aforementioned definition must be combined with the normative concept of human functioning in certain cultural circumstances. Each concept of enhancing the human condition, therefore, should entail the concept of changing the cultural surroundings of enhanced people, including reflection on new ways of communication or interpersonal relationships.

Williams's argument allows to state that from the point of view of agents potentially subjected to modification, radical enhancement that carries the possibility of them losing their perspective would be unjustified, whereas in the case of other enhancing interventions, the burden of proof, involved with reconciling impartial calculation of benefits with individual projects of these agents, would remain on the shoulders of the proponents of change (Patrone 2013).

11.4 Conclusion

The reasoning presented in this chapter does not allow to reject all possible enhancing interventions. The category of 'general incapacity', however, can be used to specify the difference between medical and enhancing activities, especially in the context of the moral enhancement project. From an impartial point of view, the loss of the human perspective is only a cost that has to be considered when weighing the risks and benefits. From the point of view of an agent, the loss of 'one's own' or 'our' point of view is comparable to an existential catastrophe. In this context, bioconservative reasoning presented by Habermas, Sandel, or McKibben can be interpreted not as an example of the *status quo* bias, but as a demand to take serious account of the perspective of agents, such as us, in the discussion on which biomedical interventions to allow for wide application.

Acknowledgements

The article originally appeared in Polish in: *Ethics in Progress Quarterly* vol. 6 no. 1 (2015): 72–84. Translated from Polish into English by Aeddan Shaw.

References

Agar N (2010) Humanity's end. Why we should reject radical enhancement. MIT Press, Cambridge, MA.

Agar N (2014) Truly human enhancement: a philosophical defense of limits. MIT Press, Cambridge, MA.

Bostrom N, Ord T (2006) The reversal test: eliminating status quo bias in applied ethics. Ethics 116:656–679.

Buchanan AE (2008) Enhancement and the ethics of development. Kennedy Institute of Ethics Journal 18:1–34.

Buchanan AE (2011a) Better than human: the promise and perils of enhancing ourselves. Oxford University Press, New York.

Buchanan AE (2011b) Beyond humanity? The ethics of biomedical enhancement. Oxford University Press, Oxford.

DeGrazia D (2007) Human-animal chimeras: human dignity, moral status, and species prejudice. Metaphilosophy 38:309–329.

Douglas T (2015) The harms of enhancement and the conclusive reasons view. Cambridge Quarterly of Healthcare Ethics 24:23–36.

Fukuyama F (2002) Our posthuman future: consequences of the biotechnology revolution. Profile Books, New York.

Habermas J (2003) The future of human nature. Polity Press, Cambridge.

Hainz T (2012) Value lexicality and human enhancement. Technoethics 3:54–65.

Harris J (2010) Moral enhancement and freedom. Bioethics 25:102–111.

Häyry M (2010) Rationality and the genetic challenge: making people better? Cambridge University Press, Cambridge.

Jonas H (1984) The imperative of responsibility. University of Chicago Press, Chicago.

Kahneman D (2011) Thinking fast and slow. MacMillan, New York.

Kahneman D, Tversky A (1979) Prospect theory: an analysis of decisions under risk. Econometrica 47:263–291.

Kass L (2002) Life, liberty, and the defense of dignity. Encounter Books, San Fransisco.

Manson NA (2002) Formulating the precautionary principle. Environmental Ethics 24:263–74.

McKibben B (2004) Enough: staying human in an engineered age. St. Matin's Press, New York.

Patrone T (2013) In defence of human prejudice. International Journal of Technoethics 4:26–38.

President's Council on Bioethics (2003) Beyond therapy: biotechnology and the pursuit of happiness. President's Council on Bioethics, Washington, DC.

Sandel M (2007) The case againstperfection: ethics in the age of genetic engineering. Harvard University Press, Cambridge, MA.

Savulescu J (2009) The human prejudice and the moral status of enhanced beings: what do we owe the gods? In: Savulescu J, Bostrom N(eds) Human enhancement. Oxford University Press, Oxford, pp. 211–247.

Savulescu J, Persson I (2012) Unfit for the future: the need of moral enhancement. Oxford University Press, Oxford.

Singer P (1995) Animal liberation. Pimlico, London.

Singer P (2009) Speciesism and moral status. Metaphilosophy 40:567–581.

Sunstein C (2005) Laws of fear: beyond precautionary principle. Cambridge University Press, Cambridge.

Williams B (1993) Ethics and the limits of philosophy. Fontana, London.

Williams B (2006) The human prejudice. In: Williams B (ed) Philosophy as a humanistic discipline. Princeton University Press, Princeton, pp. 135–152.

Żuradzki T (2014) Nowa liberalna eugenika: krytyczny przegląd argumentów przeciwko biomedycznemu poprawianiu ludzkiej kondycji fizycznej lub umysłowej. Diametros 42:204–226.

Wojciech Lewandowski

12 Procreative autonomy in the context of person-affecting and impersonal reasons for human enhancement

According to common sense, one of the fundamental principles parents should be driven by is the principle that imposes caring of their child's well-being. By definition, this principle is rarely conflicted with the parental autonomy principle that says that parents are the agents who have the primary right to decide over the well-being of their child. The parental autonomy principle requires that others should refrain from the actions that can infringe the well-being. The factor allowing the avoidance of most conflicts between the autonomy of parents and a child's well-being is the assumption that the parents are more than obliged to take care of their child and it is their primary goal. Among the conflict situations discussed today, the greatest number of them does no refer to the parents' attitude to the child's well-being, but the possible lack of competence when it comes to defining the good, in particular in the context of biomedical choices. Among those situations one can enlist the refusal of a child's medical treatment (Hickey & Lyckholm 2004, Diekema 2004) or the refusal of a mandatory vaccination.

One of the specific types of parental autonomy is procreative autonomy, understood as the possibility and entitlement to a free decision regarding the circumstances of having children (when, with whom), their number, their features, the kind of procreation (natural vs. supported) or their own role in this process (gamete donation, surrogating) (Dworkin 1994, Buchanan et al. 2006, Robertson 1996). Whereas the first of the aforementioned examples does not arouse any controversy, the remaining ones are subjects of many heated disputes. Also the conflicts between procreative autonomy and a child's well-being seem to be even more difficult to solve, since in the moment of making the procreative decisions their addressee does not exist. On one hand, this fact is in favor of the assumption that potential parents should have more freedom in deciding over the future life of their children in comparison with the parental autonomy connected with the responsibility over already an existing child. On the other hand, procreative decisions can have much bigger impact on the life of afuture child than in case of the action regarding children that already exist. One of the most commonly discussed examples of such decisions is the agreement for the preconception genetic diagnosis or the pre-implantation genetic diagnosis. The above-mentioned assumption makes many contemporary authors formulate the thesis that it is the parents'obligation to make such decisions that would result in giving birth to ababy that would have possibly the best life, e.g. through the selection of genes that would allow the child to have better physical, cognitive or moral skills than in case of making another choice (Savulescu 2001). One of the basic problems regarding the justification of this obligationis connected with the interpretation of the character of the principles which the obligation is based on. The first of the two opposite interpretations says that the obligation of the improvement of the future child's condition is impersonal and therefore refers only to the improvement of the possible value of the future state of affairs. The second interpretation of this obligation gives it a person-affecting character that dictates the avoidance of harm and the improvement of the child's benefit as an entity that comes into being as an effect of agiven decision.

Resolving the above-mentioned problem is crucial for the possibility of answering the question of the relation of the obligation of improving the future child's condition and the procreative autonomy. In this article I will present the analysis of the relation between both the person-affecting and impersonal reasons that this obligation is based on and the procreative autonomy. In the first part I will describe the non-identity problem which is the starting point for the discussion between personal and impersonal views. In the second part, in the light if these statements, I will analyze the arguments of the supporters of aiming at the possibly best quality of a future child's life. The third part will include the analysis of the possibility of comparing person-affecting and impersonal reasons in the context of improvement obligation related with procreative autonomy.

12.1 The non-identity problem vs. the improving interferences

The non-identity problem was formulated by Derek Parfit in the context of searching an answer for the question which moral principles can be formulated in relation to decisions the existence and identity of future human beings are dependent on (Parfit 2007). Most of the discussions regarding the non-identity problems are connected with the question of deciding over possible harm that was an effect of actions or negligence leading to a birth of a child suffering from serious diseases. One of the examples that can illustrate the problem is the situation of a woman suffering from rubella. If she decides to conceive a child, she takes the risk of serious complications and congenital defects of the child. If she postpones the procreative decision by three months, until the time of curing the disease, she will give birth to a different, healthy child (Parfit 1976)[1]. The essence of the non-identity problem is the lack of possibility of comparing both discussions in relation to a particular child, and, at the same time – the lack of possibility to judge whether a given decision is good or harmful for the child.

In the discussion on the evaluation of actions the non-identity problem is related with, there are two opposite solutions based on impersonal and person-affecting points of view. The first ones leave aside the identity of children that can come into being depending on the decision made and are based on the value of the state of affairs that will exist as an effect of a given decision only. This value is most often determined on the basis of the function of life quality and the number of people existing in the give state of affairs. The solutions of the second type consist in the attempts to justify the harm or benefit of a child, i. a. through the limitation of the scope of future people whose quality of life is being compared (Roberts 1998) or through the use of the concept of 'threshold harm' (Różyńska 2013).

Regardless the difficulties of trying to solve the non-identity problem, they all apparently assume the common-sense conviction that potential parents are first and foremost obliged to avoid the decisions that could be connected with the harm of their future children. The situation that results in the birth of an ill child and that can be the effect of egoist motives the parents were driven by, or the negligence they were guilty of, seems analogical, at least in this aspect, to every situation in the parent-child relation. Following this assumption, the prohibition of harming an already existing child affects parental autonomy in the same way the order of minimizing possible harm of future children influences procreative autonomy.

According to some authors, the obligation of avoiding possible harm is an insufficient restriction of procreative autonomy (O'Neill 2002). Another part the above-described discussion is held on possible in the near future problems connected with the evaluation of action or negligence that result in a healthy child being born, but if some biomedical enhancements were applied (e.g. through genetic selection at the stage of pre-implementing genetic diagnosis or the interference that took place before or during pregnancy), the child might have been bigger, stronger or more intelligent. Such a possibility would make the child live better than the child's that was actually born. The above-mentioned possibilities triggered adiscussion on the question of people making procreative decision and the problem if they should take into consideration not only the

---

1 Modified versions of this example formulate Boonin (2014) and Wilkinson (2013).

obligation of avoiding harm, but also apossible obligation of maximizing the quality of life. Similarly to the previously described discussion, at this point the non-identity problem can appear too, illustrated by the hypothetical example presented below.

Two programmes of improving human abilities: Programme E_1 includes the use of a substance, which, taken 3 months before conceiving, improves significantly the probability that the child's IQ will be higher than average. Programme E_2 consists in a regular stimulation of the child's brain over the pregnancy period, which, similarly to the previous example, improves significantly the probability that the child's IQ will be higher. If the potential parents decide to participate in Programme E_1, the mother will give birth to a child that in the future will have the IQ results above average. If the parent decides to participate in Programme E_2, a different child will be born and its future IQ results will also be above average.

Can the participation in one of those two programmes be considered a moral obligation? According to the impersonal view, the choices of either of those programmes does not differ morally, because the state of affairs in the two examples is identical, even if finally different children are the beneficiaries of programmes E_1 and E_2. The parents who would aspire to provide their future children with possibly best life, would have complete freedom of choosing one of those programmes. The situation is different when considered from the person-affecting point of view, since the necessity to postpone the planned conception by 3 months is connected with the fact that finally the child having higher IQ will be a different child that the one that would be born in the originally planned scenario. The selection or rejection of Programme E_2 has an influence on the life of a particular child, so only in this case one can say about possible benefits or their lack in the child's life.

Conversely to the discussion on possible harm connected with procreative decisions, where the obligation of minimizing the harm of future children raises no doubts, and the difficulties are only connected with judging whether the actions of parent are really harmful to someone, the problem of enhancements improving the child's life additionally has to answer the question whether the obligation of aiming at the existence of a 'best possible' child exists at all, and the question of its impersonal or person-affecting is of secondary importance.

12.2 Arguments in favor of the obligation of enhancement

One of the most prominent supporters of the obligation to apply enhancement thesis is Julian Savulescu. According to him, parents would be obliged, for example, to use pre-implantation genetic diagnosis to select such an embryo whose genetic endowment would give the biggest chance of the best life, in comparison with the possible life of other embryos.

The principle that dictates the maximizing of the possible future quality of a child's life is named the Principle of Procreative Beneficence (PB). The same principle allows the justification of the obligation of selecting one of the programmes of human abilities enhancement described above. The selection of one of the programmes is dependent on interpreting PB as an either person-affecting or impersonal principle. For quite along time the supporters of the enhancement obligation claimed that the matter of the obligation's character, person-affecting or impersonal, is of secondary importance.

We do not take a stand on this difficult philosophical issue. As we have tried to show, our moral intuitions about timing of conception recognize reasons to select future children. PB is an account of the content of these reasons, not an explanation of what might ground them (Savulescu & Kahane 2009, 277).

Applying PB to two medical programmes does not allow to state unequivocally which of them would constitute the moral obligation. It may suggest that the principle is of impersonal character and obliges the potential parents to choose any of them. Morally incorrect would be only the lack of choosing any of the enhancement programmes. However, Suvalescu and Kahane allow the possibility of the wide person-affecting interpretation of PB.

Like competing principles of procreative ethics, PB is compatible with different accounts of reasons to select future children. It can take either a wide person-affecting form or an impersonal form. According to the wide person-affecting version, our reason to select the child with better prospects is that that child will benefit more than the other would by being caused to exist. According to the impersonal version, our reason is that selecting the most advantaged child would make the outcome better, even if it is not better for the child created (Savulescu & Kahane 2009, 277).

One should notice that this argument helps justifying the obligation in case of the pre-implantation selection example quoted by Savulescu, but it gives no criterion of choice between Programmes E_1 and E_2. PB understood as both a wide person-affecting principle and impersonal principle would impose the choice of any of those programmes. The lack of defining the person-affecting or impersonal character of PB does not allow to justify the relation between the obligation of striving to have a possibly best child and procreative autonomy. It is apparently one of the reasons why Savulescu's arguments were considered the most controversial, even from the point of view of other supporters of the enhancements. One of the most frequently quoted allegations suggests that the above-formulated moral obligation to provide the child with the best life would be too demanding for potential parents, and would practically make them resign from the accomplishments of their own interests (Buchanan et al. 2006, 161–2; Glover 2006, 54). According to Robert Sparrow, this would lead to justifying a state's strong interference in the procreative autonomy of potential parents to avoid the negative outcomes of the cumulated individual procreative decisions. According to Sparrow's arguments, the lack of such interference would result in potential parents commonly applying the principle dictating to select such features that improve the future child's chances for high social and economic status. As a result, after some time the whole society would consist in white, handsome, heterosexual males (Sparrow 2014, 143).

The above-mentioned argument is dismissed by the statement that the state should apply a constraint in relation to individual decisions only when they can cause harm. If the non-identity problem does not allow justification of harm in case of applying the enhancements, the state should apply neither prohibition nor obligation of those enhancements. Following this line of argumentation, the impersonal principles or even a wide person-affecting principle do not allow the interference of a state. However, Sparrow notes that the interference does not have to be justified by a possible harm of a group of people only. The interferences aiming at the limitation of environment pollution can be justified by any references to the identity of future people. Analogically: the impersonal principles or a wide person-affecting principle can be the basis for the legislative introduction of the limitation of procreative autonomy and the obligation to select the best child (Sparrow 2014, 145).

The defense of Suvalescu is based on the thesis that PB designates only a *prima facie* obligation, identified by the author with a moral reason, whose power has to be compared with the power of other moral reasons. It is the result of this comparison that designates the action the potential parents would be obliged to (Savulescu 2014, 171–172). In relation to this view there is an allegation formulated that the categories of obligation and reason are confused (Sparrow 2007). An enhancement cannot be considered even a *prima facie* obligation, since many decisions made by parents regarding the quality of their children lives have no moral character. An example of such a decision outside the moral spectrum, which does not maximize the quality of a child's life is buying a car with worse security devices instead of a car with better ones.

According to Savulescu, the decisions that are connected with the results that can cause small, predictable and avoidable risk are moral, but referring to them such categories like guilt or punishment is not right. He claims that even if one assumes that those decisions are not moral, one can justify the moral obligation of a child selection in case of the decisions that can significantly improve the quality of life. According to Savulescu, on this basis one can justify that harm can be the handicap the child acquires in a car accident and which is caused by the wrong installation of a car seat. Analogically, the selection of embryos regarding the features that significantly influence the quality of life would be a moral obligation too. The criterion of the significant influence on the quality of life constitutes the basic justification of the symmetry between the reasons in favor of avoiding harm and those in favor of maximizing the positive quality of life[2]. However, this criterion cannot be applied in case of the two enhancement pogrammes, since when choosing E_1 or E_2 the influence on the quality of life of a future child will be identical. The auxiliary criterion of designating the strength of a reason can be the division into person-affecting or impersonal character of the reason. The criterion would allow also a comparison of the reasons in favor of the improvement of the life quality of future children and the reasons in favor of the respect for procreative autonomy.

12.3 Comparison of person-affecting and impersonal reasons

According to Savulescu, one can for sure agree that among our moral reasons there are both person-affecting and impersonal ones. The former refer to the actions towards people whose identity is defined, whereas the latter refer to future people, whose existence and identity depend on our decisions. To illustrate this, Savulescu analyzes three detailed examples of an obligation formulated 'you should do a in order that X have a good life':

> *Helping.* You have a moral obligation to help John who is starving in Africa. You should do a in order that John lives a good life (A = give money, time, expertise, etc.).
> *Selecting.* You have a moral obligation to select the best embryo of the embryos available. You should do a in order that James exists and lives a good life (A = IVF plus PGD, or some other selection procedure). [...]
> *Conservation.* You have a moral obligation to reduce carbon emissions. You should do a so that people exist in the future with good lives (A = reducing air travel, using clean energy, etc.) (Savulescu 2014, 172).

The first obligation has a person-affecting character – there is someone affected by our action. The third obligation is impersonal – a moral judgment of this action cannot be formulated with reference to a particular person. The selecting obligation seems the most problematic. On one hand, there is a dispute over the moral status of embryos, on the other hand, regardless the assumption concerning the

---

[2] The possibilities of avoiding the thesis on the symmetry of those duties are discussed by Żuradzki (2008).

status, the question of their personal identity is still subject of discussion due to the possibility of dividing an embryo or merging two embryos in one. Savulescu's line of reasoning looks as follows: if one has a person-affecting obligation to influence the enhancement of life quality of a given person, one also is obliged to select the best embryo. If one has an impersonal obligation of preserving natural environment, one is also obliged to select the best embryo. Therefore, regardless the character of the obligation – person-affecting or impersonal – according to Savulescu the obligation certainly exists. Interestingly, he still does not introduce the criterion that unambiguously allows to name the obligation person-affecting or impersonal. The criterion is, however, introduced in the same text in connection with the allegation of the restriction of procreative autonomy.

To avoid the allegation that the obligation of having the best child leads to the restriction of procreative autonomy, Savulescu supports the thesis saying that person-affecting reasons are stronger than the impersonal ones (Savulescu 2014, 177). He proves the thesis stating that most people would consider the action that causes deafness of an already existing child worse than the genetic selection which results in the birth of a deaf child. Also procreative autonomy should be restricted in the first case, but not in the second one. Regarding the remaining examples, it turns out that one should prefer helping John over the environment protection and Programme E_2 over Programme E_1, since, both in case of help and Programme E_2 it is possible to ascribe the benefits resulting from our action to particular people.

Leaving the previously declared suspension of the judgment regarding the person-affecting or impersonal character of PB allows Savulescu to defend procreative autonomy. Non-use of enhancements would be unjust in the sense of not-fulfilling the impersonal obligation, but would not be harmful to anyone. However, the restriction of procreative autonomy through a legislation assuming an obligation regarding these interferences would be in accordance with impersonal reasons, but would be harmful for potential parents. If the person-affecting reasons are stronger than the impersonal ones, one should resign from this kind of legal regulations.

Another interesting consequence of supporting the thesis that person-affecting reasons are stronger than the impersonal ones is the statement that the non-fulfillment of impersonal obligation should not be connected with guilt or social ostracism. It is of particular importance in the discussion on the moral evaluation of the decision of non-applying preconception diagnosis or pre-implementing genetic diagnosis. The parents of a disabled child, who previously made such a decision, should not, according to Savulescu, be criticized as follows: 'you should have done anything to have a different child', since in the moment of its existence the child deserves equal respect. On this basis the author comes to a conclusion that PB has a prospective and not retrospective function, which means that it can be a reason in favor of action before it is taken, but cannot be the criterion of evaluating the action after it is taken.

Nevertheless, the disambiguation of the character of PB does not dismiss all allegations that were formulated since it has appeared in the discussion for the first time. Rebecca Bennet pays attention to the fact that the attempts to find the impersonal X theory, based on the convincing function of life quality and the number of future persons, which do not lead to paradoxical and absurd consequences, failed, and without this theory the obligation cannot be justified. According to Bennet, the authors refer only to simple intuitions and emotional reactions to a given example that can be quite easily undermined (Bennett 2014). However, it seems that this allegation is too strong. Ethicists quite often refer to such feelings as guilt, regret or shame as auxiliary criteria that allow to state whether the action that caused such a feeling was in fact connected with the non-fulfillment of moral obligation. For sure, it would be difficult to decide over the person-affecting or impersonal character of the obligation only on this basis.

The problem in Savulescu's argumentation is the prospective and retrospective approach to the reasons in favor of the enhancement of future children. In the prospective approach, which is the moment when the child does not exist, the only person-affecting reasons the parents can take into consideration are their own interests. The remaining reasons would be connected with the impersonal value of the future state of affairs[3], but in this case they would be weaker. Therefore, this approach allows a very broad procreative autonomy. In the retrospective approach, the evaluation of the actions of parents who decided on natural procreation, ready for taking care of a disabled child, if they will have one, is exactly the same as the evaluation of the action of parents who strive for having a disabled child to derive benefits from the social help. If both couples of parents will fulfill their moral obligations to the already existing children, there is no possibility to prove a moral difference between their decisions. In both cases the impersonal value of a given state of affairs is identical, and in both cases, according to Savulescu's assumptions, it would be wrong to state: 'You should not have aimed at having this child'. However, it seems that in the above-mentioned

---

3   I skip the person-affecting reasons regarding the already existing people and connected with the social costs of giving birth to a disabled child, since, firstly, the costs are the basis for designating the impersonal value of the future state of affairs and, secondly, in accordance with the above-discussed assumptions, the reasons connected with these costs are not strong enough to restrict the procreative autonomy.

examples there is a significant difference connected with the parents' moral intentions. The impossibility to connect the moral evaluation of intentions and results of the parents' actions seems to prove a point against the possibility of differentiating the prospective and retrospective approaches to moral obligations connected with procreation.

The thesis on the priority of person-affecting reasons over the impersonal reasons allows avoiding the non-identity problem, justifying the broad scope of procreative autonomy and respecting disabled people. The main consequence of the thesis is making the moral evaluation of enhancement of human condition connected mostly with the intentions of parents (see Chapter 11). Due to this fact one should consider more important the arguments of bioconservatists, like Michael Sandel (Sandel 2007) or Peter Herissone-Kelly (Herissone-Kelly 2006), who pay particular attention to this aspect of the problem.

Acknowledgements

This text originally appeared in Polish in: Warmbier A (ed) (2016) Spór o podmiotowość: perspektywa interdyscyplinarna. Księgarnia Akademicka, Kraków. Translated from Polish into English by Aeddan Shaw.

References

Bennett R (2014) When intuition is not enough. Why the Principle of Procreative Beneficence must work much harder to justify its eugenic vision. Bioethics 28(9):447–455.

Boonin D (2014) The non-identity problem and the ethics of future people. Oxford University Press, New York.

Buchanan A, Brock DW, Daniels N, Wikler D (2006) From chance to choice. Genetics and justice. Cambridge University Press, Cambridge.

Diekema D (2004) Parental refusals of medical treatment: The Harm Principle as threshold for state intervention. Theoretical Medicine 25:243–264.

Dworkin R (1994) Life's dominion. An argument about abortion, euthanasia, and individual freedom. Vintage Books, New York.

Glover J (2006) Choosing children: genes, disability, and design. Oxford University Press, Oxford.

Herissone-Kelly P (2006) Procreative beneficence and the prospective parent. Journal of Medical Ethics 32:166–9.

Hickey KS, Lyckholm L (2004) Child welfare versus parental autonomy: medical ethics, the law, and faith-based healing. Theoretical Medicine and Bioethics 25(4):265–276.

O'Neill O (2002) Autonomy and trust in bioethics. Cambridge University Press, Cambridge, New York.

Parfit D (1976) Rights, interests, and possible people. In: Gorovitz S (ed) Moral problems in medicine. Prentice-Hall, Englewood Cliffs, NJ, pp. 373–374.

Parfit D (2007) Reasons and persons. Oxford University Press, Oxford.

Roberts MA (1998) Child versus childmaker: future persons and present duties in ethics and the law. Rowman & Littlefield, Oxford.

Robertson JA (1996) Children of choice: freedom and the new reproductive technologies. Princeton University Press, Princeton, NJ.

Różyńska J (2013) Złe geny, 'złe życie' i koncepcja krzywdy progowej. Etyka 47:50–66.

Sandel M (2007) The case against perfection: ethics in the age of genetic engineering. Belknap Press, Cambridge, MA.

Savulescu J (2001) Procreative beneficence: why should we select the best children? Bioethics 15(5/6):413–426.

Savulescu J (2014) The nature of the moral obligation to select the best children. In: Akabayashi A (ed) The future of bioethics. International dialogues, Oxford University Press, Oxford, pp. 170–182.

Savulescu J, Kahane G (2009) The moral obligation to create children with the best chance of the best life. Bioethics 23:274–290.

Sparrow R (2007) Procreative beneficence, obligation, and eugenics. Genomics, Society and Policy 3(3):43–59.

Sparrow R (2014) Ethics, eugenics, and politics. In: Akabayashi A (ed) The future of bioethics. International dialogues, Oxford University Press, Oxford, pp. 139–153.

Wilkinson D (2013) Death or disability? The 'Carmentis Machine' and decision-making for critically ill children. Oxford University Press, Oxford.

Żuradzki T (2008) Genetic engineering and the non-identity problem. Diametros 16: 63–79.

Wojciech Lewandowski

13 Intrinsic and instrumental values in the assessment of human enhancement

One of the objections against bioconservatism is that it insufficiently distinguishes between the various degrees of human enhancement. Taking drugs to improve memory or concentration is regarded in the same way as embryo selection for cognitive enhancement, and this, in turn, in the same way as creating an enhanced brain-machine interface. Advocates of human enhancement claim that there are no reasons strong enough to justify the prohibition of all enhancing interventions. According to them, the reasons for and against various interventions should be balanced against each other to formulate a moral judgment about the permissibility or impermissibility of a given intervention.

The debate on the strength of reasons in the assessment of human enhancement is usually based on one of the following distinctions of reasons. The first one is a distinction between person-affecting and impartial reasons. It concerns the effects of actual decisions about using enhancing technologies on the existence, identity, and number of future people. Predominantly, it is assumed that in the situations in which it is possible to show that a given intervention would be beneficial or harmful for a future person, the person-affecting reasons are stronger than impersonal ones (see Chapter 12). The main problem is that many actions taken in the context of human enhancement, e.g. procreative decisions and embryo selection, can hardly be viewed as person-affecting harm (Saunders 2015). The second distinction is between agent-relative and agent-neutral reasons. The former are based on the agent's perspective – they concern her own well-being, her relations with other people, and obligations which only that individual agent has. Agent-neutral reasons abstract from the agent's perspective and concern general well-being and obligations to all those with moral status. The latter are viewed as stronger in theories in which impartiality is an essential element of morality, however, many authors are trying to justify human enhancement by reference to both kinds of reasons (Savulescu & Persson 2012). The third distinction divides reasons into those based on intrinsic and instrumental values. The common understanding of these values is that the proper way of referring to instrumental values is to use them for the realization of further ends, and the proper way of referring to intrinsic values is to promote or respect them. From this point of view, it would be simple to see reasons based on intrinsic values as essentially stronger than those based on instrumental values. It should be noted, however, that not all intrinsic values are seen to have absolute superiority. The best example are attempts at balancing both kinds of values in environmental ethics. Analogically, if it is possible to justify that actual human nature is intrinsically valuable, then the risk of loss of this value may draw the line beyond which the reasons for increasing instrumental values through the enhancement of human capacities may cease to prevail. This kind of argumentation is formulated by Nicholas Agar in his book *Truly Human Enhancement*. He shows that some ways of enhancing our cognitive capacities or prolonging life are undesirable as they raise these traits to an excessively high level (Agar 2014, 2). What differs his argumentation from the bio-conservative view is an attempt to formulate and justify a model of balancing instrumental and intrinsic values based on the category of 'transformative change' which allows for a differentiated approach to various kinds of human enhancement. In this paper I am going to analyze the possibilities of building a general model of balancing these values in the context of human enhancement.

13.1 Transformative change as the boundary for enhancing interventions

Nicholas Agar uses the criterion of degree of enhancing interventions to distinguish between radical enhancement, which improves significant attributes and abilities to levels greatly exceeding what is currently possible for human beings, and moderate enhancement, improving significant attributes and abilities to levels within or close to what is currently possible for human beings. These significant attributes and abilities may be defined by their prudential value, i.e., how they can promote our interests or well-being. Prudential value may be viewed from one of two points of views: objective or anthropocentric. From the objective perspective, prudential values are instrumental values, dependent on the results of actions taken with the use of human attributes and abilities. Enhanced cognitive capacities have greater instrumental value because they enable us to solve increasingly more difficult and complex problems, and enhanced strength increases efficiency in physical activities. Prudential value seen from the anthropocentric perspective is an intrinsic value, independent of the results of the use of our capacities, and corresponding to the engagement in the exercise of these capacities (Agar 2014, 17–18, 28).

The distinction proposed by Agar is inspired by Alasdair MacIntyre's conception of goods internal and external to the practice. 'By 'practice' I am going to mean any coherent and complex form of socially established cooperative human activity through which goods internal to that form of activity are realized in the course of trying to achieve those standards of excellence which are appropriate to, and partially definitive of, that form of activity, with the result that human powers to achieve excellence, and human conceptions of the ends and goods involved, are systematically extended.' (MacIntyre 2007, 187).

According to this definition, the arts, sciences, complex games, politics, or the making and sustaining of family life are practices, and such activities as playing tic-tac-toe or bricklaying are not. Goods external to practices are those goods which may be achieved differently than by a given practice. When they are achieved, they remain individual property and may constitute the object of competition. On the other hand, goods internal to a practice may be defined only by the concepts taken from the given practice and may be recognized only through participation in this practice. The achievement of these kinds of goods is a good for the whole community (MacIntyre 2007, 190–191).

It may be noted that the possibility of enhancement of future people's capacities is a challenge for MacIntyre's view. Raising the IQ of a handicapped child, who so far couldn't participate in the practice of chess-playing, would enable him to achieve both goods internal and external to this practice. Further improvement of his intelligence – allowing him to play on Samuel Reshevsky's level – would increase his chance of achieving more goods external to the practice, while maintaining the same level of goods internal to the practice. Problems arise when the child's intelligence is raised to a level so high that playing chess would not offer him any challenge, being comparable in difficulty to tic-tac-toe. Continuous victories over world's best players would not constitute a good for the whole community and may even entail the loss of some internal goods. From the point of view of advocates of human enhancement, in order to avoid negative consequences such as the alienation of enhanced individuals, as many people as possible should actually undergo enhancement, which would lead to the formation of new practices and provide opportunities to achieve new goods internal to them. The prospect of a future society consisting of individuals whose capacities significantly exceed the current abilities of actual people, and who are engaged in practices completely different from current ones, including a different approach to morality, may be compatible only with the objective point of view, as it collides with the anthropocentric perspective. *Our own* practices and goods internal to them matter *to us* more than any future practices of enhanced people. How to balance both kinds of values? According to Agar, 'We arrive at a final reckoning of the prudential value of an enhancement by appropriately balancing the instrumental and intrinsic value of the resulting capacity.' (Agar 2014, 27–28). The key criterion is the threshold set by 'transformative change'.

> A transformative change alters the state of an individual's mental or physical characteristics in a way that causes and warrants a significant change in how that individual evaluates a wide range of their own experiences, beliefs, or achievements (Agar 2014, 5–6).

This proposition of a criterion for the limit of human enhancement presented by Agar is based on the individual's point of view. The main threat for the individual is a fundamental change in the way in which she evaluates her life.

From this point of view, the main argument against interventions leading to transformative change concerns the potential threat for our identities, as these interventions may affect the psychological connections between our past and actual selves by altering our assessment of our autobiographical memories. If before enhancing our physical abilities our participation in a marathon was memorable as a valued achievement, then after enhancement the same achievement may be unimpressive and not worth remembering (Agar 2014, 64). It should be noted that such argumentation would only concern the individuals who actually have some autobiographical memories from a time before the transformative change, and hence it wouldn't help to resolve problems concerning procreative decisions, embryo selection, or interventions performed on fetuses or infants. Furthermore, this argumentation requires a justification of the concept of identity based on autobiographical memories.

The second argument against radical enhancement is based on the fact that a transformative change may be irreversible. Radical cognitive or moral enhancement may lead to an outcome in which the enhanced person possesses extremely different beliefs and moral dispositions as compared with those from before the transformation. Changing the basis for moral valuations may have the effect that the person who decided to implement this change will not have a chance to recognize a possible error and regret her decision. According to Agar, this constitutes a good reason to avoid such modifications (Agar 2014, 14). Objections to this argument consist primarily of attempts to demonstrate that the individual may have reasons for irreversible transformative change, even beyond the context of human enhancement. According to Nicholas Bostrom and Toby Ord, growing up is such an irreversible process (Bostrom & Ord 2006, 671). Although this transformative change is not discontinuous, there is a clear difference between beliefs and valuing standards possessed by the person in childhood and the same person after reaching adulthood. The fact of this difference cannot be a reason for a child against this kind of transformative change. Agar's reply is based on the thesis that radical enhancement differs from growing up in that the child may assign significant value to his practices, but he cannot assign a value to the fact that these practices are valuable for him. In contrast, adult people can connect their practices into the whole project of their lives and assign value to being a human adult (Agar 2014, 74–75; Agar 2010, 188–189). It seems that this argument can be defended only from the 'human point of view' understood as the point of view of rational human beings participating in practices considered as valuable. In this case, however, the previous argument based on individual perspective and focused on the threat for individual identity loses its strength, and at the forefront stands the species-relativism view, according to which 'certain experiences and ways of existing properly valued by members of one species may lack value for the members of another species.' (Agar 2014, 188–189). The main argument against radical enhancement then turns out to be based on the risk of loss of intrinsic values significant from the 'human point of view'.

The argumentation presented above is not exposed to the speciesism objection as it does not assume that the intrinsic values of members of the *homo sapiens* species are objectively superior to the possible values shared by potential rational members of other species. It also does not say that the participation in the common valuable practices of rational beings belonging to different species is impossible. It says only that rational beings of one species, having different ideals, may not want to participate in some practices of rational members of other species.

The main challenge for species-relativism is justifying why the way of assigning value would depend primarily on biological species membership and not, for example, on having certain cognitive capacities or ways of experiencing the world. Another possible objection against basing intrinsic values on species-relativism is that it requires the abandonment of a universalist approach in moral theory. It is significant that one of the most famous defenses of human values against enhancement is formulated by a prominent representative of the antitheory approach (Williams 2006). MacIntyre's view, on which Agar's argumentation is based, is also far from universalism, which makes an attempt to create an objective model of evaluating potential enhancing interventions by balancing intrinsic and instrumental values even more difficult.

13.2 Balancing instrumental and intrinsic values

On the basis of the idea described above, there can be distinguished the following criteria and categories for comparing instrumental and intrinsic values (Table 13.1).

Tab. 13.1: The comparison of the objective and anthropocentric ideals

Objective ideal		Anthropocentric ideal	
Instrumental value of human capacity		Intrinsic value of human capacity	
Goods external to practices		Goods internal to practices	
The criterion of positive or negative outcomes of the use of a given capacity		The criterion of compatibility with current human standards of valuation	
Q^-	Q^+	I^-	I^+
Decrease of the quality of life	Increase of the quality of life	Lesser possibility to engage in practices compatible with the current human standards of valuation	Greater possibility to engage in practices compatible with the current human standards of valuation

How could the four above categories be compared? One of the possibilities is to apply the concept of lexical superiority of values. The strong lexical superiority of value A over value B means that *any* amount of a value is better than *any* amount of B value. The weak lexical superiority of A over B means that *some* amount of a is better than *any* amount of B (Arrhenius 2011, 291). The most popular illustration of the concept of lexical superiority is John Stuart Mill's famous quote: 'it is better to be a human being dissatisfied than a pig satisfied.' (Mill 1998, 57)[1]. Abstracting from hedonistic axiology, if applied to the problem of human enhancement, this sentence may be interpreted in following way:

$$I^+Q^- > I^-Q^+$$

> – strong lexical superiority

Applying this to the problem of human enhancement, it would mean that, with respect to the actual human condition, every enhancing intervention which would increase the quality of life while simultaneously decreasing the possibilities of achieving goods internal to valued practices would be worse than an intervention which increases the opportunities to participate in these practices

---

1 The problem of whether Mill's thesis may be interpreted as applying lexical superiority is discussed by B. Saunders (2010). Analysis of relationships between strong and weak superiority discusses G. Arrhenius and W. Rabinowicz (2005). Possible interpretations of lexical superiority in the models of social choice are analysed by J.H. Moldau (1992, 142–143).

despite the reduction of the quality of life. Paraphrasing Mill's words: it is better to be a human being dissatisfied than a post-human satisfied.

Assuming that I^0Q is the actual state of intrinsic and instrumental values, the model for evaluating decisions concerning the enhancement of human capacities based on strong superiority of intrinsic values would be as follows:

$$I^+Q^+ > I^+Q^0 > I^+Q^- > I^0Q^+ > I^0Q^0 > I^0Q^- > I^-Q^+ > I^-Q^0 > I^-Q^-$$

The assumption that compatibility with current human standards of valuation sets the lexical threshold makes it possible to claim that no matter how great the potential growth of instrumental value would be, the choice of a given intervention is better than refraining from it only when it is associated with the maintenance or increase of intrinsic values. Using this model might be advantageous, as it may lead to solutions of some common problems when assessing enhancing interventions. Furthermore, it could help to avoid the '*status quo* bias' objection, as lexical superiority of intrinsic value may provide a good basis for the preservation of actual human capacities on the current level (see Chapter 11).

There are, however, many problems which should be resolved before the adoption of this model. First of all, it is necessary to answer the question of whether it can support deontological constraints against performing enhancing interventions which lead to the loss of intrinsic values. On the one hand, the strong lexical superiority view seems to be perfect ground for these constraints, because it makes it possible to justify the claim that all options leading to a loss of intrinsic values are impermissible, and at the same time, it also allows for a gradation of the other options that set the intrinsic value at least at the initial level. The task of authors defending the bio-conservative position would be to justify the connection between the axiological thesis that decisions promoting intrinsic values are better than others and the normative thesis that these values should be respected and protected.[2]

The second problem is constituted by the possible implausible implications of strong superiority of intrinsic values. The classic example is a situation when a huge loss of values from the lower level is accompanied by only a slight increase in the values of the higher level (Griffin 1989, 83–89). In the context of human enhancement this situation would occur in the case of a rapid increase of suffering with a slightly improved possibility of achieving goods internal to practices. According to Agar, such a view would be bio-conservative extremism.

---

2   One of the possible ways of justifying the universal normative character of intrinsic values is basing them on virtues. The difficulties of this approach are analysed by E.D. Pellegrino (1995).

Mankind has developed many practices which allow it to face pain, suffering, and death, however, it doesn't seem that the prospective increase of such virtues as compassion or heroism during a war or a natural disaster would justify allowing these catastrophes Agar 2013, 93–94). Furthermore, there are possible situations in which the prevention of extreme social injustice or of the extinction of human species would justify giving up some intrinsic values (Pugh, Kahane & Savulescu 2013, 343). A possible answer to this objection is that the first situation concerns the necessity of balancing two different kinds of intrinsic values and the second is a situation in which both intrinsic and instrumental values are endangered. According to Francis Fukuyama, 'no one can make a brief in favor of pain and suffering,' but 'the highest and most admirable human qualities... are often related to the way that we react to, confront, overcome, and frequently succumb to pain, suffering, and death.' (Fukuyama 2002, 173). This claim is accompanied by the thesis that 'our good characteristics are intimately connected to our bad ones' and that 'violence and aggression are often needed to defend ourselves, the feelings of exclusivity are needed to be loyal, without jealousy we could never feel love and our mortality allows us as a species to survive and adapt.' (Ibid). This argument, however, seems to miss the point as it assumes the radical impossibility of the human condition which excludes aggressive behavior and discrimination without excluding defense against aggression, loyalty and love. It should rather be said that human virtues should work in good times and in bad, which means that there should be the possibility of achieving internal goods both in favorable conditions and in the face of pain, suffering, and death. Furthermore, the earlier mentioned combination of this model with deontological constraints would permit claiming that the necessity of avoiding wars and natural disasters is justified not only by balancing values, but also by human rights (Caney 2009, 165). Another answer to the problem of conflict situations might be to apply this model only to decisions assuming a positive quality of life. The argument for this solution is that most of the human enhancement projects assume a positive quality of life at the starting point, and conflict situations of the kind described earlier would occur only in therapeutic decisions which need more complex models of ethical assessment. This answer requires the assumption that participation in practices is to some extent dependent on quality of life. If so, then the option in which quality of life falls below the minimal level needed to participate in a given practice should never be preferable.

The third challenge for this model is a matter of clarifying how to define the current level of intrinsic values and the criteria of growth or loss of these values. If this model is to be applied to political decisions concerning the implementation of technologies improving human capacities, and not only to individual decisions whether or not to use these technologies, then the obvious criterion would be the risk of elimination of a given valuable practice from social life. The easiest way to estimate these changes is by referring to the number of people with the capacities needed to participate in this practice. The downside of this model is 'anthropocentric eugenics', because on this basis we could claim that the existence of enhanced people whose capacities and traits are not compatible with actual human standards of valuation is undesirable. More plausible would be a reference to the existence or absence of a given practice. The problem here, however, is the lack of precision in identifying those practices which should be preserved. It seems that many examples given by Agar or MacIntyre would hardly be seen as intrinsic values lexically superior to the values of improving the quality of life. Playing chess or running a marathon certainly have intrinsic value, however, it is difficult to consider them to be common values from the anthropocentric point of view. The main task, then, is clarifying and narrowing down the concept of intrinsic values related to participation in a practice.

In the next part of this chapter I will analyze two possibilities of doing that: basing intrinsic value on human commitment to ground projects and on interpersonal relationships.

13.3 Ground projects and interpersonal relationships after transformative change

According to Roduit, Baumann, and Heilinger, a good framework for assessing enhancing interventions is Martha Nussbaum's list of ten capabilities fundamental for human beings: life; bodily health; bodily integrity; senses, imagination, and thought; emotions; practical reason; affiliation; other species; play; and control over one's environment (Nussbaum 2011, 25). The prognosis about how human enhancement may affect human life in these respects can play both a constraining and guiding role in the assessment of such interventions, since the Capability Approach provides us both with ten thresholds which demarcate the levels under which human life would be seriously impoverished and with a holistic account of human life (Roduit, Baumann & Heilinger 2015, 629). The problem is that decisions about individual or species transformative changes are made from an agent's perspective. In order to assign intrinsic value to these capabilities and compare them with instrumental values they need to be referred to some more fundamental values in the agent's perspective.

Consider an example of transformative change of sensual experience given by Laurie Paul: 'Imagine that neuroscientists and engineers invent a microchip that, when implanted in the brain, gives humans a new sensory ability, a sixth sense in addition to the usual five. If this sense is truly new, rather than a combination of more familiar senses, before getting the chip, we cannot know what it would be like to experience the new, sixth, sense. With respect to this sensory ability, anyone without the chip would be in the same position as a person who is blind from birth, or a person who has never been able to hear: there would be a human sensory ability that some people have and others don't, but those without the chip would not know what it is like to have it until they experience it.' (Paul 2014, 6). The Capability Approach needs a justification of the role which having five senses instead of six or more plays in our lives. That means that assessment of transformative change should be first-personal.[3] In contemporary ethical debate there are two widely discussed sources of intrinsic values which could serve as a holistic view on the value of capabilities: ground projects and special relationships.

The first proposition which supports strong lexical priority of intrinsic values over instrumental ones is inspired by Bernard Williams' reflections on the agent's integrity (Williams 1973, 116–117). If the possibility of satisfying one's categorical desires is a condition of integrity, then it is a natural consequence to accept the claim that commitment to ground projects has value which is lexically superior to instrumental values.

$$I_p^+Q^+ > I_p^+Q^0 > I_p^+Q^- > I_p^0Q^+ > I_p^0Q^0 > I_p^0Q^- > I_p^-Q^+ > I_p^-Q^0 > I_p^-Q^-$$

I_p – intrinsic value of commitment to ground project

The main argument for this proposition is that the reduction of value of ground projects to values based on maximization of utility leads to counter-intuitive conclusions. Objections against consequential theories are often illustrated by cases in which the agent has an obligation to sacrifice his own projects in order to maximize general well-being. Williams' view on the connection between integrity and identity seems to support strong lexical superiority, as there is no level of quality of life high enough which could outweigh our commitment to everything which makes us *us*. In the context of human enhancement, a great increase in the quality of life is never worth abandoning our human values (Williams 2006, 149–152).

The problem of this justification is the difficulty of determining the nature of lexical superiority of ground projects' value. Not all projects seem to have such a

---

3 According to Paul, the main criterion for this kind of decisions is the subjective desirability of revelation (see more in Chapter 6). It seems, however, that also the desirability of revelation should be balanced against the possibility or the lack of possibility of participating in practices compatible with the current human standards of valuation.

value. Technological advances have led to the elimination of many practices and thus – many intrinsic values have been abandoned in order to give way to the growth of instrumental values. More and more human practices are carried out through information technologies. In the future new practices will appear and future people will have the possibility of choosing old and new life projects and achieving them without effort (Schermer 2008, 363). A model based on strong lexical priority of intrinsic values of ground projects should assume the possibility of mutual comparison of these values. The criterion of compatibility with current human standards of valuation is insufficient on its own. According to Joseph Raz, even now it is difficult to compare the intrinsic value of the career of a lawyer and of an artist, because both of these practices contain some subjectively chosen project (Raz 1986, 342). For the same reason it would be difficult to justify the obligation to preserve a specific profession in the society, or the demand for the capacities or traits related to this profession.

An attempt to defend the strong superiority of ground projects' intrinsic value could be based on a classic conception of human nature, in which the agent's ground project is pursued to its ultimate end. In this perspective, perfection is the fullest development of the agent's traits according to natural human inclinations. This approach could include human enhancement, provided that the interventions preserve the ability to act in harmony with natural human inclinations and do not modify these inclinations themselves (Eberl 2014). According to MacIntyre, the rejection of the claim that people have their ultimate end is the main source of the failure of the Enlightenment Project to create universal moral standards for resolving practical problems (MacIntyre 2007, 52). In the context of the human enhancement problem, the lack of consideration about the end towards which human practices are aimed, or the reduction of this end to the category of well-being, causes consecutive, contradictory proposals to arise for new directions of enhancing human capacities, and the arguments formulated by each faction appear to be equally compelling. Furthermore, the lack of the category of an ultimate end would make it impossible to differentiate between the practices which require commitment and make life meaningful and mere consumption (Borgmann 1984, 219). The main foundation for lexical superiority of the ground projects' value would be, therefore, the fact that any attempt to balance one's projects against the quality of life would constitute self-corruption and a threat to one's integrity.

It should be noted that the above arguments can be applied not only to a defense of the model involving the lexical ordering of values, but also against it, as they could support the view opposing any attempt to build a theoretical framework for comparing different kinds of values. Such a framework would require conceiving the ultimate end of human life as clearly as possible in order to determine which practices may lead to this end. If the commonsense view on perfection is that it should be based on practical wisdom rather than on theoretical models, then building these models for the optimal balance between intrinsic and instrumental values should be viewed as another doomed-to-failure consequence of the Enlightenment Project described by MacIntyre. It could also be said that there is no possibility of even formulating a comprehensive project of human life, the implementation of which would allow for the achievement of perfection (Slote 2011). Human life may rather be viewed as a creative search for a way to realize a whole range of different kinds of practices, with the possibility of abandoning some projects, starting others, or returning to the previous ones.

A compromise between these positions would be the acceptance of the weak superiority of intrinsic values.

$$I_p^+Q^+ > I_p^+Q^0 > I_p^+Q^- > I_p^0Q^+ > I_p^0Q^0 > I_p^0Q^- > I_p^-Q^+ > I_p^-Q^0 > I_p^-Q^-$$

› – weak lexical superiority

According to this version, the possibility of a sufficient increase of instrumental values or the prevention of their decrease might outweigh the growth of intrinsic values or the prevention of their decrease. The degree of the superiority would not be defined once and for all, but it would be dependent on individual practical wisdom. If technological progress could help avoid some catastrophic decrease of instrumental values at the expense of the elimination of some practices which were sources of intrinsic values, then it would only depend on the agents' view concerning the significance of that practice whether a future without this value would be better than with it.[4]

It seems that the best candidate for such a significant practice which could generate values that outweigh a great decrease of the quality of life are the practices related to some interpersonal relationships, such as family ties or friendship. This would be more consistent with deontological constraints than the integrity view, since special relationships seem both to have intrinsic value and to generate obligations (Raz 1989, 19, Scheffler 2004, 260). Furthermore, it can serve as an easy justification of why some transformative changes are undesirable. If cognitive enhancement led to a great increase of the quality of life, but at the cost of the lack of possibility to engage in practices developing previous relationships

---

4 This case abstracts from other considerations concerning obligations or duties which may affect the ultimate judgement.

and to act in accordance with one's obligations generated by these relationships, then one would have strong reasons not to undergo this change. From a general point of view, the possibility of engaging in these relations can be seen as a fundamental condition of the acceptance of enhancing interventions.

Given that previous arguments against strong lexical superiority may also be applied to intrinsic values from practices related to interpersonal relationships, the new version of the model would be based on weak lexical superiority:

$$I_R^+E^+ > I_R^+E^0 > I_R^+E^- > I_R^0E^+ > I_R^0E^0 > I_R^0E^- > I_R^-E^+ > I_R^-E^0 > I_R^-E^- \quad (14.5)$$

I_p – intrinsic value of commitment to interpersonal relationships

A possible objection to this model is similar to the previous one: how to formulate a list of special relationships which are sources of the intrinsic value of a practice? The answer here may be more plausible than previously: though it is impossible to define special relationships, there is almost universal agreement that at least some of them, like family or friendship, should be taken into account in all ethical considerations. This claim, however, doesn't resolve the second problem: whether special relationships are a source of intrinsic values irreducible to the quality of life or other values. The value of a relationship may be dependent on, e.g., its quality or the degree of commitment to it. According to Simon Keller, these relationships can have only extrinsic value, even though they are agent-relative, irreplaceable, immense, and not straightforwardly dependent upon some other value (Keller 2013, 55). Suppose we discover a society in which a certain kind of special relationship is entirely absent. Imagine that children in this society are raised communally and that there are no special loving bonds between children and their parents. Suppose that the communal arrangement appears to work very well and that the society functions no less successfully than ours. People in this society, as compared to ours, seem just as happy, just as virtuous, just as secure, just as respected, and so on (Keller 2013, 58–59).

If we imagine that the society described by Keller is a consequence of some kind of human enhancement, then according to the proponents of these interventions it is hard to maintain that the model of lexical superiority may be based on rational assumptions. It should be noted, however, that from the anthropocentric point of view the question is not about the objective value of possible future societies, but about what kind of society we have most reason to pursue. If the future society is built through individual procreative decisions, then one of the most important reasons for having children is to build a special relationship with them. The model of weak lexical superiority may be one of the possible ways of conceptualizing these reasons.

13.4 Conclusions

Assessing human enhancement with the models for comparing intrinsic and instrumental values makes it possible to avoid some problems in contemporary dispute. Using these models indicates that at least in theory some types of interventions may have positive effects for the preservation of intrinsic values. This also makes it possible to show that bioconservative arguments against human enhancement may rely not on an incorrect estimation of the future value, but on an assumption of the primacy of intrinsic values over instrumental ones. Finally, it makes it possible to justify the claim that a predicted increase in the quality of life shouldn't be the only criterion for the assessment of human enhancement. At the same time, these models cannot constitute an independent criterion for the assessment of human enhancement, as they should also be accompanied by deontological constraints. Using these models also requires an axiological framework to explain the relation between the intrinsic value of capacity and the intrinsic value of relationships and individuals. Furthermore, the superiority of these intrinsic values is justified in this model only by assuming the priority of the agent-relative and anthropocentric perspective over the agent neutral. Finally, it should be still justified that the strength of reasons to pursue or refrain from pursuing some end through enhancing interventions is proportional to the lexical superiority of intrinsic values over the instrumental ones.

Acknowledgements

This paper has been previously published in: A. Warmbier (ed), The idea of perfection and human enhancement, Peter Lang, 2018.

References

Agar N (2010) Humanity's end. Why we should reject radical enhancement. MIT Press, Cambridge, Mass.

Agar N (2013) Radical human enhancement, and what's wrong with it. In: Sandler RL, Basl J (eds) Designer biology. The ethics of intensively engineering biological and ecological systems. Lexington Books, Lanham, pp. 87–104.

Agar N (2014) Truly human enhancement: a philosophical defence of limits. MIT Press, Cambridge, Mass.

Arrhenius G (2011) Superiority in Values. In: Rønnow-Rasmussen T, Zimmerman MJ (eds) Recent work on intrinsic value. Springer, Dordrecht, London, pp. 291–304.

Arrhenius G, Rabinowicz W (2005) Millian Superiorities. Utilitas 14(2):127–146.

Borgmann A (1984) Technology and the character of contemporary life: a philosophical enquiry. Chicago University Press, Chicago.

Bostrom N, Ord T (2006) The Reversal test: eliminating status quo bias in applied ethics. Ethics 116(4):656–679.

Caney S (2009) Climate change, human rights and moral thresholds. In: Humphrey S (ed) Human rights and climate change. Cambridge University Press, Cambridge, pp. 163–177.

Eberl JT (2014) A Thomistic appraisal of human enhancement technologies. Theoretical Medicine and Bioethics 35(4):289–310.

Fukuyama F (2002) Our posthuman future. Consequences of the biotechnology revolution. Farrar, Straus and Giroux, New York.

Griffin J (1989) Well-being. Its meaning, measurment and moral importance. Clarendon Press, Oxford.

Keller S (2013) Partiality. Princeton University Press, Princeton, NJ.

MacIntyre A (2007) After virtue. A study in moral theory. Notre Dame Press, Notre Dame.

Mill JS (1998) Utlilitarianism. Oxford University Press, Oxford.

Moldau JH (1992) On the lexical ordering of social states according to Rawls' principles of justice. Economics and Philosophy 8(1):141–148.

Nussbaum M (2011) Creating capabilities: the human development approach. Belknap Press, Cambridge, Mass.

Paul LA (2014) Transformative experience, Oxford University Press, Oxford.

Pellegrino ED (1995) Toward a virtue-based normative ethics for health professions. Kennedy Institute of Ethics Journal 5(3):253–277.

Pugh J, Kahane G, Savulescu J (2013) Cohen's conservatism and human enhancement. Journal of Ethics 14(4):331–354.

Raz J (1986) The Morality of Freedom. Clarendon Press, Oxford.

Raz J (1989) Liberating Duties. Law and Philosophy 8(1):3–21.

Roduit JAR, Baumann H, Heilinger JC (2015) Ideas of perfection and the ethics of human enhancement. Bioethics 29(9):622–630.

Saunders B (2010) J.S. Mill conception of utility. Utilitas 27(1):52–69.

Saunders B (2015) Why procreative preferences may be moral – and why it may not matter if they aren't. Bioethics 29(7):499–506.

Savulescu J, Persson I (2012) Unfit for the future: the need of moral enhancement. Oxford University Press, Oxford.

Scheffler S (2004) Projects, relationships and reasons. In: Wallace RJ (ed) Reason and value: themes from the moral philosophy of Joseph Raz. Oxford University Press, Oxford, pp. 247–269.

Schermer M (2008) Enhancements, easy shortcuts and the richness of human activities. Bioethics 22(7): 355–363.

Slote M (2011) The impossibility of perfection: Aristotle, feminism and the complexity of ethics. Oxford University Press, New York.

Williams B (1973) A critique of utilitarianism. In: Williams B, Smart JJC (eds) Utilitarianism. For and against. Cambridge University Press, Cambridge, pp. 77–150.

Williams B (2006) The human prejudice. In: Williams B (ed) Philosophy as a humanistic discipline. Princeton University Press, Princeton, N.J., pp. 135–152.

Wojciech Lewandowski

Concluding remarks

In this book we have presented a combined pluralistic approach to the moral problems concerning genetic selection and human enhancement. It consists of two combinations and both approaches are, in turn, linked to one another. The first joins the individual perspective of a parent with the social perspective expressed in moral assumptions towards legal regulations. The second one is a combination of principles and virtues in moral reasoning. Individual and social reasons are expressed in the form of principles such as procreative beneficence, procreative nonmalaficence, the principle of reproductive autonomy or the acceptance of a child. In many cases, the principles formulated from these two perspectives support each other, but their radical dissimilarity makes potential conflicts harder to resolve. The clash of these two perspectives provides the opportunity to discover the proper meaning and the scope of moral principles concerning procreation based on the intrinsic value of the parent-child relationship and that of the child himself, with both values being complementary. The value of the relation is what makes potential parents want to create it, even before the child exists and hence without the necessary reference to the existence and identity of the child. In the social aspect, the intrinsic value of the relationship allows one to justify the legal protection of embryos, foetuses and the relationship itself. It also limits some of the possible enhancing interventions involved in the transhumanist and posthumanist projects as it gives an axiological meaning to some of the biological and psychological aspects of human nature, such as hugging or breast-feeding. The advantage of grounding the moral principles of procreation in the value of the relationship is that it avoids the non-identity problem, is complementary with a virtue approach but it is also easy to put in legal terms and broad enough to embrace the full process of reproduction, from preconception up to the postnatal phase. The main problems lie in defining the essential value of this relationship. Consequentialism recognizes this value on the basis of the impartial view of the amount of happiness possible to achieve from being in the relationship. This is both the reason for the existence of the relationship and any changes that may occur in it, including the enhancement of one or both parties through biomedical interventions. The pluralistic approach assumes that we cannot resign from the view from within relationships as a referencing point. The test for our recognition of this value are situations in which the relationship is confronted by suffering, disability or disappointed expectations. The thought that they do not alter anything in terms of the axiological status of the relationship can give us the motivational strength to confront them.

The value of the relationship cannot be the only basis for moral principles. A clear example in which we need another grounding is that of sex selection. Even if we accept the irreducible value of the parent-child relationship, the possibility of sex selection puts us in conflict with the reasons of beneficence, appropriate sex balance (in the family or in the society), of avoiding sexism and of the unconditional acceptance of a child. The solution to these conflicts lies in the thought that, ultimately, they seem to be based on the child's value seen from different perspectives and that the true meaning of a child's traits must take into account the fact that all of them depend on this value and not vice versa. Views about sex selection, selection to disability or preventing disability and about human enhancement should take this relationship into account since without a strong assumption about the importance of the personal perspective, there is a danger that the true meaning of a child's life will vanish in ethical neutrality. As such, this is only a small step from neutrality to indifference. Projects of enhancement will remain blind if they do not take into consideration the shared life history, commitments and value experiences of both parents and children.

The pluralist position we defend can deal with the conflicts between different perspectives without giving up the importance of any of them by referring to the category of virtues. The moral character of a parent is shaped in a specific, individual perspective and network of relationships. Without understanding oneself as a moral agent, it is impossible to give one's child the chance to live a good life. At the same time, an important element of moral character is the disposition to see one's decisions, including procreative ones, from a distanced and impartial point of view. Positions permitting a wide range of interventions in human procreation and those imposing restrictions must assume that the primary precondition of the moral value of procreative decisions is that they should be made in good faith by virtuous agents or at least those trying to be such, avoiding causing harm or reducing a child's life to the function of fulfilling one's own unfulfilled desires. Justice in the social perspective is expressed by avoiding the dominance resulting from the privileged position of the present generation over the next one. On the one hand, this reflects the individual relationship of parents to children and, on the other, the solidarity of all existing individuals for whom existence is a fundamental good. The meaning of procreation from this perspective can be seen as a free market of existence in which there are no prerequisites to join and which is regulated by the most valuable characteristics of human nature.

Index

A

Adams, Robert 131–133
Agar, Nicholas 39, 48, 155, 177, 184, 222, 255, 257, 272–275, 277–279, 284
Aiken, William 33, 224
Akabayashi, Akira 269
Ando, Hideki 99
Andorno, Roberto 23, 32, 110, 114
Andrews, Lori B. 177
Angrist, Misha 21, 32, 167, 177, 194, 222
Annas, George J. 164, 167, 168, 177, 192–194, 222
Aquinas, Thomas 112, 197
Archard, David 142, 149
Arendt, Hannah 187, 188, 192, 209, 223
Ariail, Kiley 9, 18
Aristotle 32, 112, 114, 164, 177, 191, 195–221, 223, 286
Arnhart, Larry 186, 223
Arrhenius, Gustaf 276, 284, 285
Asch, Adrienne 27, 34, 101, 105, 106, 111, 114, 115
Aslin, Richard N. 186, 225
Audi, Robert 200, 204, 206, 223
Augustine, St. 134, 187, 219, 220, 223

B

Bartels, Dianne M. 33, 34
Bartlett, Robert C. 32, 114, 177, 223
Basl, John 284
Baumann, Holger 279, 285
Beauchamp, Tom L. 18, 22, 32, 178, 179
Becker, Gay 86, 100, 150
Bellemare, Charles 175, 178

Benatar, David 40, 48, 128, 133, 149
Bennett, Rebecca 114, 233, 244, 267, 268
Berger, Roni 149
Bergh, Torbjörn 151
Berkowitz, Jonathan M. 56, 63, 67
Berlin, Isaiah 12, 13, 17
Biesecker, Barbara B. 21, 32
Bigelow, John 142, 149
Birnbacher, Dietrich 91, 99, 104, 114, 155, 163, 164, 178, 192, 223
Blount, Sally 175, 178
Blustein, Jeffrey 142, 149
Blyth, Eric 136, 144, 149
Boivin, Jacky 151
Bolt, L.L.E. 217, 218, 223
Bonu, Maria 149
Boonin, David 261
Bordet, Sylvie 9, 17
Borges, Edson 150
Borghesi, Francesco 226
Borgmann, Albert 281, 285
Borini, Andrea 149
Bostrom, Nick 13, 17, 69, 155, 178–181, 184, 223, 248, 249, 257, 258, 274, 285
Botkin, Jeffrey R. 27, 32, 33, 96, 99
Braga, Daniela P. 150
Brennan, Samantha 133, 134
Brock, Dan 33, 39, 48, 67, 99, 114, 178, 193, 223, 268
Broome, John 38, 48
Buchanan, Allen E. 24, 28, 33, 39, 48, 56, 57, 59, 67, 88, 89, 91, 92, 99, 102, 114, 156–159, 162, 164, 166, 167, 169–172, 178, 192, 193, 223, 247, 250, 251, 257, 259, 264, 268

Burges, Anthony 206, 223
Butler, Anneliese 150

C
Campbell, John 149
Caney, Simon 278, 285
Caplan, Arthur L. 29, 33, 34
Caplan, Bryan 43, 48
Cattoli, Monica 144, 149
Chadwick, Ruth 178, 223
Chesterton, Gilbert K. 194, 223
Childress, James 22, 32
Churchland, Patricia 185, 223
Cohen, Gerald A. 169, 178, 285
Collins, Francis C. 183, 224
Collins, Susan D. 32, 114, 177, 223
Congregation for the Doctrine of the Faith 135, 149
Cook, Thomas 121, 133
Crosby, John F. 134
Crosby, John Henry 134
Cserne, Peter 180
Curlender, Shauna 82, 100

D
Dahl, Edgar 56, 67
Dancy, Jonathan 46, 49
Daniels, Ken 150, 158, 163
Daniels, Norman 33, 39, 48, 67, 99, 114, 136, 178, 223, 268
Darwin, Charles 15, 183, 184, 197, 203–205, 221, 226
Dasgupta, Partha 123, 124, 133
Davies, Kevin 22, 33
Davis, Dena S. 24, 27–29, 33, 45, 46, 63, 67, 210, 211, 224
DeGrazia, David 155, 157, 163–165, 178, 186, 192, 215–217, 224, 241, 233, 254, 257
de Lacey, Sheryl 136, 149, 150
de Lissnyder, Evi 151

de Melo-Martin, Inmaculada 60–63, 65–67
DePoe, John M. 131, 133
Descartes, René 220
de Sousa Bonetti, Tatiana C. 150
de Sutter, Petra 151
de Waal, Frans 185, 224
Devlin, Albert J. 206, 224
Devolder, Katrien 235, 244
Dhont, Marc 151
Diamond, Cora 12, 17, 103, 104, 106, 115
Diekema, Douglas 259, 268
Dinopoulou, Vasiliki 49
Dodds, Susan 149
Dods, Marcus 223
Donagan, Alan 140, 150
Dougherty, Trent 130, 133
Douglas, Thomas 125, 133, 185, 216, 224, 233, 235, 240, 244, 251, 257
Draper, Heather 137, 150
Dréze, Jean 56, 67
du Preez, Elisabeth 150
Dworkin, Ronald 12, 17, 23, 33, 63, 67, 191, 224, 259, 268
Dyson, Esther 21

E
Eberl, Jason 281, 285
Eisenkopf, Gerald 178
Elliott, Carl 218, 224
Elshtain, Jean Bethke 179, 226
Elwyn, Glyn 151
Engelhardt, H. Tristram 22, 33

F
Fabre, Cécile 64, 67
Fehige, Christoph 134
Feinberg, Joel 23, 33, 74–76, 80, 81, 88, 92, 93, 99, 214, 224
Föllmi-Heusi, Franzisca 178

Frankfurt, Harry G. 217–219, 224
Freedman, Benjamin 47, 49
Friese, Carrie 150
Fischbacher, Urs 175, 178
Frith, Lucy 149
Fukuyama, Francis 156, 178, 184, 192, 224, 247, 250, 257, 278, 285

G

Gaita, Raimond 17, 115
Galjaard, Hans 55, 68
Gauthier, David 38, 49
Geach, Mary 146, 150
Gelhaus, Petra 30, 33
Gerris, Jan 151
Gerth, Hans H. 50
Giannaris, Dimitros 49
Gizbert-Studnicki, Tomasz 93, 99
Glantz, Leonard H. 177
Glover, Jonathan 156, 178, 264, 268
Goedeke, Sonja 136, 144, 150
Gordijn, Bert 114, 178, 223
Gormally, Luke 150
Gorovitz, Samuel 269
Gould, Stephen J. 156, 178
Green, Ronald M. 92, 99, 179, 185, 190, 224, 231, 243, 244
Greenberg, Julia 179
Greene, Joshua 185, 190, 224
Griffin, James 277, 285
Gutmann, Amy 116
Guyer, Paul 225

H

Habermas, Jürgen 29, 33, 44, 45, 47, 49, 156, 165, 178, 184, 188, 192, 194, 204, 205, 208–210, 212–214, 217, 221, 224, 226, 247, 249, 257
Hainz, Tobias 253, 257
Haberko, Joanna 78, 99
Haidt, Jonathan 185, 218, 224
Hamann, Katharina 179

Handa, Hiroshi 99
Hannan, Sarah 133, 134
Hare, Richard M. 91, 99, 102, 103, 115
Harris, John 42, 43, 49, 56, 68, 157, 159, 160, 172, 174, 179, 184, 194, 206, 208, 224, 225, 233, 235–237, 240, 244, 251, 258
Harsanyi, John 39, 41, 49
Hart, Herbert L.A. 165, 179
Havel, Valcav 176, 179
Häyry, Matti 45–47, 49, 231, 244, 258
Heilinger, Jan-Christoph 279, 285
Hélen, Ilpo 29, 33
Herissone-Kelly, Peter 49, 233, 244, 268
Heyd, David 117, 123, 124, 126, 127, 133
Hickey, Kenneth S. 259, 269
Hodge, James G. Jr 9, 17
Holland, Stephen 31, 33, 79
Holm, Søren 55, 57, 58, 60, 61, 68
Holtug, Niels 130, 133
Hoptman, Laura 114, 115
Hotke, Andrew 106, 107, 115
Hotta, Kentaro 99
Hume, David 204
Humphrey, Stephen 285
Huxley, Aldous 183, 203, 206, 221, 225
Huxley, Julian 183, 188, 205, 221, 223, 225
Huxley, Thomas Henry 183, 188

I

Iaconelli, Assumpto 150
Imamura, Yoshimasa 99
Isasi, Rosario M. 9, 17, 177
Ito, Takumi 75, 99

J

Jaeger, Werner 32, 33
Johnson, D. Gale 133

Jonas, Hans 252
Juengst, Eric T. 101, 115
Justyński, Tomasz 75, 76, 81, 83, 86, 97, 99

K
Kahane, Guy 11, 18, 106–108, 116, 185, 207, 226, 227, 229, 232, 245, 263, 269, 278, 285
Kahneman, Daniel 248, 258
Kamm, Frances M. 11, 17, 39, 49, 58, 59, 62, 68, 91, 99, 102, 105, 110, 115, 157, 172, 179, 192, 193, 209, 225
Kandel, Michael 225
Kant, Immanuel 13, 15, 16, 187, 203–211, 217, 219, 221, 223, 225
Kass, Leon R. 30, 34, 42, 43, 49, 141, 150, 156, 179, 184, 225, 247, 250, 258
Keller, Simon 125, 133, 283, 285
Kevles, Daniel 156, 179
Khan, Jeffrey P. 178, 179
Kidd, Celeste 186, 225
Kilner, John F. 179, 226
Kirkman, Maggie 136, 150
Kitcher, Philip 92, 99
Knoppers, Bertha M. 9, 17
Kolodny, Niko 141, 150
Kołakowski, Leszek 197, 204, 205, 225
Kołodziejczyk, Sebastian T. 227
Könczöl, Miklós 180
Korsgaard, Christine M. 203–206, 217, 218, 225
Kröger, Sabine 178
Kramer, Matthew 200, 225
Kuhse, Helga 34, 48, 68, 116
Kymlicka, Will 102, 104, 106, 115

L
LaFollette, Hugh 33, 224
Lang, Wiesław 84, 99

Lecce, Steven 118, 119, 133
Lee, Ronald D. 133
Lem, Stanisław 222
Leonard, John 226, 244
LeRoy, Bonnie S. 33, 34
Levy, Neil 56, 68
Lewis, Clive Staples 156, 179, 194, 195, 225
Locke, Don 90, 100
Locke, John 13, 215
Lohse, Karoline 181
Lotz, Mianna 119, 133, 134
Lyckholm, Laurel 259, 269

M
MacDougall, Kirstin 150
McDougall, Rosalind 31, 34
MacIntyre, Alasdair 110, 112, 115, 188, 189, 197, 225, 272, 273, 275, 279, 281, 282, 285
Madaschi, Camila 150
Magnusson, Erik 118, 119, 133
Makrakis, Evangelos 37, 49
Manson, Neil A. 251, 252, 258
Marcus, Ruth B. 147, 150
Marsh, Jason 130, 134
Mason, H.E. 150
Mastroianni, Anna C. 178, 179
McBrayer, Justin P. 133
McCarthy, Thomas 49
McConnell, Terrance C. 143, 150
McDowell, John 199, 200, 225
McKibben, Bill 247, 257, 258
McKie, John 116
McMahon, Catherine A. 151
Melamed, Rose M. 136, 150
Melis, Alicia 181
Mill, John Stuart 71–73, 96, 100, 204, 226, 276, 277, 285
Miller, Paul 245
Milton, John 206, 226, 236, 244
Minor Hippias 30

Mitchel, C. Ben 161, 179, 188, 226
Moldau, Juan H. 276, 285
Müller-Hill, Benno 156, 179
Murdoch, Iris 113, 115
Murray, Robert F. Jr. 10, 17, 21, 22, 34, 168, 179

N
Nachtigall, Robert D. 136, 150
Nagel, Thomas 188, 209, 214, 219, 226
Nelson, James L. 142, 150
Noor, Liesbeth H.W. 55, 68
Nussbaum, Martha 109, 115, 169, 178, 179, 279, 285

O
Ogaura, Toshihiko 99
O'Neill, Onora 23, 34, 63, 68, 95, 100, 261, 269
Ord, Toby 248, 274
Overall, Christine 119, 134

P
Palmeri, Holly 186, 225
Papio, Michael 226
Parens, Erik 27, 34, 105, 106, 111, 115
Parfit, Derek 28, 34, 89, 90, 100, 125, 134, 215, 225, 226, 232, 244, 260, 261, 269
Pargetter, Robert 149
Parker, Michael 233, 244
Parry, Sarah 136, 151
Pascal, Blaise 220
Patrone, Tatiana 256, 258
Paul, Laurie A. 280, 285
Paul, Marylin S. 149
Pellegrino, Edmund D. 27–32, 34, 173, 179, 180, 226, 277, 285
Pennings, Guido 151

Persson, Ingmar 155, 180, 184, 190, 207, 226, 234, 236–240, 244, 245, 254, 258, 271, 285
Peterson, Martin 38, 50
Pico della Mirandola, Giovanni 201, 202, 226
Piłat, Robert 185, 198, 199, 203, 213, 226
Pinker, Steven 111, 115
Plantinga, Alvin 188, 226
Plato 169, 173, 180, 191, 200, 202, 220
Pollock, John L. 38, 50
Post, Stephen G. 17, 18, 32, 34, 116
President's Council on Bioethics 51, 52, 57, 61–64, 66, 68, 213, 218, 226, 247, 258
Prior, Elisabeth 84, 149
Provoost, Veerle 136, 151
Prusak, Bernard 141, 142, 144, 151
Pugh, Jonathan 209, 226, 278, 285

Q
Quaid, Kimberly A. 9, 18

R
Rabinowicz, Wlodzimierz 276, 285
Rae, Scott 179, 226
Ramsey, Paul 167, 180, 210, 226
Rawls, John 38, 39, 49, 50, 108, 109, 115, 165, 166, 168, 170, 180, 285
Raz, Joseph 281, 286
Reiman, Jeffrey 89, 91, 92, 94, 100, 108, 115
Reeve, C.D.C. 180
Richardson, Jeff 116
Riva, Massimo 226
Roberts, Melinda A. 261, 269
Robertson, John A. 56, 63, 68, 259, 269
Roche, Patricia A. 177
Roduit, Johann A.R. 279, 285

Rønnow-Rasmussen, Toni 284
Rothstein, Mark A. 179
Rose, Steven 233
Różyńska, Joanna 261, 269
Rulli, Tina 141, 151

S

Saenz, Carla 31, 34
Safjan, Marek 84, 97, 99, 100
Sandberg, Anders 185, 226, 245
Sandel, Michael 13, 18, 28, 30, 34, 43, 65, 68, 98, 100, 109, 111, 112, 115, 158, 173, 180, 194, 213, 225, 226, 233, 245, 247, 250, 257, 258, 268, 269
Sandler, Ronald L. 284
Sanger, Alexander 54, 68
Saunders, Ben 271, 276, 285
Savulescu, Julian 11, 13, 14, 17, 18, 49, 56, 64, 68, 69, 97, 100, 106–108, 116, 155, 178–181, 184, 185, 190, 207, 226, 227, 229–234, 236–240, 243–245, 250, 254, 255, 258, 260, 262–267, 269, 271, 278, 285
Schaefer, G. Owen 207, 227
Scheffler, Samuel 104, 106, 116, 141, 151, 282, 286
Scheler, Max 187, 188, 220, 227
Schermer, Maartje 281, 286
Sen, Gita 69
Shaw, Margery 81, 100
Shklar, Judith N. 109, 116, 169, 170, 180
Shapiro, Ian 175, 180
Sidgwick, Henry 142, 151
Silver, Lee 162, 163, 165, 180
Singer, Peter 34, 48, 59, 68, 69, 91, 92, 100, 102, 103, 105, 116, 127, 134, 164, 179, 180, 205, 227, 254, 258
Skąpska, Grażyna 99
Slote, Michael 282, 286

Smart, John J.C. 286
Snyder, Jack W. 56, 63, 67, 151
Solomon, Andrew 112, 113, 116
Soniewicka, Marta 9, 10, 12, 14, 16, 18, 21, 22, 24, 26, 28, 30, 32, 34, 51, 52, 54, 56, 58, 60, 62, 64, 66, 68, 71, 72, 74, 76, 78, 80, 82, 84, 86, 88, 90, 92, 94, 96, 98–102, 104, 108, 110, 112, 114, 116, 155, 156, 158, 160, 162, 164, 166–168, 170, 172, 174, 176–178, 180, 183, 184, 186, 188–190, 192, 194, 196, 198, 200, 202, 204, 206, 208, 210, 212, 214, 216, 218, 220, 222, 224, 226, 227
Sorenson, James R. 29, 34
Spaemann, Robert 86, 87, 100, 191, 192, 196, 199–201, 209, 210, 214–217, 219, 220, 227
Sparrow, Robert 39, 50, 264, 269
Stein, Edward 63, 69, 104
Strawson, Peter 219, 227
Stróżewski, Władysław 220, 227
Steinbock, Bonnie 61, 69, 78, 92, 97, 100, 115
Stiel, Mareike 151
Stoller, Sarah E. 106, 116
Styron, William 42, 50
Sunstein, Cass 252, 258
Suzuki, Takayuki 99
Svanberg, Agneta S. 144, 151

T

Taupitz, Jochen 163, 180
Taylor, Charles 109, 110, 116, 187, 189, 191, 202, 208, 214, 215, 220, 227
ter Meulen, Ruud 11, 18, 226, 245
Thomasma, David C.
Thorpe, Mark 27–32, 34, 173, 180
Tomasello, Michael 179, 181, 186, 191, 201, 227

Turda, Marius 223
Tversky, Amos 248, 258

V
van de Velde, Annemie 151
van Soest, Arthur 178
Velleman, David 130, 134
Vernon, Richard 133, 134
von Hayek, Friedrich 170, 181
von Hildebrand, Dietrich 122, 134

W
Wachbroit, Robert 22, 34
Walker, Mark 185, 195, 196, 198, 203, 227
Wallace, R. Jay 286
Walter, James J. 102, 116
Walters, LeRoy 178, 179
Walzer, Michael 98, 100, 112, 116, 173, 176, 181
Warneken, Felix 175, 179, 181
Warnock, Mary 100, 226
Warren, Mary Ann 51, 69
Wasserman, David 22, 34, 118, 122, 131, 134
Watt, Helen 146, 151
Weber, Max 36, 41, 44, 50, 175, 181

Weil, Simone 113
Weirich, Paul 38, 50
Weschka, Marion 163, 180
Wessels, Ulla 134
Wielenberg, Erik J. 131, 134
Wikler, Daniel 33, 39, 48, 67, 99, 114, 165, 178, 181, 193, 223, 268
Wilsdon, James 245
Wilkinson, Dominic 261, 269
Wilkinson, Stephen 51, 56, 57, 60, 61, 69
Williams, Bernard 108, 116, 248, 254–256, 258, 275, 280, 286
Williams, Tennessee 206, 224
Winch, Peter 17, 115
Wood, Allen W. 225, 269
Wright Mills, Charles 50
Wyeth, Andrew 114, 115

Y
Yamaguchi, Yuki 99
Young, Robert 149

Z
Zimmerman, Michael J. 284
Żuradzki, Tomasz 40, 41, 50, 249, 258, 265, 269